THE NEW FATHERHOOD

THE NEW FATHERHOOD

Why Everything They Told You About Being a Dad Is Wrong, and How Embracing It Will Transform Your Life

Kevin Maguire

New York Boston

The tools and information presented herein are not intended to replace the services of trained health professionals or be a substitute for medical advice. You are advised to consult with your health care professional with regard to matters relating to your health, and in particular regarding matters that may require diagnosis or medical attention.

Details relating to the author's life are reflected faithfully to the best of their ability while recognizing that others who were present might recall things differently.

Balance
Hachette Book Group
1290 Avenue of the Americas
New York, NY 10104
GCP-Balance.com
@GCPBalance

First Edition: May 2026

Balance is an imprint of Grand Central Publishing. The Balance name and logo are registered trademarks of Hachette Book Group, Inc.

Interior illustrations by Tony Johnson.
Print book interior design by Sheryl Kober.

Library of Congress Cataloging-in-Publication Data has been applied for.
ISBNs: 978-1-5387-7306-2 (trade paperback), 978-1-5387-7307-9 (ebook)

Printed in the United States of America

LSC-C

Printing 1, 2026

For Padme, who opened my eyes,
and Bodhi, who opened my heart

The nature of rain is the same, but it makes thorns grow in the marshes and flowers in the gardens.

—Arabian Proverb

Everyone thinks of changing the world, but no one thinks of changing himself.

—Leo Tolstoy

CONTENTS

THE NEW FATHER HOOD

INTRODUCTION

When Fatherhood Doesn't Go to Plan

Let me start with a story. About how fatherhood felt, second time around. The first time, with my daughter, it went mostly to plan. With my son, not so much.

In the months after Bodhi was born, at around eight p.m. every evening, both kids tucked up safely in bed, I'd take the dog for a walk—just the two of us. I'd walk through Barcelona, the city I call home, the warmth of a balmy Mediterranean evening on my face, distant yelps from children descending a metal slide too hot for their bare legs, an idyllic orange glow slowly setting on the horizon. I'd head to a park—one far enough from home to prevent bumping into someone I knew, but close enough not to arouse suspicion—to sit on a bench. And I would start to cry.

I spent the summer of 2019 wondering what was wrong with me and why I didn't love my son. He was born three months earlier: happy, healthy, and everything we could have asked for. After settling into the unique cadence new parents face—moving abruptly between adorable vignettes and incessant sleep deprivation—I started to sense something wasn't right. The thought didn't arrive fully formed—it began as a dull background static, which I initially attributed to exhaustion. But when it stubbornly remained, even after the occasional decent night of sleep, I started to question what I was feeling. A darkness had crept up on me since his birth. I was angry, all the time, over the smallest things. I didn't want to be around my wife. Didn't want to play with my daughter. Didn't want to talk to friends and family. Getting through each day was a struggle, like wading through mud with a hundred-pound rucksack strapped to my back. And, most painfully of all, I didn't want to be near my newborn son.

Hearing him cry was akin to fingernails scraping down a chalkboard. And he cried—a lot. At least I thought he did, though I now realize—writing this, six years later—my mind was blowing this small thing out of proportion, just as with everything else; molehills transformed into mountains, trapping me in their valleys. I gave up trying to get him to stop, because my mind told me it was useless—he'd only be moments away from starting to shriek again. What was the point? I did the only thing I knew how. I shrank away. From being a husband. From being a father. I retreated into an illusion of comfort, finding solace in a dark place. As I sat on that park bench crying, my eternally sad basset hound watching tears run down my face, I tried to get my head around what was happening. With hindsight, I realize how fortunate I was that this was my second child—I had a benchmark to compare against. After a few months of existing in this void of meaning, I concluded that this wasn't "normal" and I started hunting down clues as to why I was feeling this way. While Googling things like "*new dad sad*" and "*why I am crying new dad*," I came across an article written about a doctor struggling to connect with his second child. Here was a medical professional articulating exactly what I was struggling to name:

> *"He cries as soon as I walk in the door," Dr. Levine told his wife, who pointed out that the baby was too young to hate anyone. Feeling isolated and rejected, Dr. Levine became "verbally vicious" to his wife and demeaned his son constantly. As the weeks went by, his thoughts and feelings about and toward his son got darker. "I hate him. I wish we'd never had him," he told his wife.*

I read these words and felt an odd sense of relief. The symptoms were listed, and all too familiar: Ongoing feelings of anger toward your partner and child. Feeling numb and empty. Increased irritability. Increased use of alcohol and substances. Significant weight gain or loss. Loss of interest in work or hobbies. Feeling sad. Crying for no reason. And the reason? A collection of words I knew but had never seen combined: **paternal post-partum depression**.

I had no idea it existed. I was aware of postpartum depression (PPD). All dads-to-be are. We're warned about its dangers, advised to be on the lookout for telltale signs in our partners. But there is scant thought given to a father's mental health after a baby enters his life. Back in 2019, when I was searching on the World Health Organization's website for *paternal mental health*, it returned the entirely unhelpful *Did you mean: maternal mental health?* Paternal postnatal depression (*PPND*, the term used in the UK) still returns zero results on the website for the National Health Service (NHS), although they did add *It can also affect fathers and partners* to the postnatal depression page at some point in the years since. In the years since, I've learned of a mental health charity that, until very recently, wouldn't allow male writers to use the term as it led to complaints from female donors. They were told to call it "depression for dads."

Looking back on photos from that time, I don't recognize the man in the picture. I was physically there, but that's about it. There is visual evidence of me holding my son and smiling—I knew well enough to put on a happy face when the camera was watching. But there are other photos. The ones where I don't know I'm in the background and have been captured as part of a mise-en-scène. And that man looks broken. Truly defeated. Empty. Shattered, in every meaning of the word. I look at him and realize what my wife must have felt, seeing a man she loved so far removed from the person she fell in love with. I needed help. As I started to understand what might be happening to me, I opened up to her. I'm forever grateful she was there. We figured it out together. Worked on a routine to get back on track. I started therapy, a daily meditation practice, and exercising regularly. Cut out the bad habits and negative loops that were keeping me stuck in a dark headspace. I learned to identify the triggers that led me to break down; to notice the tics—like the scratching of my arms—that were external manifestations of internal turmoil, that were my body's way of telling me I wasn't doing okay. And I purposefully spent time with my son: wearing him on the street, having fun on our own, building the belief that I could do this.

Therapy was an essential part in rebuilding a healthy internal dialogue. My therapist told me, "Eventually, you will love your son, and your connection will be all the stronger because of what you went through to get there." I still think about this weekly. Even as he insists I lie down on his bed while he falls asleep, even as he continues to catch me as I do my best earthworm impression sliding out of the room, hoping he doesn't notice. I remember all I did to feel that warmth inside my chest as his sleepy hand is draped over it. I worked hard for this. And I didn't do it alone.

It all started by opening up. First, with my wife. Later with family and friends. It was opening up to the dads in my life that provided the greatest revelations. Because when I started talking to friends about these feelings, I realized I wasn't alone. When I first diagnosed that paternal postpartum depression might be the cause of my ills, I began searching for other dads who'd been through it. Knowing that dads would be much less likely to speak up about mental health problems, I assumed I'd work my way through most of my phone book to find a friend who could help. How wrong I was. The very first friend I spoke to told me he knew of two other dads who had been through the same. Would I want to talk to them? This was a pattern I saw repeated as my net was cast wider. In private, men would tell me what they went through. In public, you'd hear nothing but crickets. Conversations with dads around me couldn't have been further from what I'd been led to believe.

I got better—I'll tell you all about it later. I also made it a habit to reach out to friends who had recently become dads, making sure they were doing okay—and telling them it was fine to talk about it if they weren't. I believed that opening up about my own struggle would reduce any shame that friends feeling the same way might be experiencing. My hunch was right. Wondering how to do this for more dads, and dismayed with the lack of resources out there for dads struggling with their mental health, I wondered if I could put something out there—an SOS beacon, an SEO honeypot—that might help those searching for answers like I once had. These essays, which I began sharing online in 2021 as a weekly newsletter titled *The New Fatherhood*, grew to become one of the most popular fatherhood newsletters on the internet, with tens of thousands of dads reading it across more than 150 countries.

It started with a short email, sent out to a few dozen people I knew. I asked friends who were working at various tech companies and ad agencies to share a message on their parenting Slack channels or message boards:

> *Being a dad isn't easy.*
>
> *We're expected to do more, and be more, than any generation of dads before us.*
>
> *Be the rock of the family. Be more vulnerable. Be successful. Be ever-present.*
>
> *It ends up feeling like we're doing a terrible job of everything.*
>
> *We know moms don't have it any easier. But moms have one thing that we don't: They have each other. Check-ins. Texts. Calls. Coffee.*
>
> *Moms talk to other moms. They share their struggles. They look out for one another, building support networks to shield and lift each other up during life's biggest transitions.*

Us dads? We need more of that. The world needs dads looking out for dads.

Outside of a digital deluge of PowerPoint decks, I had done little to convince myself I could write. And what I was choosing for "my beat" would mean venturing into uncomfortable territory. Opening up, becoming a dad who discusses his feelings, would mean pushing back against what felt—and still feels!—like generations of history, societal beliefs, and cultural conditioning. It would take a few months of essays before I would work up the courage to share an early version of what you read across the last few pages. I was, like so many other men, trained to see vulnerability as a weakness: something to be taken advantage of by an unscrupulous co-worker or soon-to-be-former-friend on their way to the top. From birth, and into business, we are taught to keep the cracks in our armor hidden away. This works, until it doesn't. Until becoming a father forces us into a reckoning with all that we've pushed down. I wasn't the first man, and I surely won't be the last, who had hitherto navigated the world utterly oblivious to what lies beneath. Becoming a parent activates a primal element, bringing us in direct contact—and conflict—with emotions we may have spent decades avoiding. All those years spent building walls between yourself and the world? Now you've got to tear them down, for you and your kids. If you're heading into fatherhood unaware of the emotional turbulence to come, then buckle up, buddy, because this ride is gonna get bumpy as hell.

My battle with paternal postpartum depression broke me. But I came back better. I learned to open up and ask for help. It inspired me to start writing, to show other dads a way out of the hole they might have fallen into. It taught me how essential it was to unlearn the inherited behaviors that my father passed on to me, as his father passed down to him, as men have unknowingly done for as many generations as we've walked the earth. It taught me the immense power of vulnerability, how little we see men model it in modern society, and that through telling our truth, and beginning to expose our soft underbellies, we can help others do the same.

This isn't a book about how to navigate paternal postpartum depression. But it was this moment that changed the trajectory of my life and acted as a gateway to a broader truth—that fatherhood itself is undergoing a fundamental transformation. My battle with depression revealed the chasm between how we talk about fatherhood and how it actually feels. Recognizing this gap—and finding few resources to bridge it—forced me to put into the world what I couldn't find. Those essays grew beyond anything I could have imagined and led to the book you're reading right now. A weekly newsletter offered me the opportunity to trace the transformations happening across fatherhood, to report on modern masculinity from its front lines, following the trail of fathers investigating curious sounds of internal rumblings, questioning why fatherhood doesn't feel right: the expectations of a changing society meeting the harsh light of reality. It's hard to put your finger on—this paternal dissonance, the funny feeling that pervades life after becoming a dad. Because we stand on the precipice of a monumental shift in fatherhood. And we're not just standing: We are being invited—no, implored—to hurl ourselves over its edge; to surrender to it in the hopes of survival, to dramatically reshape our sense of self for the greater good.

As men take more active roles in the upbringing of their children—with many attempting to co-parent equally, or the increasing number choosing to become stay-at-home dads—we're shouldering the burden of sleep deprivation, the pressures to be both a perfect parent and productive employee, and dozens of other battles that mothers have been fighting for decades, if not centuries: attempting to navigate the tightrope between everything society expects from you and all you're able to give, and the struggle to maintain a sense of self beyond being a parent.

This book is a chronicle of my attempt to make it through this labyrinth, my best attempt to leave a red thread for other brave adventurers seeking help on their own journey. (If you'd like a reference that's not almost three thousand years old, think of each of these chapters as a bloody spot in a FromSoftware game, where I left a note before inevitably getting flattened by the hidden boulder around the corner.) This is a book about parenting the same way *The Odyssey* was a book about sailing. It is a book that will tell you're not being selfish in thinking about yourself, at least not this time, because every ounce of effort you put into this herculean task of becoming a better father will be paid back tenfold, with generations of your lineage thankful for the work you do here, even if they aren't aware of it. And what could be more resonant to a parent than knowing your offspring didn't value all the effort you made? They may grow up and never even realize, but no matter, no mind: Know that, in developing a better relationship with yourself, and working through that emotional cardboard box of bullshit you promised you'd clean out ages ago, you can have an cascading impact on your life, as well as the lives of your partner, your children, and—if we haven't entirely fucked up the planet by then—the generations that may once roam the earth after you have transitioned to dust.

We stand amid the rubble and stubborn remains of an archaic definition of fatherhood. Our safe harbor of breadwinner status has been torn from us, with no new port to call home. Hitting your children has been widely condemned by society and outlawed by governments since the 1990s, but Homer Simpson was still strangling his son Bart until 2020. We're questioning the decisions our parents made, habits inherited from thousands of fathers before us, as society is only beginning to permit us to feel the full range of our emotions. And, unbelievably—when the deck is so clearly stacked against us—the bar for fatherhood remains so low that we're in danger of tripping over it every time we leave the house to push a baby down the street in a stroller. (An experience that will give you incontrovertible truth—if any were needed—on how society sees the role of dad. "Daddy daycare, is it?" one passerby may note. "Your day to babysit?" "Giving Mom a break?")

We need to do better. We need better role models. A connection to something deeper: community, presence, purpose. The spirit is willing, the stomach is hungry, but the nourishment on offer is weak; we turn to a blue Australian cartoon dog like an oasis in the desert, hoping he can raise all boats while asking, "What Would Bandit Do?" You may have arrived at the sleep-deprived shores of fatherhood on the back of success in other areas of your life—a happy marriage, a career path the envy of your high school friends—but checked into the hospital feeling woefully under-prepared. You may have been someone who, for years, was excelling in your professional life, only to be thrust into a new world where none of the tools and techniques you spent years perfecting are useful. We're lost, asking fundamental questions about what life means now. Can't find the answers? Then throw yourself back into work, or who knows where. Holding a child in your arms—this living, breathing, defecating manifestation of love who will frustratingly not respond to instruction or input, with no rhyme or reason, crying incessantly, even given your best shot at making them stop—can feel like standing up in a room full of your bosses, armed solely with a PowerPoint clicker that emits a high-piercing shriek every time you try to advance to the next slide.

I've spent a decade as a dad, obsessed with my two children. I've spent the last five years studying fatherhood with more intensity than anything my ADHD-riddled brain previously hyperfixated on during the forty-something years I've been spinning around on this earth with you. I've read enough peer-reviewed parenting papers to fill a university library, and the evidence is clear and consistent, echoes in a cave pointing a path forward: Fatherhood literally changes our brains, reshapes our hearts, and transforms who we are at a fundamental level. Becoming a father will change you—that much is certain. And while the shift will never be entirely under your control, it can, with the work, be under your influence.

I believe the book you hold in your hands is unlike any fatherhood book that came before it. Most of the genre focuses on how to support the mother and baby, and rightly so—this is your number one job before the birth and will remain essential in the years afterward: this brave new world where you'll be required to keep another human being alive *and* turn them into an upstanding member of society. But fewer books ask us to turn the mirror on ourselves, and to realize that to succeed in this domain will require a different approach. Those books were about them; this one is about you. It is an invitation to think about the kind of parent you want to be, the dad you want your kids to remember. This probably isn't the first book you've read in an attempt to be a better version of yourself. Maybe you've got a shelf full of books bought in this hope: productivity books you read on how to be more effective with your time, next to philosophy books that tell you you're barking up the wrong tree. Perhaps you plowed through stacks of business books to give you an edge at work and then, like Icarus, flew a little too close to the sun and burned out, before landing back in the inevitable mindfulness section of the store in the hope you might find inner peace and drag yourself away from the edge.

What got you here won't get you there, as they like to say. Fatherhood comes along, and though your drive may be the same, your time and focus are diminished. The new normal means men are taking a more active role in the lives of their children than any generation before. This means you're going to be home more than any father before you, and in this place, the rules are different. What worked so well in the office falls apart on first application in the safety of your home. Harder, better, faster, and stronger aren't welcome here. Being a dad cuts differently today, and these wounds are fresh. What's required is a perspective shift—that we begin thinking about fatherhood the way we've previously thought about our careers, and ourselves: to understand how to get better at what is the most important job we'll ever do, to find opportunities for meaningful "training" to help us identify and improve on our weaknesses, to seek out mentors who have been through it all before and can offer us just the right advice at just the right time. Because this ain't your old man's fatherhood. Things are different this time. And you have the chance to play a part in a once-in-an-era change that will redefine the heart of fatherhood as surely and inevitably as it will change yours.

The initial idea for this book came together thirty-five thousand feet in the air. A vignette of modern fatherhood manifested itself in the aisle ahead of me: A man was rocking a small baby backward and forward, his son doing his damn best to scream our metal bird into the ground. I had found myself on a plane without my kids for the first time in a long time, traveling for work, and was hoping for a few hours of peace. Instead, 11C was the seat of your worst nightmare. But I wasn't mad—I felt nothing but empathy. We've all been there. I recalled twelve hours between London and San Francisco, holding the hands of a stubborn, almost-walking toddler who was determined to spend the entire transatlantic flight doing laps of a Boeing 787. I looked at this father walking up and down the aisle, shushing his son midflight, and had a revelation: In just a single generation, the experience of being a dad had transformed so fundamentally that, only decades ago, it would have been Mom's sole responsibility to keep the baby from erupting while Dad remained in his seat, possibly even smoking a cigarette. Planes move fast. But fatherhood, for this generation, moves even faster.

The rules have changed, the new ones yet to be set in stone. In order to understand The New Fatherhood, and our place in it, first we need to recognize the water in which we swim, the history of fatherhood, and how it's shaped our current predicament. Then we'll examine how to break harmful cycles and forge new paths. We'll confront the societal forces that work against the engaged, emotional father. And then we'll turn inward, developing a framework to identify how fatherhood impacts your career, health, emotional life, belief systems, and beyond. We'll explore tools for navigating these waters, turning potential challenges into opportunities for growth. Then we'll get practical with tools and techniques on how to thrive as a father in the modern world—redefining success, mastering time, nurturing relationships, and finding a sustainable rhythm to be present for your children without sacrificing your own well-being.

This isn't a manual—it's a manifesto.

It's our collective attempt to define the new rules of fatherhood.

And it's just the start.

THE NEW RULES OF FATHERHOOD

#1. **Old rule:** *Survive.*
New rule: *Thrive.*

#2. **Old rule:** *Dad knows all.*
New rule: *Dad's figuring it out.*

#3. **Old rule:** *Go ask your mother.*
New rule: *Come talk to your dad.*

#4. **Old rule:** *Hide your weaknesses.*
New rule: *Vulnerability equals strength.*

#5. **Old rule:** *You are what you do.*
New rule: *You are not your job.*

#6. **Old rule:** *Religion as an obligation.*
New rule: *Faith as an invitation.*

#7. **Old rule:** *Children limit possibilities.*
New rule: *Children expand horizons.*

#8. **Old rule:** *Maximize every minute.*
New rule: *Lose track of time.*

#9. **Old rule:** *Dad bod decline is inevitable. Accept it.*
New rule: *Your health is a gift to your family.*

#10. **Old rule:** *Push it down.*
New rule: *Bring it up.*

#11. **Old rule:** *Control their behavior.*
New rule: *Understand your own.*

#12. **Old rule:** *Tough it out.*
New rule: *Tune it in.*

#13. **Old rule:** *Drugs are bad.*
New rule: *Open your mind.*

#14. **Old rule:** *Focus on noise.*
New rule: *Find the signal.*

#15. **Old rule:** *Success is measured by salary.*
New rule: *Success is measured by quality of life.*

#16. **Old rule:** *MAN UP.*
New rule: *Man down!*

#17. **Old rule:** *Fight or flight.*
New rule: *The dad abides.*

PART I

THE STATE OF THE NATION

In order to define a new fatherhood, we need to know not only where we're going but where we've been: how we arrived at this moment of paternal flux and our role in breaking, and remaking, what has been provided by the lineage of fathers that came before us.

CHAPTER 1

The Case for Abundancy

The real voyage of discovery consists not in seeking new landscapes, but in having new eyes.

—Marcel Proust

Old rule: *Survive.*
New rule: *Thrive.*

If you've been gifted this book on becoming a new dad: congratulations! You're in for the wildest ride of your life. You've no doubt got hundreds of questions regarding the next few weeks and months and throughout the first year, and you're hoping to learn everything you need to know to navigate those initial milestones—to understand exactly what's going to happen, and when, with your baby. And I'm happy to tell you that all these answers, and many more, can be found...in another book.

It's called *Your Baby Week by Week: The Ultimate Guide to Caring for Your New Baby* by Caroline Fertleman and Simone Cave. I don't know what witchcraft they pulled, which cauldron was used to concoct the potion that produced this eerily accurate play-by-play. The book offers more than insight—you'll have foresight, the uncanny ability to predict exactly what is going to happen, when it's going to happen, almost down to the day. It will put your mind at ease with alarming regularity in the first year of your child's life. If you don't own it, go buy it. It's okay, I can wait. Grab your phone, tap the smiley box icon, and get them to drop it off at your house tomorrow. Yeah, I know you're still paying for Prime, even though you said you were going to cancel it. No judgment here. Next-day delivery is a new-parent lifeline.

Are you back? Then let's begin. You may have bought this book of your own free will. You may have been gifted it from a well-meaning friend—another dad with knowledge of what lies ahead. You may have been given it by your significant other, which could mean the chips are already stacked against me. Maybe you're standing, right now, wondering if you should add this to your paternity tsundoku pile. How many parenting books have you read so far? Am I your first? Or did you get here after spending time with Emily Oster, Dr. Becky, Philippa Perry, maybe even Armin Brott if you ventured beyond "parenting" and dipped your toe into the "fatherhood" genre?

You may be approaching this book with a sense of trepidation. I know I would be. Life is too short to read bad books, and the fatherhood shelf is sadly littered with them. Because while there are great parenting books—ones that make it all mercifully easier—far too many miss the mark. And when written for a male audience, they seem compelled to position themselves as "survival guides," promise "basic training for new recruits," attempt to turn you from "dude to dad," or offer a "playbook on the biggest game of your life." (All taken from real books, I regret to inform you.) To quote just a few of the reviews from these books (without singling out a particular offender), "In this book all the men are dumb and all the women are mean," "This is what it would look like if a frat-boy tried to write a pregnancy book," and "If I wanted advice on how to raise a child like they did in the 80s, I would have bought a book from back then."

These books feel like relics from the past. Because they exist within an old-world mentality, aimed at dads wondering how they're going to *get through* fatherhood. They operate from the primary perspective of what psychologists call the "scarcity mindset," a way of thinking centered on all the resources we don't have enough of. Scarcity Fatherhood focuses on everything we'll lose upon becoming a parent—our money, our time, our freedom. Scarcity Fatherhood looks toward the past, at the men you grew up around, who had a more traditional, seemingly easier job. From this mindset, fatherhood is a black hole whose inescapable gravitational force must be resisted as it attempts to rip you away from life's main plotline: to win at work, to chase the American Dream, or whatever local flavor of it you inherited. This thinking makes raising children feel secondary, a side quest to fill your XP meter, a distraction from the essential narrative of the story. Dads have been permitted to think like this for generations, to work hard and parent light, so long as they performed what today's start-ups would call Minimum Viable Parenting: stick around, play rough, offer occasional advice, keep the family in line. Anything outside of this? Don't worry, your wife can figure it out.

But the world no longer ticks this way—at least in the cross-section of society I suspect most readers of this book will occupy. If we gaze over from the opposite side of the scarcity chasm—from the viewpoint of Abundant Fatherhood—we see that having children is additive, not reductive. It doesn't take you away from where you were heading but offers a path to somewhere altogether new. To a place where, whisper it, life might even be better. But embracing abundance means breaking away from negative framings of fatherhood that have fossilized over generations. You know what I'm talking about—dads who warn you of approaching doom: Here be dragons, come prepared. As if the zombie apocalypse is approaching, and here's your ten-step checklist guide to battening down hatches, calculating rations and fuel, wondering whether you'll make it through the winter without having to start carving chunks out of each other. Pregnancy becomes just one on the list of mini-bosses to be felled before the inevitable final battle arrives; a never-ending to-do list to be tackled as the timer ticks toward zero. These dads tell you: "Welcome to the end of your life!" and that "Parenting isn't living—it's surviving. It's keeping your head above water."

It's little wonder fatherhood is suffering from an identity crisis. Scarcity Fatherhood is a surefire path to dissatisfaction—if we only measure the experience through the doors it closes, we'll always end up coming up short and resenting the time we spend with our kids. But viewed with a different lens—one I'll spend this book outlining and investigating—fatherhood is a gift. In 2023, Bloomberg reported that $6.3 trillion was spent globally on wellness—all those dollars changing hands in our attempts to look, think, and feel like better versions of ourselves. What if the answer was hiding in plain sight? Ask any dad what the most transformational experience of his life was, and he'll almost always tell you: becoming a parent. Yes, it is the most challenging job we'll ever do. It's an eighteen-year-long (at least!) project with no guaranteed ROI, zero performance-related bonuses, and a grueling schedule. As comedian Jim Gaffigan wrote, "It may be a thankless job with ridiculous hours, but at least the pay sucks." It can make you, it can break you, it'll do both, in succession, on repeat, during a twenty-four-hour period. There's no linear career progression. It's never clear who is in charge. It's an endeavor we choose to undertake, knowing it will continue to morph into the unexpected—even as you envision that wild future when your children may one day have children of their own, a concept that seems so remote today you'll wonder how your own parents ever came to grips with it. It's all of this, all at once, and so much more.

Abundant Fatherhood means tuning in to the idea of raising children as a point of leverage to radically transform all aspects of your life. Every experience you have—kids, partner, friends, career, purpose, passions, interests, and health—will shift upon becoming a dad. By approaching fatherhood as an opportunity to thrive—and not simply survive—we can be better: for our kids, for loved ones, and for ourselves. Pointing inward, we can discover more than we previously believed possible and use this to grow. And we can begin to enjoy, and not just endure, the trials and tribulations of turning these defenseless babies that we've had a hand in creating—even if it was, as an Italian friend once told me, "only three minutes and a cigarette"—into fully grown adults. But, just as throughout life, your experience will be entirely dictated by how you view it. "The universe is change," wrote Marcus Aurelius in *Meditations*. "Our life is what our thoughts make it."

The future sounds of fatherhood can be heard with your ear to the ground, but you must tune out the deafening noises from those who desperately want it to remain in the past. You'll hear it codified in different ways: social media comments where AlphaDad84 will reminisce about "a time when men could be men," politicians who promise a return to "traditional values" where they are freed from the responsibilities of home. This common refrain is a thinly veiled wish for society to return to a period when men could say and do whatever they pleased. The world has changed, but those with the right perspective can see we have been provided with a springboard, not a setback: a place where modern men can navigate new breadths and depths of their lives with open minds and hearts.

While you can lead a horse to water, you can't make it drink. Seeing this change as a seed of opportunity requires stepping up, in presence and purpose. Dads are playing a more active role at home than ever before. But in a country like the United States, around 40 percent of dads don't take the full amount of paternity leave offered, and 2019 data showed that less than a third of dads in the UK took any. This is partly due to employers and governments slowly catching up to the needs of modern families. But how society sees the role of the father, and how we view fatherhood ourselves, is as much to blame. Studies have shown that men who lean into fatherhood consistently deliver positive outcomes in the well-being of children: One Swedish study found that children whose fathers took paternity leave were less likely to experience behavioral and emotional problems later in life; another from the University of Oslo revealed that couples who shared parental leave equally experienced increased satisfaction in their relationship and had a higher chance of remaining married. It follows logic—and leading research—that dads who take longer paternity leave are more likely to be engaged in childcare activities later on, and form stronger bonds with their children as they grow. And how much time we spend with our newborn children is just another parenting pressure point where radical change is required, just one of the huge shifts we've witnessed with front-row seats.

Fail We May, Sail We Must

My path to Abundant Fatherhood wasn't a straightforward one. It started in Manchester, England. It was 1983, and I was the firstborn son of a working-class family—born into a stratum of society that Margaret Thatcher, then prime minister, was actively dismantling through policy and rhetoric. I've always considered myself a born-and-bred Mancunian, but it would take starting preschool and socializing with local kids before I would develop the northern twang the Gallagher brothers would eventually make famous around the world. Before then, I delivered my sentences with a distinctly Irish accent, having learned to speak by listening to my parents and their friends. A few years before I was born, they left the small town of Dromore, in the middle of Northern Ireland, scant miles from "the big town" of nearby Omagh—the same streets that would later become the scene of the deadliest incident of the Troubles in 1998, an IRA bomb that killed 29 people and injured 220 others. My parents left behind a country of conflict, crossing the short waters to put down roots of their own, and spent the early years of their marriage—the honeymoon period, if not the honeymoon itself—living in a rented caravan in Scotland. They moved where the work was, where other Irish immigrants had paved the way before them, and ended up in the North West of England, plying their trade in the construction industry.

My dad spent the early years of my life driving up and down the length of the United Kingdom in a Ford Transit van, through sleet, snow, and shite, laying cable in the ground, getting compensated by the mile. At the end of the week, his hard labor would directly correlate to a stack of cash delivered at five p.m. on a Friday, in a small, square manila envelope with various deductions scrawled across the front. He'd head home on Friday evening after a week of work—probably via the pub, this final deduction into the hands of the barman rather than the taxman—with that lifeline in hand. Sometimes it would be enough money to get through to next week. But not always. Living week to week, working-class dads did what they could to keep a roof over the heads of their families. They were forced to ruthlessly battle at the bottom layers of Abraham Maslow's *hierarchy of needs*—the rainbow-colored pyramid that helped humankind understand our motivations like never before. It would be much later in life when my parents could begin working toward the upper layers of self-actualization—back then, there were bills to pay and mouths to feed. I remember my dad coming home one weekend, dirt underneath his fingernails, the smell of tarmacadam pervading the house, and showing me what he was getting paid to put into the ground: a black cable the width of your index finger, which sprouted at the cut end into a bouquet made up of hundreds of transparent threads, each as thin as a human hair. "Fiber optic cable," I was informed when I asked what it was. What was it for? "Some new kind of telephone," he offered, unaware of the future he was literally paving the way for, that his blood, sweat, and tears would enable his son to eventually learn a trade, build a career, make a family, and—much later—start a newsletter.

My parents worked hard. They learned how to work their way up the ladder and secure better-paid jobs to support their growing family. When I grew up, I followed the same pattern they had: I studied, traded one job for another, and experienced a perfect alchemy of hard work and good luck that eventually landed me the job I'd dreamed about since I was a teenager—fiddling with ones and zeroes across those fiber optic cables but doing it for Google. This job took me and my family from London to the other side of the world: to the golden sunsets of California, the new center of the universe, a supposed utopia driven by a silicon revolution.

It wasn't long until things started to fall apart. It looked like everything had gone right. So why did it feel so wrong? I'd become a dad, had been successful in my career, followed the rules I'd heard my entire life—put the hours in, provide for your family, get a job (if you like it, all the better, but don't consider it a necessity), don't complain, get on with it. I'd done what dads had always done, ad infinitum: Go to work, come home, be the best dad you could with whatever was left in the tank. We grow up witnessing these behaviors, internalizing them, and allowing them to ossify into absolute truths. Over time, we've accepted a common narrative around fatherhood: While it opens the aperture of your heart, it limits your career, increases stress levels, makes your relationship with your partner worse, distances you from your friends, places you further from your goals, divorces you from your passions, and turns you into a shell of the person you once were.

But what if the opposite is true? Abundant Fatherhood means questioning what we've inherited and accepted, the same rules crumbling beneath our feet, as our role at home and across society undergoes a once-in-an-era change. This means accepting that the transformative effects of fatherhood might be measured in more than just love, and that tapping into new levels of empathy might see us hitting new highs in our careers and forever altering what success means as we head into the second halves of our lives. It nudges us toward a world where we can believe, contrary to popular opinion, that our closest relationships could become stronger than ever and that some friendships—not all, but enough—will become deeper and more meaningful. And it brings us face-to-face with the stark reality that raising a child means weaving together the disparate elements of the man you are today with the boy you once were, allowing you to grow in ways you never thought possible.

Fatherhood can act as a gateway to an entirely new way of living. But that mindset requires letting go as much as leaning in. To get there will mean doing the work: playing your part in understanding, breaking, and then carefully repairing the chains that have been passed down by generations of men before you. This is the most important and—I'm devastated to inform you—emotionally grueling work you'll ever do: to discern the difference in what an unbroken line of fathers have passed along over centuries, some of it useful, most of it not. To take your place in history and illuminate a path forward for the sons and daughters who will follow in our wake. And to do this under a spotlight as the people we love and live with, and society at large, expect more from us than at any point before.

"Fail we may, sail we must," as was tattooed across the arms of DJ and producer Andrew Weatherall. But thankfully, for this generation of dads, we don't have to navigate these seas alone. Men are—finally, mercifully—starting to do the impossible: to open up to each other. Throughout this book, you'll hear from some of the thousands of dads I've met along the way. Because while my name is on the front cover, this is the work of a collective: every man working intentionally to push fatherhood forward, to reject those who attempt to drag it into the past. By reading this book, you're becoming a part of this community, this group of salmon swimming upstream, all part of The New Fatherhood. Many of them found their way to the newsletter over the years: like Anthony, a dad from the North West of England (somehow they make all the best people there), just one of the many I've gotten to know since I started bombarding inboxes all those years ago. He once told me, "The best parenting books are the ones that help me change myself. The kids are fine; I am the bottleneck."

We're going to spend the next few hundred pages together, but don't expect advice on how to "survive" fatherhood. I won't tell you how to change a diaper or when you need to start saving for college. (If you're reading this in the United States, you're probably already late on that second one. My apologies.) Where we're heading is uncharted: a place where we'll learn to surf the waves of fatherhood that threaten to drag us across the reef, and believe in their ability to carry us to better shores. This is for every man committed to doing the work—standing side by side, trying to raise better humans while working to be better dads. The days will be long, the years will be short; you will have less time, less money, less energy, and less headspace than ever to figure this out.

So let me help you with some help of my own—all the dads I've met along the way.

Let's hear it from the dads on...shifting to abundance

The biggest surprise in becoming a father was just how much I love being a dad. Maybe it's because I was the last out of my friends to be a dad and had years of their horror stories to lower my expectations. I expected it to be difficult—and maybe I'm just lucky or maybe I've got a good perspective on things—but it just hasn't been as difficult as my friends made it out to be. On the other hand, we just welcomed our second boy into the world a few weeks ago and a lot of those same friends told me how difficult two would be. They were right on the money with that. **Justin**

I didn't expect how long "it" would take to grow on me. It's something to be a dad (and looks like I'm not too bad at it so far), to be a cool daddy, or to be a partner to your partner. It's another entirely to stop feeling foreign to the new person that joined your family cell. Without the motherly hormonal boost, it can take years. And it's okay. Because once they start interacting more, that bond? Yeah, pretty hard to escape. **Martin**

I used to pride myself on speed—moving fast, getting things done, always on the go. Fatherhood slowed me down in a way that felt painful at first. Suddenly I was spending twenty minutes watching a snail cross the pavement with my toddler. But in that slowness, I started noticing more. Life feels less like a race, more like a walk I don't want to end. My kids give me new eyes on the world. I was worried I'd run out of myself to give. Instead, I've ended up with more than I started with. **Leo**

CHAPTER 2

The History of Fatherhood

Boys don't hunger for fathers who will model traditional mores of masculinity. They hunger for fathers who will rescue them from it. They need fathers who have themselves emerged from the gauntlet of their own socialization with some degree of emotional intactness. Sons don't want their father's "balls"; they want their hearts.

—Terry Real, *I Don't Want to Talk About It*

Old rule: *Dad knows all.*
New rule: *Dad's figuring it out.*

There's a photograph I own, taken at the tail end of the 1980s, that is unique among all others.

Within its frame are three people: me, my father, and his father. Three generations of Maguire men huddled around a single seat in my grandfather's living room in Ireland. The framing is terrible—we see an equal amount of ceiling as we do of my grandfather, a foreshadowing of how it would feel to FaceTime my parents decades later. Jack, my grandfather, sits up straight, his face proud, wearing a cardigan that I look at enviously as an adult today. Over his left shoulder is my father, Kevin Senior, a few years shy of his thirtieth birthday. Over his right, a small boy, to whom the guard is being passed, who wears a crisp white shirt and looks toward the camera, blissfully ignorant.

I often think about what fatherhood meant for those two men, and all the other dads that came before them. My dad once boasted that he never dealt with a shitty diaper. If you heard a father say this today, you'd pity his poor wife. My dad worked hard. That was what was required. Back then, it was so simple, with three words that defined a father's role for millennia: **Protect, Provide, Preside.** This trinity, the Three Anchors of Traditional Fatherhood, encapsulated the entire responsibility of the father and was shaped by evolution and hardwired into our DNA long before we had language to describe it.

There is a genetic and evolutionary basis for these anchors. Men are, on average, physically larger and stronger than women—typically by 15 to 20 percent. Since we roamed Eurasia in our loincloths, fathers have had a clear role: bring meat home; ensure that wives and children were safely inside the cave when the sun went down; lead the tribe to safety and prosperity. "Protect, Provide, Preside" is a pattern that reappears throughout much of the animal kingdom—humans included—as the father's primary role, from the days we learned to walk on two feet, right up to the rear bumper of the present day.

All female mammals provide milk to their offspring to keep them alive; humans are no exception. This role—an articulation of Provide that none of us would be here without—has always fallen to the mother. Archaeological evidence supports this division of labor extending deep into our evolutionary past—Neanderthal milk teeth, discovered in Belgium in 2013, indicated that most children were typically weaned at seven months old (which aligns with the six months that the World Health Organization still recommends new mothers breastfeed for). Women have given up their bodies, for millennia, to keep humanity's children alive. Our job was to ensure that they were protected. To use our bigger bodies to protect their smaller ones from danger.

Provision followed naturally. The male body, optimized through evolution for strength and endurance, became the primary resource-gathering machine. Anthropological studies of hunter-gatherer societies consistently showed men traveling farther from home base to secure resources while women maintained closer proximity to children. This old paradigm of men-only hunting groups has come under scrutiny—in 2023, Seattle Pacific University found that 79 percent of sixty-three historical societies had evidence of female hunters. Still, this pattern established the foundation for what would later become formalized as "Dad as the breadwinner."

As the individual responsible for protection and provision, the father also assumed final decision-making authority—presiding. This leadership function extended from immediate family to broader community structures, with patriarchal systems emerging—and some might say stubbornly persisting—across diverse cultures and continents with remarkable consistency for millennia. Father as the head of household: the final authority, making decisions and maintaining order, through faith or fist, "my way or the highway." Father as judge, jury, and executioner, all rolled into one—and good luck to any plaintiff hauled in front of that kangaroo court.

That traditional trinity wasn't arbitrary—it evolved from biological realities and environmental pressures that have shaped societies for thousands of years. Its persistence reflected its evolutionary utility. But it meant that fatherhood was reduced to responsibility rather than relationship—dads defined within a rigid framework of physical capability rather than their ability to connect with their children emotionally. This functional model of fatherhood dominated history with remarkable stability—from ancient civilizations through the pre-industrial era. Historical texts—Aristotle's writings, Confucian teachings, biblical passages—consistently emphasize this triumvirate of paternal responsibilities. Everything outside it could be abandoned, or worse; it was deemed to be unmanly, emasculating, a woman's job. If the Three Anchors once moored us to solid ground, when did the rope begin to fray?

The Historical Evolution of Fatherhood

From the moment *Homo* became *erectus*, pretty much up to when you were born, the role of the father was consistent. Up until the eighteenth century, dads of old had another *P* in their bow that the nineteenth-, twentieth-, and twenty-first-century dads would not: Presence. Until the Industrial Revolution, fathers were primary parents in ways we rarely acknowledge today. They worked from or near home—as farmers, craftsmen, merchants—with children serving as apprentices or helpers in the family trade. Robert Bly outlined this in *Iron John*, a book on the history of men: "The traditional way of raising sons, which lasted for thousands and thousands of years, amounted to fathers and sons living in close—murderously close—proximity, while the father taught the son a trade."

Men took an active role in raising their children by passing them a job, along with a surname. This father was moral compass, educator, and disciplinarian. His role was clear: to prepare his children—especially his sons—for adulthood by teaching them both practical skills and moral values. He was leagues away from even the worst twentieth-century dads in terms of emotional availability—the historical record and popular literature from the time suggests these fathers were stern authority figures—but they were at least present in a way that would soon become impossible for many men. Because coming down the canals of Lancashire and Yorkshire was the Industrial Revolution, which would see the biggest-ever decline in the number of self-employed, trade-from-home dads.

Complex machinery was being constructed in textile factories, and staff were needed to run and repair it. Manchester, the city where I was born and raised, became "Cottonopolis," the center of this transformation, with other British cities following suit. (No pun intended. Well, maybe a small, bespoke one.) These factories also needed workers to deal with the administrative tasks of running the business, optimizing the workforce, and selling their output—and before long, we had our first office jobs.

As work moved from home to factory and office, something profound happened: Fatherhood became defined primarily by absence. For the first time in human history, a father's key contribution was reduced almost entirely to economic provision. Trades passed on for generations were left to wither; the father who left at dawn and returned after dark became the norm. His authority, on paper, was intact, but his daily influence waned. This physical separation created an emotional distance that, for many families, would persist for generations. Says Robert Bly, again: "By the middle of the twentieth century, a massive change had taken place: the father was working, but the son could not see him working. Now a man takes up desk work in an office, becomes a father himself, but has no work to share with his son and cannot explain to the son what he's doing."

Early-twentieth-century parenting manuals reflect this shift, with fathers encouraged to maintain distance and discipline. Consider this advice from a 1928 book, *Psychological Care of Infant and Child*, in which behavioral psychologist John B. Watson tells us: "The father has a powerful voice. You have everything ready to produce a conditioned fear reaction." The book continues with guidance that would be a pretty solid AI response to "how to raise your kids so they'll definitely need therapy":

> *There is a sensible way of treating children. Treat them as though they were young adults. Dress them, bathe them with care and circumspection. Let your behavior always be objective and kindly firm. Never hug and kiss them, never let them sit in your lap. If you must, kiss them once on the forehead when they say goodnight. Shake hands with them in the morning. Give them a pat on the head if they have made an extraordinarily good job of a difficult task.*

These beliefs stubbornly persevered. As recently as 1994, authors Michael and Debi Pearl were advising parents to think of their children more as pets than progeny in *To Train Up a Child*: "By taking control and teaching them to control their emotions and to instantly obey, your children will be cheerful and pleasant." When I first picked up this book, I expected it to be a holdover from the Victorian times, or at least the early 1900s: I didn't expect it to have been released the same year Mufasa told his son that "everything the light touches will be yours," the same year Aphex Twin graced us with the genius of *Selected Ambient Works Volume II*. What does a dad do when being distracted by a son trying to grab his glasses? Let's ask Michael and Debi Pearl:

> *Again say, "No," and thump or swat his hand with a light object so as to cause him a little pain, but not necessarily enough to cry. He will pull his hand back and try to comprehend the association of grabbing the glasses with the pain. Inevitably, he will return to the bait to test his new theory. Sure enough, reaching for the glasses again causes pain, and the pain is accompanied with a quiet, little "No." It may take one or two more tries for him to give up his career as a glasses snatcher, but he will. Through this process, the child will associate the pain with the word "No." There quickly comes a time when your word alone is sufficient to gain obedience.*

It is bleak to think that this was still a viable model of fatherhood in our lifetime. But in the sixty-six years between the publication of Watson's and the Pearls' books, something shifted. It was fundamental. It was remarkable. As writer Stephen Marche eloquently noted in 2014 in *Esquire* magazine:

> *A single small but vital fact distinguishes men of the past fifty years from all other men in history: Most of us see our children being born. It's one of those changes to everyday life that we take for granted but that have the most radical consequences. Up until the mid-1960s, the*

> *mysteries of birth were mainly the preserve of women. Then, suddenly, they weren't. The new father is an engaged father by instinct. Witnessing birth was the beginning of a widening intimacy. The new father holds his babies. He bathes them. He reads to them. The new father knows that the role of the father is not merely to provide food and shelter. The role of the father is to be there, physically and mentally.*

This shift—from pacing in waiting rooms to standing beside our partners during the most vulnerable and powerful moment of human experience—fundamentally altered our relationship with our children and ourselves. We were no longer receiving them after they arrived; we witnessed their entry into the world. This impact was profound but not instantaneous. Cultural lag meant many men present at the birth of their child still parented in accordance with old scriptures—but something had begun to crack in the foundations that had defined fatherhood for generations.

The Dads We Watched: From Bumbling Idiot to Bandit

You can't be what you can't see. And while fatherhood was experiencing a change in homes across the world, it wasn't reflected in what we watched—at least at first. When I think of the fathers my father watched, I see the stoic, silent type: Howard Cunningham from *Happy Days*, or Pa Ingalls from *Little House on the Prairie*. These dads were loving and supportive, dispensing advice from kitchen tables and armchairs with calm detachment. They were the moral compass of the family but rarely let their guard down in vulnerable moments.

The 1980s and 1990s saw the emergence of the "transitional father," men caught between old models and new possibilities: craving deeper connections than they had with their own dads but lacking a clear road map or template to achieve it. Their struggle played in living rooms and on our television screens, where pop culture began documenting—and shaping—this evolution in real time. A new archetype began to emerge: the bumbling dad. Homer Simpson, Al Bundy, Tim "The Tool Man" Taylor, Hal Wilkerson—men whose incompetence was played for laughs. They may have been good at their job, they may not. ("You'll have to speak up, I'm wearing a towel.") These dads tried—and often failed—at parenting, their missteps softened by good intentions, moments of accidental wisdom and stealth mentorship. Lowering the bar for competence opened space for deeper engagement: It gave men permission to fail at fatherhood without being failures as men, stumbling as they were into territory their own fathers never entered. But this portrayal came with a cost—the bumbling dad trope suggested that men were inherently ill-equipped for nurturing, further cementing the idea that the emotional heft of parenting should remain in the mother's domain while men could only clumsily imitate.

This was never more apparent than how TV explained fatherhood to our children. *Peppa Pig* was first shown on British TV in 2004 before captivating children in over 180 countries. It became so popular it led to problems in the United States as children would arrive at preschool with British accents, in what was termed the #PeppaEffect (especially prominent in kids arriving in school after the COVID-19 pandemic). Peppa Pig, while fairly innocuous in the escapades of the children, was a damning portrayal of the family patriarch. Daddy Pig is an oaf, a bumbling idiot, and the source of all—if solution to a few—of the family's many mishaps.

A pivotal change occurred, at least from my vantage point, in the early 1990s—around the time Michael and Debi Pearl were telling us to raise our children like we train our dogs. In *The Fresh Prince of Bel-Air*, Uncle Phil showed us that fatherhood could transcend biology, and tough love and tenderness could coexist without conflict. Fatherhood began to be positioned as a site of personal transformation: In *Mrs. Doubtfire*, Robin Williams disguised himself as a nanny to spend time with his children after a divorce. The film dramatized a profound shift: a father willing to reinvent himself entirely to maintain a connection with his children. Over the course of the movie, Williams moved from unreliable, fun-time dad to dependable, fully engaged dad: cooking, cleaning, helping with homework, and attending to all emotional needs. Williams showed us that being a better dad wasn't emasculating, even if you needed to dress up as a sixty-year-old Scottish woman to do it, and that fatherhood itself might be redemptive—that through raising children well, we might discover capacities we never knew we had.

A direct line can be traced through to 2006, and *Friday Night Lights*'s Eric Taylor—a man who straddled masculine authority and emotional availability in ways that felt revolutionary. He represented fatherhood with clear eyes and a full heart. He wasn't just raising a daughter—he was father figure to an entire team, many without a strong paternal presence at home. As we entered the 2010s, TV dads continued to evolve, and no one embodied this better than *Modern Family*'s Phil Dunphy. He represented something genuinely new—a dad defined by neither stoic authority nor comedic incompetence, but by endless enthusiasm and vulnerable goofiness. His famous "peerenting" philosophy (being both a parent and a peer) captured the tightrope many of us walk daily. He showed up for his kids and made them a priority. What made Phil revolutionary wasn't that he never fumbled or bumbled—he certainly did—but that his missteps came from trying too hard rather than not trying enough.

As TV grew up, so did its portrayal of fathers. The era of the antihero was closely shadowed by the portrayal of the anti-father. These roles leveraged the tension that sits between work and family—even when work meant cooking meth or whacking wise guys. Tony Soprano and Walter White justified their crimes as necessary sacrifices for their families: "I'm doing it for my kids" became both motivation and absolution, even when it was all done to massage their own ego. These characters, initially celebrated, were revealed to be deeply broken men, and the gulf between what they believed they were providing for their kids and what they were actually taking away was insurmountable.

Phil Dunphy and Coach Taylor ran so Bandit Heeler could play. In 2018, *Bluey* burst onto our screens, and with it Bandit—a revolutionary father, the archetypal new-fatherhood dad. Bandit is engaged, playful, emotionally available, and competent. He's neither bumbling nor distant, neither workaholic nor perfect. He gets tired, loses patience, makes mistakes, and repairs them. He's fully human while also being 100 percent dog. The show treats his involvement as normal rather than noteworthy, suggesting that perhaps culture is finally catching up to what fathers have been quietly doing for years.

The Virtuous Circle of New Fatherhood

In the decades since my father and his father held their newborn children in their arms, society's idea of fatherhood has shifted decisively. That shift continues to transform us. "Fatherhood will change you" is a phrase heard by every dad-to-be. It's so common, it's almost lost its meaning. On discovering you are to become a father, other men in your life—young or old, brand-new or lifer—will tell you some variation of the same thing: "You've never known love like the first time you hold your child in your arms." For some of us, it's true right away. For others, the road is longer, but we arrive there eventually. Your tiny corner of the world revolves around your chaotic main-character energy, but these shifts are being echoed in the tectonic plates of fatherhood and are measured in generations, not years. Three interconnected gears in motion, creating compounding effects in how we live our lives and raise our kids:

I. Fatherhood Is Changing

The modern father is more present, literally and emotionally. He's no longer assumed to be the primary breadwinner or disciplinarian. He could be single or married; gay or straight; biological, adoptive, or a stepfather. He may be back at work or staying at home as the primary caregiver. He'll spend more time with his newborn child, taking advantage of better parental leave schemes provided by his employer or government. (Again, apologies to US readers.) He's more fluid in his responsibilities and takes a more equal workload with his partner (while aware he still has a long way to go).

For some, this shift is unexpected and terrifying. It has felt inevitable for a while. It can't be tracked consistently—it is influenced by location, values, education levels, socioeconomic backgrounds, and more. To paraphrase William Gibson, The New Fatherhood is already here—it's just not evenly distributed. Is this change for the best? It depends on whom you ask. The loud voices of the traditionalists, those who reject the new responsibilities required of them, who refuse to shoulder the mental load of the women who have suffered silently with it for eons, would rather see us returned to the era of three *P*s.

II. Fatherhood Changes You

Science recently confirmed what many of us know intuitively: Becoming a father rewires your brain and body. When men hold their newborns, oxytocin—often called the "bonding hormone"—floods their system, giving them a similar chemical surge to that experienced by mothers during breastfeeding. Studies using functional MRI machines have shown that fathers' brains develop enhanced neural responses to their children's cries and expressions, creating pathways once thought unique to mothers. Research on primary-caregiving gay dads shows that their amygdala adapts in the same way as a new mother—its gray-matter volume and vigilance-related activity rising to the same level seen in women, underscoring that it's the caregiving role, not gender, that rewires the parental brain.

Meanwhile, testosterone levels take a nosedive—nature's way of turning potential competitors into nurturers. A 2011 study from Northwestern University found that new fathers' testosterone dropped by 34 percent in the first month after their children were born. This wasn't temporary—levels remained lower even after the children were toddlers. What evolutionary biologists once viewed as a "cost" of fatherhood (decreased competitiveness and aggression) is now understood as a perfectly designed neurobiological adaptation transforming hunters into caregivers. Our bodies, it seems, are beating our cultural conditioning—so long as we show up. This rewiring creates a profound dissonance for many—we push toward tenderness and nurturing at the exact moment society demands we "man up" and focus on our role as a provider.

The question isn't whether fatherhood will change you—the biology makes that inevitable. The degree to which you will change depends on countless factors: how much time you spend with your babies and children, your own childhood experiences, even your sleep patterns. The question becomes how to consciously navigate that transformation, and whether you'll spend your energies pushing back against it or embracing where it may lead.

III. You're Changing Fatherhood

Here's where it comes together—where we can begin laying new foundations for the future to bend the arc of fatherhood in the direction we want it. Because you're changing fatherhood, right now. The logic is sound—every generation of fathers carries the torch from the one before. Tomorrow's definition of fatherhood is ours to claim. Our grandfathers changed it for their sons. And our fathers changed it for us. But these shifts occurred at a glacial pace under the gaze of a society whose expectations remained consistent. Today, the rate of change has accelerated exponentially.

The decisions you make change fatherhood for the children you are raising and will be felt for generations to come. Therefore, reading this book in public can be considered a radical act. (Remember: When you see someone in public reading a book you like, it's like the book is recommending the person. If I see you reading this in the wild, I'm sure as hell going to say hello.) When your kids see you tackle a difficult situation with grace, they will build a better mental model of what a father should be. On the flip side, when they see you lose your shit over something minor and inconsequential, they'll pick up those habits too. These actions will influence the fathers that our sons might become, and the kind of men our daughters might marry. These three monumental shifts are transforming modern fathers. But it's important not to view them in isolation. Tied together, they become the Virtuous Circle of New Fatherhood.

The path here wasn't straight, just as the way forward won't be either. But understanding this evolution—with all its contradictions and complexities—gives us context for the challenges we face as we redefine what fatherhood means, slamming tracks onto the ground while the train hurtles forward. The old rules of fatherhood were clear, consistent, and externally focused. The new ones are ambiguous and evolving and require a painful degree of self-examination. No wonder so many of us feel caught, stuck between a rock and a hard place: We're too evolved to embrace the old ways and too conditioned to embody the new ones.

Protect, provide, and preside are no longer fit for purpose. While only a third of 1950s wives went to work, today it's over 60 percent of wives in opposite-sex marriages. In the United States, 29 percent of married opposite-sex couples earn at the same level, and in almost 1 in 5 marriages men watch their wives bring home the majority of the bacon. Provide is cooked, and preside is heading the same way. What was once the era of Dad as Head of the House ("Just wait until your dad gets home!") has tilted. Today, most marriages are democracies, not dictatorships. Dad as sole provider and sole presider are nixed, off the menu. These functions have been subsumed by a new *P*: partnership. The co-parenting relationship doesn't discard your previous responsibilities but fundamentally reshapes *how* things happen.

Protect, as a function, still remains primarily male-coded. When a spider walks across our living room floor, the rest of the family look in one direction, and it's not toward Mom. But with dinosaurs and saber-toothed tigers extinct, what exactly are we protecting our children from? The greatest threats to our children are no longer predators lurking in the forest or rival tribes across the valley. They're more insidious: toxic messages about body image that poison girls' self-esteem; narrow definitions of masculinity that convince boys to suppress their gentleness; digital landscapes that require careful navigation by child and adult alike. Against these threats, your physical size offers no advantage.

And here lies the central tension of being a father today: We're at a crossroads between what we inherited and what we aspire to become. The headwinds against this transformation are strong. Our culture continues to send mixed messages about what makes a "real man" and a "good father." Workplaces still reward presence over performance. Our inner voices whisper that vulnerability equals weakness, that nurturing isn't masculine, that we should somehow already know how to do this impossible task no one ever taught us. These internal and external barriers make our transformation difficult, even as we recognize its necessity. It's only by understanding the forces working against us that we can hope to break through them.

Let's hear it from the dads on... the shifting face of fatherhood

Sometimes I think about how my dad showed up for us, and it was basically just working and being strict. That was what being a father meant back then. Now I find myself second-guessing everything—am I too soft, too hard, too distracted? It's like we inherited a job description that doesn't make sense anymore. Some days that's overwhelming, but most days it feels like an opportunity to actually give my kids something better than I had. **Paul**

My granddad worked the fields. My dad worked in a factory. Now I work in an office, sat behind a laptop. Three generations, three totally different versions of what "providing" looks like. But the real difference is this: I tuck my kids into bed every night, something neither of them did. It wasn't because they weren't around; more that it wasn't expected. That feels like progress to me—not just in what I give them but in how much of me they actually get. **Elliott**

My dad never changed a diaper in his life. He thought his job was done if the bills were paid. I love him, but I don't want to repeat that script. For me, being a father is about showing up in the small, everyday moments—packing lunches, reading stories, holding them when they cry. That's the legacy I want to pass down. **Conrad**

CHAPTER 3

The Odds Are Against You

The handy thing about being a father is that the historical standard is so pitifully low.

—Michael Chabon, *Pops*

Old rule: *Go ask your mother.*
New rule: *Come talk to your dad.*

The months after my son's birth remain foggy: narratives pieced together based on occasional journal entries, small patches where fog dissipated and what seems like a real memory was retained. One moment seared in my psyche was seeing my wife read a text, a sea of words from her friend Jenny—the message stretching so far across the phone screen that my thumb ached in response.

I was worried: a message this long? Something terrible must have happened.

"Is everything okay?" I asked.

"Of course. Why?" my wife replied.

"I saw how long that message was."

"She's just checking in on me. She's got two kids, she knows how tough it is at the start."

My first feeling was relief: My wife had a solid support network to lean on. But that soon passed, and another emotion surfaced in its place. It was envy, and it was asking a simple question: "Where's *my* Jenny?"

I have friends. Many are dads. But the idea that another dad would send a message, just checking in, on how I was feeling? And an essay-length one? It wouldn't happen. For the women in our lives, it comes naturally: Through thousands of years of herd behavior, and a society that allows, expects, and (some might say) forces women to take more empathetic roles than men, mothers have developed a sixth sense toward maternal group support. Scientists and anthropologists will argue until they're blue in the face whether this is evolutionary or social, but either way, it is deeply embedded and almost inescapable during those first few weeks and months. Branches of support reach out to protect. Women understand how their friends are feeling. Men do not.

Science confirms these behaviors, again and again. A 2018 University of Cambridge study into the empathy quotient (EQ) demonstrated across forty-six thousand participants measurable differences in recognizing each other's thoughts and feelings. It confirmed that women are—on average—more empathetic than men. But this study came with a twist. It was run in partnership with genetics company 23andMe, which asked participants to provide a saliva sample for analysis. The researchers found that these empathy differences were fundamentally not rooted in our DNA; zero genetic variants contribute to different levels of empathy across the sexes. The differences stem from socialization patterns, entrenched across cultures and generations. Research repeatedly confirms it, regardless of country of birth or social status: Women more easily understand each other, think intuitively, and respond appropriately while men view the world through logic- and rule-based systems, aiming to diagnose and solve problems rather than listen to and understand them.

One is not better than the other; different activities demand different states. But during this critical moment—becoming a parent for the first time and feeling your life shift forever—moms are looking out for each other in a way that dads aren't. Jenny's message confirmed it. Looking through my own texts, I saw it echoed. "How's it going?" a friend might ask. "All good," I'd reflexively respond when I clearly was not.

The odds are stacked against us—and we dealt the cards to ourselves. Men aren't supporting each other during this tectonic plate-shifting of what it means to be a man, as we experience an eruption of emotions and memories, and not all of them positive. We lack the language, the social skills, and society's permission to discuss these feelings openly with each other. It's a classic two-sided problem: Those who need help don't ask for it, and those who could help don't know where to start. How can dads begin to pull out of this doom spiral?

The Deck Is Stacked

There is no other job in the world that you'd be hired for—and be entrusted with the livelihood of small children—without significant training. But we're thrust into parenting and expected to figure it all out on the fly. We shift into survival mode, allowing fatherhood to happen to us; we experience it as a reactive experience, not a proactive one. There are already a litany of problems to solve with friends and family, new obstacles to overcome at work, and fires that must be extinguished in every corner of our lives. And now this?

As men begin to step up to the plate more equally in raising their children, they're locked in for both highs and lows: sleep deprivation, increased stress, societal pressures to be both a perfect parent and productive employee. (Again, not new to any of the moms reading this.) Fathers face a profound lack of structured support. When your wife has her first scan, you are handed a folder of resources, pamphlets overflowing with everything she will need: breastfeeding support groups, postpartum checkups, prenatal baby yoga classes. But for Dad? A slap on the back and the assumption you'll deal with it.

Once the baby arrives, this pattern repeats. Parenting groups are overwhelmingly female, and even those open to all genders revert to female-focused discussion topics. It makes sense: Men aren't turning up in these spaces and are unlikely to open up about their problems even if they do. Women have used such gatherings for centuries. They bring their babies to a Tuesday afternoon sing-along before grabbing a cup of coffee afterward—a group of moms, talking together, about this pivotal change in life circumstance. When do dads do this? Men are, of course, permitted to join these groups. But there's a particular flavor to being the sole dad in an otherwise all-female group. (It's like storming the stage in a Union Jack dress during a Spice Girls reunion.) I attended a few of these with my daughter, and while I'm sure things have gotten better in the ten years since, I can still see myself receding into the background, like Homer Simpson slowly reversing into the hedge, before walking out with feeling that "these groups are not for me." The message is subtle but pervasive: Mothers are parents; fathers are…something else?

Structures, whether informal or intentionally defined, have—quite rightly—supported new moms for decades. The Edinburgh Postnatal Depression Scale (EDPS) is a series of questions that nurses, doctors, and social workers ask new moms in order to screen them for postpartum depression. Ten simple questions on how you've been feeling that have been used since 1987—you absolutely know a woman who has been asked these. It has proven remarkably effective, correctly identifying 70 to 85 percent of mothers who are experiencing depression, leading to a 39 percent reduction in postpartum depression rates when combined with follow-up care.

Did you get asked these questions? Almost certainly not. Even though studies have found that asking dads exactly the same questions will identify the majority of paternal postpartum depression cases—once the benchmark scores factor in men's unwillingness to talk about their emotions. This diagnostic blind spot means that untold numbers of struggling fathers simply slip through the cracks. Research on maternal postpartum depression is solid and thorough—in part because we have known about it for thousands of years. As early as 460 BCE, Hippocrates wrote about a "delirium and mania" experienced by women in the months after childbirth. It was clinically recognized as early as the 1850s, with French psychiatrist Louis-Victor Marcé treating "the insanity of pregnant women and new mothers." In 1994, upon its inclusion in the *Diagnostic and Statistical Manual of Mental Disorders*, it became formally recognized as a mental health condition in the United States.

Data consistently shows that 10 to 15 percent of new moms will deal with postpartum depression. But for dads, the ballparks remain vague at best. Early research on paternal postpartum depression in 2003 took a swing, positing it as affecting anywhere between 1 and 25 percent of dads. A 2022 meta-analysis, looking at over twenty thousand men across forty-seven studies, found that around 9 percent of new dads will develop the condition, although the authors admitted this number is likely an underestimate due to lack of routine screening, measurement tools that focus on female-presenting symptoms, and the lower likelihood of men seeking medical help. My conversations with men have echoed these findings, giving me the sense that we're at the higher end of the scale, particularly as awareness increases and stigma diminishes—albeit at a much slower pace than required.

Becoming a parent isn't just bad for your mental health—your physical health will suffer too. Forty-eight percent of parents say that on "most days" their level of stress is "completely overwhelming" (double the figure for nonparents). This stress is often managed through overeating and drinking, and exacerbated by a lack of exercise, meaning "early-onset dad bod" becomes an unintended side effect. You'll neglect your own body as you start looking after a new, tiny one. Your relationship will suffer—you should prepare to minimize these effects while also observing their inevitability. (I am reminded of those warring couples who believed that "having a baby will bring us closer together," completely oblivious that it was akin to inviting the Big Bad Wolf to come check out the ornate sand castle you'd built.)

Bringing a child into the world means going from being the most important person in each other's lives to the second-most important—an instant demotion. Just thinking about work and sport—the key areas where men experience demotion—it's clear that we don't handle it very well. When a father's parenting approach differs from a mother's—as it inevitably will—he may be corrected, critiqued, or simply nudged aside. "Don't do it like that" can become a steady drumbeat in those early months, and while not malicious—rather deeply rooted in the pressure mothers face to get everything right—the impact can be profound, and sometimes irreversible. There are only so many times you can be told you're doing something wrong before you'll stop trying to do it right, retreating into a peripheral role—the fun dad, the disciplinarian, the fixer-upper—reinforcing the very dynamics we are working to escape. Equally, we can find ourselves guilty of worshipping at the altar of untouchable motherhood, providing us with the convenient side effect of abdicating responsibility. With this vicious cycle—less involvement leads to less confidence, less confidence brings less competence, less competence justifies less involvement—ultimately all roads lead away from richer relationships with your children.

As masculinity transforms, traditional structures resist being pulled into the present with everything they have. I remember being told a story a few years ago about a boy in my daughter's class who fell over, ripped his knee open, and was bleeding everywhere. He maintained a stoic, straight face throughout. And the reason he didn't shed a tear? Because his dad had taught his three sons that "boys don't cry."

The language we use and normalize through generations sets beliefs in stone. "Man up," we are told when we talk about our feelings. "Grow a pair" when we need to be brave. "Don't be a pussy" if you try to escape the norms of the group. By the time you become a dad, you've internalized this muteness so completely that you don't even recognize it as a problem. You're just like everyone else. And then a tiny human arrives, and they need everything from you. We watch our children learn to navigate the world, forgetting that simultaneously, they're watching us do the same. No one teaches you how to raise kids. If you're lucky, you grew up under the tutelage of two great teachers—your own parents—but many weren't so fortunate. Parents are stuck in one of two mindsets: *closed parenting*, where you're fixed in your worldview, shut off from new experiences and ways of operating, parenting on autopilot, sitting in the front seat of a self-driving car and allowing fatherhood to happen to you; or *open parenting*, searching for new experiences, better ways to be, different ways to think—learning how to be a kinder father, more intentional with your time and energy, and making intentional choices to becoming a better dad. Shifting from closed to open parenting can require all of your effort to undo decades of mental programming.

I Hope This Existential Crisis Finds You Well

My wife went back to the UK with our newborn son. We were a few months into raising two children, and she wanted to see her parents. I stayed home with my daughter. I'd get her to school and back, and in the hours between I'd sit in a stupor. While men and women present some similar symptoms in postpartum depression—difficulty bonding with their children, fatigue, loss of interest, social withdrawal—there are key differences. Men manifest depression through irritability, anger, and frustration. They're also more likely to indulge in risk-taking and addictive behaviors. Men are twice as likely to get addicted to drugs or alcohol in the year after the birth of their child. It makes sense why this is less prevalent in women—when the mother is the primary carer, giver, and maintainer of life, these addictions would significantly hinder her ability to breastfeed and keep the baby alive.

Increased alcohol consumption, substance abuse, pursuing extramarital affairs, gambling, impulse purchases, and pursuing unnecessary risks are all side effects of paternal postpartum depression, behaviors that provide dopamine hits that act as escape hatches, distractions to avoid the emotional pain that new dads feel. I'm thankful that of all the addictions I could have fallen into, I ended up with one that would have a minimal impact on my family. I didn't develop a hard drug habit or lose my life savings in an online casino. Instead, with every spare moment,

I'd boot up the Xbox, and fall into an online first-person shooter called *Destiny*.

It provided a sense of forward progress in a world where I felt stagnant. When I sat down and played this game it wasn't about escapism; it was about being able to feel in control of a situation, something I felt was deeply missing in real life. I could press a button to tell a character to jump or shoot and he'd do it. But no matter what I did with my son, I couldn't stop him from crying. Julie Muncy, writing in *Wired* magazine a few months after my son was born, called this very game "catnip" for people with depression. My week without my wife and son took on a new, nocturnal cadence—out of sight from them, I was free to indulge in my worst tendencies. Night after night, I sat, locked into the sofa, grinding the game until the sun came up, before realizing with shame that I needed to pull some clothes on and take my daughter to school. Bleary-eyed, I'd make my way there, drop her off, come home, and fall into bed, before repeating the process once again the next night. When my wife came home, I told her what had been happening, that I'd found out about something called "paternal postpartum depression" and that I needed help. It was the first step in the right direction.

A few weeks later, I was talking on the phone with Justin, a close friend.

"How are you doing?" he asked.

I found myself about to drop into the back-and-forth patter men do reflexively, no matter how we're feeling: "Yeah all good, you know. What about you?" But I caught myself. I stopped. I went off-script. And I told him, "No, I'm not okay. I haven't been for a while. I don't really know what is going on, but I think I've got this thing. It's postpartum depression, but it's for dads now? I didn't even know it exists. But apparently 10 percent of new dads get it."

I was still in my early days of learning about this disorder, and that stat scared me. To get through this, I knew I'd need to open up and talk to other men. And if 10 percent of dads might have it, I'd need to open up to an entire gang of male friends with kids to find one who had been through it—and that was assuming they both had the emotional intelligence to know what was going on and were open to talking with another man about it. I was doing these calculations in my head, realizing the odds weren't in my favor, when Justin interrupted my train of thought: "I have two friends that have told me something similar. Do you want me to ask if you can talk to them?"

I couldn't believe my luck. The first father that I'd talked to about this already knew two dads who'd been through it. Justin put me in touch with Mike a few days later. Like me, Mike worked in advertising and had found it hard to adapt after the birth of his child. As I listened to him telling his story, it felt like a reflection of my own. After his second child was born, he'd been feeling angry, disconnected, just not himself. And he'd also spent an ungodly amount of time playing *Destiny*—the very video game I'd gotten hooked on.

Mike and I spoke every few weeks, our bond strengthened by difficulty and distance, the paradox of finding it easier to open up to a stranger than a friend. That connection became a lifeline for us both—a thread of understanding when the rest of the world was oblivious to what we were going through. As I scroll back through our WhatsApp history I can see our back-and-forth: We'd share how we were feeling, swap occasional news articles about fatherhood, give our opinion on upcoming *Destiny* loot drops. This simple connection—two dads supporting each other when structural systems had failed us—provided something we both sorely missed: recognition. We weren't alone. Our experiences weren't unique. The problem wasn't just us—it was everywhere. "Connecting with you was a game-changer for me," Mike told me, years later. "I think being so far apart physically allowed us to get incredibly close without judgment."

The stats, studies, and stories I share aren't academic observations; they're evidence of a system in which fathers are forced to struggle in silence. We feel the deck is stacked against us—not because we're not up to the job, but because the models of fatherhood we inherited are broken, and the support systems we need don't exist. Fatherhood is challenging beyond sleepless nights and new logistics. We are forced to recognize that no one is coming to save us, and that we must become the circuit breakers ourselves—the ones who say "enough" and slam the brakes on the cycle of isolated suffering.

Let's hear it from the dads on...opening up

The hardest part for me is to figure out how to prevent myself from passing on all of my worries and insecurities to my daughter. Last week, after I finished working and came downstairs to look after her she said, "Let's work, Dad," so we start playing, and she says, "We have to do meetings!" and starts bashing on the keyboard I gave her. And I started crying. Not for her; she's doing innocent play, modeling behavior and being a bit creative about it. I cried for me, because I am so far from fulfilled and happy with anything to do with my job, but I have to keep that to myself, because we have bills to pay. I cried, I think, because I thought about what kind of (better) dad I might be if I was happy with the other parts of my life. **Chad**

I've got a good group of friends, but we never talk about the real stuff. I could tell them every detail about my football team's chances this year, or debate the latest Netflix show everyone is watching, but I've never once said I was struggling as a dad. And that's not because I don't want to. It's because I don't even know how to start that conversation. It's like we've all agreed to build this wall between us, and even if I could find the door, I don't think I'd know how to open it. **Matt**

A mate of mine finally told me he was having panic attacks after his daughter was born. I was floored—not because he was struggling, but because I realized I'd seen the signs and said nothing. Men don't get taught how to look out for each other like that—I'd grown up for years watching my dad bottle up all his feelings; the most emotion he'd show was a thumbs-up emoji on text. Since then I've made a promise to myself: If I think a friend's in trouble, I'll ask twice, I'll push past the "Yeah, I'm fine." It still feels awkward, but I'd rather risk awkwardness than lose a mate to silence. **Edward**

CHAPTER 4

Breaking the Cycle

I wanted you to have your own life, apart from fear—even apart from me. I am wounded. I am marked by old codes, which shielded me in one world and then chained me in the next.

—Ta-Nehisi Coates, *Between the World and Me*

Old rule: *Hide your weaknesses.*
New rule: *Vulnerability equals strength.*

Philip Larkin's 1971 poem "This Be the Verse" captured parenthood's original sin: We inherit behaviors we never asked for and carry forward the unresolved wounds of those who came before us. Your parents "fuck you up," Larkin suggested, often against their best intentions, the poem acting as a cultural shorthand for inherited pain. For decades, this fatalism felt inevitable. But what if it wasn't?

During my years of writing about fatherhood, and after conversations with thousands of dads across the world, I've begun to realize there's a way to push back against everything that we inherited and put us back in control. This is a path I've walked myself and will likely continue on for the rest of my life. It is a pattern I have witnessed in the journey of countless others. It takes the form of five stages:

I. ***Recognition:*** *Identifying inherited patterns and understanding how they shape our experience of fatherhood.*

II. ***Resistance:*** *Understanding barriers, internal and external, that make change so challenging and an admission of the depth of the work that needs to be done.*

III. ***Revelation:*** *The discovery that what we feared might destroy us actually strengthens us, and that what appears to be a dark and dangerous path can become a source of great power.*

IV. ***Reconstruction:*** *The deliberate work of building something new. Not just abstaining from harmful patterns but actively creating better alternatives.*

V. ***Renewal:*** *What this new world looks like from the other side.*

This journey isn't linear. It's just as likely that you'll find yourself moving back and forth between stages rather than progressing clockwise, akin to Joseph Campbell's *The Hero's Journey*. Recognition may trigger resistance; reconstruction requires returning to revelation. But together, these five elements create a path toward breaking cycles persisting for generations. This isn't easy work—it requires confronting uncomfortable truths about both ourselves and those who raised us. But by traveling this path, we become the ones who say "the buck stops here," creating futures for our children different than the ones we inherited and making deliberate choices about the legacy we leave.

Recognition: Identifying Inherited Patterns

After my daughter was born, the first person I called was my mum. I felt a connection to her I'd never felt in my life. I was in tears—let's be honest here, I was a mess throughout—but, in that moment, I was overwhelmed with this pure feeling of love for another person. Through the sobbing, I told her, "I can't believe you did that for me."

In that moment, I saw my mother like I had never seen her before. I had spent the years running up to fatherhood reflecting on all the ways I'd be different from my parents when my time came. And then, in an instant, I was filled with empathy and understanding for what they'd done. On the day I was born, my father was three weeks shy of twenty-three years old. Twenty-three! I can't pinpoint exactly what I was doing at that age—memories are blurry, techno was blaring, we're deep in unreliable-narrator territory with no sign of escape. But it's safe to say I could barely look after myself, never mind a screaming baby.

Becoming a parent and being able to navigate through—rather than fight against—these shifts in our centers of gravity and sense of self can lead to reality-shifting perspectives. If you've ever had anyone bore you to death retelling a psychedelic experience—and don't worry, I'll be one of those insufferable people before this book is finished—then you'll be familiar with the "messages" that people come back with: earth-shattering revelations that (if I'm being mean) read like Hallmark cards or (if I'm being kind) come off like second-grade Beatles lyrics. "I went on a five-hour psilocybin trip and realized that 'all is love.'" "At the end of two nights on ayahuasca I realized that 'all we are is energy.'"

From the perspective of a new dad, I realized I'd watched my parents grow up in front of my eyes. I sat front row during a period of their development when—thinking back to myself at that age—I was only whisker clear of weekends on dance floors, self-medicating to figure out who I was and who I might become. My parents passed down to me what had been passed down to them—a generation of children growing up in Northern Ireland, my father one of fifteen siblings, a boy and girl who left the country at the tail end of the 1970s and the height of the Troubles.

There were patterns they inherited and passed on, as so many parents did before them. Much has changed in what is expected of men today, but of all the positive shifts in fatherhood over the past half century I'd personally rank one atop the pile: as of 2023, sixty-five countries—mostly European and Latin American—have outlawed acts of physical violence committed by parents toward children. Even in countries where it is still legal to hit your child, shifting attitudes mean that it is done less overall and openly admonished in public (though sadly still occurring behind closed doors).

You may have been hit as a child. It may have been a light "spanking." Maybe it was harder, and termed "discipline" or "tough love," or justified by religion and tradition. Whatever it was called, we now understand its impact. The data tells a stark story: In a 1995 study, 90 percent of US parents reported using corporal punishment on their children at least once, with 40 to 60 percent having used it within the last six months. In the UK during the same period, around 80 percent of children experienced physical discipline at home. For those born in the 1980s, spanking and other forms of physical discipline were not just common—they were the norm.

Research has conclusively demonstrated that physical punishment increases the risk of negative developmental outcomes. Not only does it lead to increased aggression, but it is also highly correlated with adult mental health problems and reduced cognitive development. Perhaps most importantly, numerous studies have established that physical punishment causes aggressive behaviors in children rather than the other way around. A landmark 2012 paper in the *Canadian Medical Association Journal* starkly noted that "no study has ever found that physical punishment enhances developmental health."

In 1999, the National Society for the Prevention of Cruelty to Children (NSPCC), the UK's leading children's charity, kicked off a groundbreaking advertising and fundraising campaign. It was a watershed moment, aiming to fundamentally shift societal attitudes in violence toward children, driving the conversation to the forefront of national consciousness and demanding action at the highest levels of government. It successfully placed child protection on the political agenda, prompting significant legislative changes and increased public awareness. The simple, yet powerful, demand was for a "Full Stop" to child abuse. The campaign's television advertisements were a cultural force. They didn't shy away from the harsh realities of child abuse. One memorable ad showed posters of a footballer, children's cartoon characters, Action Man, and even the Spice Girls covering their eyes, demonstrating our complicity in avoiding the realities of the situation. Celebrities lent their support, and people on the street wore green lapel pins as a shibboleth, indicating their membership in a group attempting to form a protective ring around the country's children, grasping toward a future world where they would be seen and heard but never hurt. Ads showed the faces of ordinary people, implied stories of suffering within our own communities, and children's voices begging their parents to stop. It was deliberately confrontational—designed to shock a country out of complacency and to force us to acknowledge the hidden pain. It was a call to action, a demand that we, as a society, say "enough is enough."

In 1654, French philosopher Blaise Pascal wrote, "All of humanity's problems stem from man's inability to sit quietly in a room alone." He wasn't wrong then, and he isn't wrong now. Generations of fathers have struggled with this stillness, preferring action—in whatever form, even violent—over the discomfort of reflection. A blown lid was an acceptable alternative to regulating emotions effectively. It's heartening to realize how dramatically attitudes have shifted toward corporal punishment. In the United States, national survey data shows a steady decline in both approval and use of spanking over the last few decades; the number of parents who admitted to using physical violence as punishment dropped almost 28 percent between 1975 and 2014. In the UK, polling has found that rejection of physical punishment has climbed sharply, with more than two-thirds of adults now saying it is never acceptable, driven by the sterling work by the NSPCC. What was fundamentally accepted—nay, encouraged—back then is increasingly viewed as harmful and unnecessary today.

British novelist Marina Warner, writing in 1989, said, "Britain was the last developed country where beating schoolchildren was respectable. This was outlawed [in 1988] by one vote in Parliament." This change compounded the difficulties dads face stepping into a redefined version of fatherhood beyond the protect, provide, and preside reward chart, golden stickers indicating our contribution to the success of the family unit. The role of disciplinarian became something that, to briefly switch into business-speak, "was a well-defined and significant part of the project that spoke to our strengths and fell within our realm of expertise." Dads looked around and saw it enabled and encouraged among their peers. They went to pray on the Sabbath and heard sermons on its importance from the altar: "Whoever spares the rod hates their children, but the one who loves their children is careful to discipline them," advised the book of Proverbs.

Swiss psychologist Alice Miller, writing in *For Your Own Good*, an exploration of parent-inflicted violence, said, "I can imagine that someday we will regard our children not as creatures to manipulate or to change but rather as messengers from a world we once deeply knew, who can reveal to us more about the true secrets of life than our parents were ever able to." (Ironically, while Miller is celebrated for exposing the hidden cruelties of childhood, her own son Martin later revealed that she was unwilling to apply those insights at home.) Breaking the cycle isn't led by rational and intellectual thoughts—it's deep, emotional work. For many men, this presents a unique challenge. We desperately need to access the very emotions we've been told to repress since boyhood.

What is expected from fathers has widened while the tools in our arsenal have—mercifully, in many cases—become limited. Yet we still lack effective alternatives. A parent raising a hand to hit a child in public today elicits the same outrage that a husband hitting his wife would have done in the 1950s when domestic violence became more widely criminalized and prosecuted. For generations, women have united to hand down the tools and techniques to raise children—how to feed, how to soothe, how to nurture, how to care, how to practice love in all its expressions. For dads, we don't know where to start. Recognition begins when we acknowledge the patterns passed down to us—both the ones we want to keep and those we need to break. Or as Karl Ove Knausgaard writes in *Boyhood Island*, the third book of his *My Struggle* series:

> *I am alive, I have my own children, and with them I have tried to achieve only one aim: that they shouldn't be afraid of their father. They aren't. I know that. When I enter a room, they don't cringe, they don't look down at the floor, they don't dart off as soon as they glimpse an opportunity, no, if they look at me, it is not a look of indifference, and if there is anyone I am happy to be ignored by it's them. If there is anyone I am happy to be taken for granted by, it's them. And should they have completely forgotten I was there when they turn forty themselves, I will thank them and take a bow and accept the bouquets.*

Resistance: Spelunking into the Well of Feelings

The books you read. The podcasts you listen to. The movies you watch. The company you keep. If it isn't blazingly clear already, throughout this book—and for as long as I live—I'll continue to bang the drum on how these cultural artifacts can offer a mirror to your own experience and unlatch doors toward change. All that's needed is to keep your mind open, follow your curiosities, and see how far down the rabbit hole they take you.

During the pandemic, my wife sent me a podcast she thought I'd enjoy. Freaky folk singer Devendra Banhart (solid start) was talking about a book he had found helpful during the 2021 lockdown (usefulness demonstrated, sign me up), exploring modern retellings of ancient Buddhist teachings (okay, sold). It was to become my first episode of Krista Tippett's *On Being*, a series of conversations I'd spend hundreds of hours with in the years to come.

One night, I lay on my son's bedroom floor, my hand through the wooden slits in his crib. I was rubbing his back to help with his pandemic baby separation anxiety, which seems to affect so many children born between 2019 and 2021—that brief window where the world was turned upside down, and most parents were always home, navigating uncharted territory while trying to wind down at the end of yet another unprecedented day. I had put the podcast on to help nod me off on the roll-out mattress. But it had the opposite effect: I was hooked, wired in, rewinding over and over so I didn't miss a beat. Banhart read the words of Pema Chödrön, the Tibetan Buddhist nun, advising us what to do *When Things Fall Apart* and how navigating difficult times can bring us closer together:

> *Awakening is frequently described as a journey to the top of a mountain. We leave our attachments and our worldliness behind and slowly make our way to the top. The only problem with this metaphor is that we leave all the others behind—our drunken brother, our schizophrenic sister, our tormented animals and friends. Their suffering continues, unrelieved by our personal escape. In the process of discovering "bodhichitta" (a noble or awakened heart), the journey goes down, not up. Instead of transcending the suffering of all creatures, we move toward the turbulence and doubt. We jump into it. We slide into it. We tiptoe into it. At our own pace, without speed or aggression, we move down and down and down. With us move millions of others, our companions in awakening from fear. At the bottom we discover water. Right down there in the thick of things, we discover the love that will not die.*

We remain obsessed with individual achievement, always equating success with elevation: "climbing the ladder," "scaling my Everest," "being on top of the world." But Chödrön offers a different path: What if going higher isn't the goal? What might be found when we head deeper? What lies beneath? Many men never discover, because they are warned away from the Well of Feelings at an early age. "It's dangerous," young boys are told. "Don't look down there. Stop crying. Don't get emotional." We learn to stay away from the well. We stick a big warning sign next to it: **BEWARE. STAY OUT.** We nail it closed with old wooden planks, to be avoided at all costs. As we grow older, our fear of what is inside strengthens. Maybe you saw other boys get bullied for playing near it: holding a baby doll, talking about their feelings, crying on the playground. For acting "like a girl."

And then you find yourself with a kid. Back to the well you go. Face-to-face with these unavoidable feelings. These tiny humans bring you cautiously back, wondering what was down there all along, carefully prying the nails out of the old boards that kept you out—or that kept something else in. And you realize this place is beautiful, somewhere where, as Karl Ove Knausgaard wrote, "All that was left was emotion, and it was stark, you were looking straight into the essence of human existence, the very nucleus of life, and thus you found yourself in a place where it no longer mattered what was actually happening."

We're programmed to believe that fatherhood will be in direct competition with our goals, our career, our ambition, our passions and hobbies. Choose success in your job or choose to be a great dad. Because you can't have both. If you want to climb the ladder, there will be late nights, early mornings, missed bedtimes, and busy weekends. We're force-fed success stories of childless men who get up at five a.m. and do an hour of emails, forty-five minutes of Wim Hof breathwork, and then ninety minutes on the Peloton. If you've got kids? Forget about it. Forget about success. It's over.

Fatherhood begins to look like a weakness. A loss of your killer edge. Something that brings you further from "the top." (Again with the elevation!) But the Well of Feelings changes all of that. Because when you head down there, it doesn't take away. It's additive. As you go deeper down, you learn more about yourself. You conquer the fears you had, freeing the chains they placed on you. When you descend to the bottom, it's a real

Bruce Wayne moment. Because it's not a well—down below is a Batcave, a subterranean HQ filled with cool shit that can bring a new perspective to every aspect of your life. Empathy. Tenderness. Emotion. So much power that you can put back into your career and passions: how you create, how you communicate, how you understand. Your ability to connect with others becomes your superpower.

Revelation: Opening the Empathy Valve

The journey into the Well of Feelings isn't simply personal exploration—it's biological transformation. When men become fathers, our bodies and brains quite literally change to prepare us for caregiving. Testosterone levels drop, oxytocin production increases, and neural pathways associated with empathy and emotional responsiveness strengthen. Science has confirmed what many fathers have felt for years: Fatherhood rewires us for connection. This physical shift mirrors a psychological one—where once we maintained emotional distance, New Fatherhood forces proximity. Where we once saw weakness in vulnerability, we discover its immeasurable strength. This revelation—that the qualities we were taught to suppress can become our greatest assets—transforms not just how we parent, but how we move through the world.

Listening to Banhart and Tippett talk through Chödrön's book, it wasn't lost on me that Bodhi—my son's name—is a central concept to Buddhism, representing the state of enlightenment. There is a direct line that runs from my experience learning to love him years ago to writing this book. Having a son brought me deep into the well in a way that having a daughter never did, and forced me to confront the generations of men who had come before me. It made me realize the work I needed to do to break these cycles, and the power I could take from what I found down there.

Chödrön herself showed an innate understanding of fatherhood's ability to unlock empathy:

The father of a two-year-old talks about turning on the television and unexpectedly seeing the bombing of the federal building in Oklahoma City. He watched as the firemen carried the limp and bloody bodies of toddlers from the ruins of the day-care center on the building's first floor. He says that in the past he was able to distance himself from other people's suffering. But since he's become a father, things have changed. He feels as if each of those children were his child. He feels the grief of all the parents as his own grief. This kinship with the suffering of others, this inability to continue to regard it from afar, is the discovery of our soft spot.

I have felt this. I am sure you have too. I have come to think of it as the opening of a valve marked *empathy*. I don't recall exactly when it happened, though in hindsight it feels more like a gradual loosening than the flick of a switch. Now that I'm a parent, everything feels more, all of the time. And that can be hard. But it's also a direct route to experiencing more daily moments of joy. As we move toward "the discovery of our soft spot" together, we must remember: This path is treacherous, but few are more impactful and emotionally rewarding. Empathy and vulnerability, the emotional yin and yang to shift the most important relationships in your entire life, are essential in your interactions with your children and partner. Empathy helps you understand their feelings. Vulnerability makes it easier for them to understand yours.

We arrive on the shores of fatherhood having traveled through different waters. Some alight after smooth sailing. Others have had wave after wave crash upon their boat, have weathered storms leaving indelible marks on both ship and sailor. If your childhood was far from ideal, becoming a father will bring long-dormant emotions and experiences to the surface, waves that must be navigated before all are consumed in their wake. An increased capacity for empathy means being more emotionally impacted, more often. You'll feel higher highs and lower lows—a ping-ponging common to new parents. Science tells us that this is worth it: People with higher levels of empathy live longer, happier lives with stronger social connections and better physical health outcomes. They recover more quickly from setbacks and demonstrate greater resilience in the face of adversity. And guess what? You're in luck. Becoming a father and forming strong emotional bonds with your children is a fast track to empathy in every aspect of your life. More empathy in the world can only be a good thing—even if it means crying at Pixar movies more often than you used to.

Reconstruction: The Japanese Art of Kintsugi

I opened up to Kam, a close friend, from the better side of my depressive episode. "It's strange," I told him, "after how tough it all was, I'm grateful for it. Putting myself back together made me realize how strong I could be."

Nietzsche famously said, "What doesn't kill you makes you stronger." I know you're rolling your eyes as you read this, because I'm rolling mine as I write it. It's so far beyond the line marked cliché that it crossed the city limits an hour ago. But it's a phrase that remains with us, almost 150 years later, because it resonates deeply. It is a profound human truth, speaking of progress, healing, and resilience.

I was moved to write after going through one of the darkest periods I've ever faced, in a life with enough of them already. I came out of the other side and was staggered that there weren't more men talking about it. But as soon as I started talking to them privately, I found dads who had been through it too. And as I started to write about it publicly, I've had hundreds email me from across the world and share their experiences. I've had close friends open up, realizing that they'd been through the same thing themselves, and how their reactions and behaviors nearly tore their families apart during those tender, fragile months. If there's any chance at all that we're going to become better men, better husbands, and better dads, the only hope in hell we have is by starting to show our scars to each other. Only this will enable us to escape the avalanche of baggage we bring to fatherhood—whether it was passed on to you by all the dads that came before you, or by society itself.

When a pot breaks, the first thing you do—after realizing which kid did it—is throw it away before it can cause any injuries. If it's one you like, you might bust out the superglue in an attempt to make it good as new. But practitioners of the Japanese art of kintsugi will try another approach. They will create a lacquer mixed with powdered gold and repair the item, with these golden seams visible to all, the process of repair inseparable from the object itself (in Japanese, 金継ぎ literally translates as "golden joining").

What was broken is reborn anew, more compelling than it was before. It is imbued with a sense of history, a new beauty, where the rupture becomes part of the story, and the process of repair becomes as important as the craft of construction: damage acknowledged, beauty restored. As Leonard Cohen's song "Anthem" suggests, these flaws become essential openings for light. Bonnie Kemske, author of *Kintsugi: The Poetic Mend*, called the practice "an intimate metaphoric narrative of loss and recovery, breakage and restoration, tragedy and the ability to overcome it. It speaks of fortitude, uniqueness and the beauty in survival, leading us to a respectful acceptance of loss and hardship."

Men are trained to see weakness and vulnerability as two synonyms that exist inside the bubble of business—trapped inside a modern-day Matrix where we can't see the world as it is but only as a representation of the world our captors use to keep us placated. It's no wonder we hide our weaknesses away. We pretend they don't exist or work quickly to "fix" them, ensuring that they remain invisible to all but the keenest observer. But these cracks are the making of us. They are proof we are fallible, that we can come back from any bad hand we've been dealt. We all have a set of scars unique to us, and it's only by exposing them and making our repairs visible to the world that we help others do the same. As Hemingway wrote, "The world breaks everyone and afterward many are strong at the broken places."

Keeping my golden seams visible and sharing them publicly reminds me how far I've come and the work it took to get there: gathering the support of my wife, friends, and family; devoting time to many forms of therapy; engaging in the weekly public healing of writing a newsletter for dads navigating these waters together; exploring meditation and mycology; the conversations with other dads who reveal their repairs to me.

These cracks are mine: my struggles, my imperfections, my vulnerabilities, my restoration. I wear them with pride. And I use them to move forward with purpose.

Renewal: New Models for Modern Fathers

When I started looking for help during my dark stretch, searching for fathers with similar experiences in paternal postpartum depression, I found next to nothing. As I came out the other side, I did what felt impossible at the time—I started writing about it. It was 2021, and the humble newsletter was undergoing a resurgence. I committed to writing once a week and seeing where it led. If nobody read it, that would be fine. Still, I'd do it for a year. What happened soon after stunned me: emails flooding in from fathers around the world, each one carrying a similar message: "I thought I was the only one." Men I'd never met wrote paragraphs that could have been pulled from my own diary. Fathers from different continents, cultures, and backgrounds all described the same feelings of disconnection, despair, and the crushing guilt that came with it. These weren't isolated incidents or anomalies. They were evidence of a silent epidemic—men suffering behind closed doors, believing their struggle meant they were failing at fatherhood before they'd barely begun.

"This Be the Verse" became Philip Larkin's most popular contribution to culture. He joked that he expected to hear it recited in his honor by a thousand Girl Guides before he died. Its interpretation of parenthood is a grim one: If harm is inherited, then the only safe move is to opt out entirely. Parents must make a binary decision: Either pass forward their flaws (alongside whatever else they've picked up along the way), or decide against having children. That fatalism felt inevitable in 1971. But today, for a new generation of fathers, an alternative is coming into focus. We can—nay, we must—do the necessary work to prevent what we inherited being passed down forever, unwillingly, stacking the deck against our children.

Old models are being dismantled, without clear new ones to take their place, leaving fathers grasping to make sense of this liminal space: Who am I, if I am not my job, my strength, my ability to benevolently rule over my wife and children? The fathers who commit to making these changes aren't doing it because it is easy. They are doing it because it is difficult. They're asking the crucial question Larkin never considered: What if the pain stops with us? What if fatherhood could be reimagined, not as an inevitable passing down of psychic damage, but as an opportunity for healing?

When we challenge long-held beliefs, we can reduce the influence they exert, and imagine new futures, a world where fathers are no longer seen as secondary caregivers but become equal and essential—their bond with children just as vital as the mother's, and this new world is reflected in parental leave policies and societal attitudes. Where we are freed from the pressure of being sole providers, able to attain a new sense of identity outside our work, becoming humans with depth whose value extends far beyond income generation. Where we are no longer deemed emotionally stunted in their relationships, can talk about their feelings rather than fight them, and practice vulnerability in their own lives, acting as emotional guides for their children. And where we might move beyond being harsh disciplinarians, break with the evil-headmaster archetype, and become nurturing boundary setters who protect rather than punish.

We are the first generation of men fundamentally rejecting aspects of masculinity that don't serve us while holding on to the ones that do. This suggests the transformation we're witnessing isn't so much the replacement of an old model but the reimagining of a new one, expanding the definition of what modern masculinity can encompass. This broader, more flexible understanding of fatherhood creates natural pathways into previously unexplored domains of life we'll discover in the chapters ahead.

Fatherhood is changing—that much is clear. This generation of men are realizing they can learn to ride this wave rather than be crushed under it. Our journey offers hope, an alternative to misery passed through the bark of the family tree, an inheritance transformed. But what's required is a mammoth undertaking—a complete rethinking of the rules of fatherhood. It's no longer enough to identify our limiting beliefs and blame the past for the present. We need new rules to replace them; ones fit for purpose. Soon we'll talk about how we can update the entire operating system of fatherhood. But first, we must understand and audit the internal narratives that we bring to it.

Let's hear it from the dads on…breaking the cycle

I think that there is something in being a dad to a son in particular that can be quite challenging and it has left me feeling vulnerable at times. I found everything came quite naturally with my daughter, but with my son, I've felt a bit different, and it's certainly brought up some old insecurities and vulnerabilities that I've not dealt with, and that on reflection my dad never dealt with either. A lot of it is image stuff and feeling oddly threatened by a one-month-old baby! Which sounds ridiculous to type out (but I guess that's why these things fester because we are too scared to admit them!). I think that part of it is in being a son, they're more comparable to you. Which is definitely something that people love to do—particularly in the early days. **Paul**

Your writing on postpartum depression helped me more than you will ever know. My second-born were identical twins and everyone kept tell me what a gift I received. About three months in I remember telling my wife that they took everything from us and I wished they were never born. There are descriptions and things you put in the article that I literally completely understand, and spoke to me well beyond what you can even imagine. Playing *FIFA* until 4 a.m., sleeping forever and still being tired. Calling myself a loser because I can't process this on my own. How you don't recognize the man in the pictures. Random fog and completely detached from everything—the list goes on. I got to a point where I asked for help, lots of it. We celebrated their third birthday last weekend. I woke up crying and hugged my wife. Everything has been clicking for about eight months after I got help. I don't know if I could have done it without your essay. **Nick**

Thank you, my friend. Today was the first time when I had the courage to research what the hell happened to me in the last two years. I cried reading your essay and it was somehow relieving. Maybe I will find the courage to also share my story and seek help because I am in a really dark place now. But thank you again! I really thought I was alone in this. **Charles**

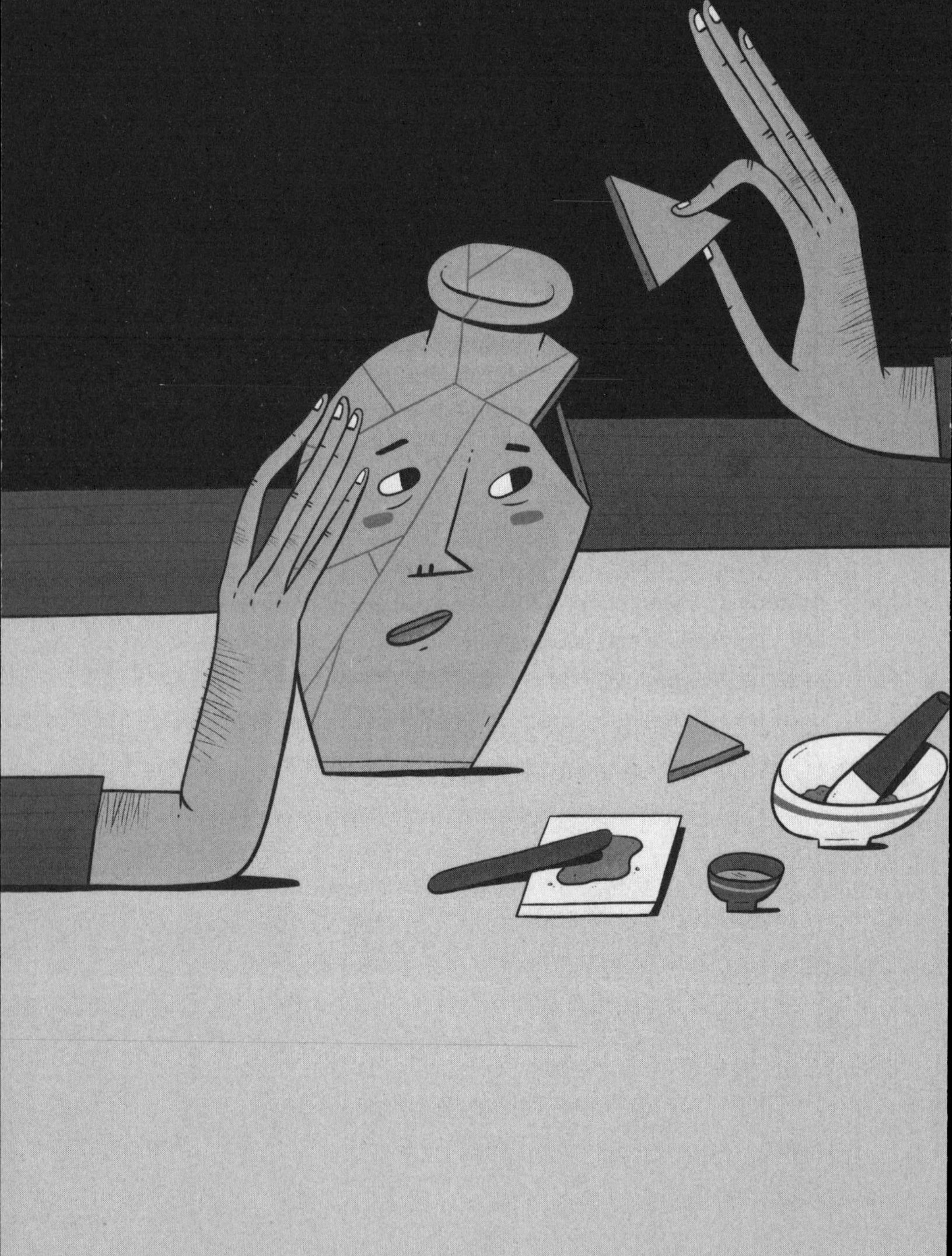

PART II

ALL THE PIECES MATTER

Understanding the history of fatherhood is not enough. We must honestly examine the beliefs that drive it—the interconnected set of personal priorities and societal systems that makes us feel like passengers in the car and not drivers at the wheel.

CHAPTER 5

You Are Not Your Job

Recovering alcoholics talk about needing to hit rock bottom before they are able to climb out. The paradox for the workaholic is that rock bottom is the top of whatever profession they're in.

—David Chang

Old rule: *You are what you do.*
New rule: *You are not your job.*

"So, what do you do?"

There it is. The most annoying, most prevalent, and most "second" question in the world today. (The most "first" question is still "What's your name?" But I wouldn't bet on it being #1 forever.)

It doesn't matter where you are. Out for dinner. Drinks with friends. House party. School pickup. Weekends on playgrounds. Hiking up to the peak of Yosemite's Half Dome. It's all anyone wants to know. And why? Because of a deeply entrenched belief in the United States, now spreading its tentacles across the world: Your job is the most important thing about you and defines who you are.

It's not just cities like New York, London, and San Francisco. It's everywhere. We inherited it from our fathers, and their fathers before them. They were the breadwinners. They went to work. You were left home with Mom. (Ever ask your dad how much time off he got when you were born? Go try it sometime.) These men went out, worked hard, saw their kids on evenings and weekends. They did a job—probably one job, for a long time—and they did it well.

If you go back far enough, jobs didn't define our identities—they became them: Smith, Taylor, Dyer, Slater, Miller, Baker, Spicer, Cook, Fisher, Shepherd—a short selection of surnames and jobs you're familiar with. This naming convention spans cultures: in India, Mehta (accountant) and Lohar (blacksmith); in Russia, Kuznetsov (smith), Popov (priest), and Melnik (miller); and in the Arab world you'll find Al-Najjar (carpenter), Al-Haddad (blacksmith), and Al-Sabbagh (dyer).

When the time came, their sons would take up their tools along with their name. Jesus was the son of God, but he was also the son of a carpenter and followed his dad, Joseph, into the trade. Our ancestors' professions became permanent markers of family identity, passed down through generations, tools and trade for the next son in the lineage. Fathers handed down well-worn livelihoods and successful family businesses to their children who—ready or not—would take the reins. It still happens: I know a handful of people who run (or are in the process of learning to run) their father's business today.

For generations of men that came before us, it wasn't just the type of work you did that defined you—it was how long you did it too. How many had a dad who stayed in the same job most of his life? That was what you did. You worked hard, racked up the years (and the pension), and then bowed out with a gold watch and hopefully enough to die with. If the shit hit the fan, you'd get a new job. But—with hope, and a bit of good luck—it was steady as she goes.

Or steady as she went. Because times have changed. According to the US Bureau of Labor Statistics, men born in the years 1957–1964 (both of my parents are right in that sweet spot) had an average of twelve jobs throughout their entire careers. Twelve jobs across four decades. I'd worked in more places by the time I hit thirty. Once I add up my first few bar and retail gigs (I'll skip the paper route) along with early "foot in the door" advertising jobs, I was well on my way. We're working our way through more roles at younger ages. The days of being sole providers are behind us, as we are expected—and desire—to be equal co-parents too, playing a more active role in fatherhood than any generation of dads before. These factors lead to new feelings and opportunities. Søren Kierkegaard famously saw anxiety as "the dizziness of freedom." And Uncle Ben made sure we never forgot that "with great power comes great responsibility."

In order to reconstruct what fatherhood means today, it's essential to grapple with the concepts that tether it to previous terra firma. That's why we're talking work first, before we dive into the other elements of your life. It's an essential sacred cow we need to diagnose, dissect, and sacrifice: the totemic father as the breadwinner, finding meaning in work and little else. Our sense of purpose and meaning has been historically and intrinsically tied to the work we do, and our inability to feel success without it holds our ability to change in stasis. And all too often we can, as Esther Perel writes, "bring the best of ourselves to work while bringing the leftovers home."

It's only natural that becoming a parent leads to questioning the outsized role that work plays in our lives. We're taught terms like *work-life balance*, which gives these two elements a false equivalence, sitting on opposite sides of a scale, when *work* is in fact a smaller circle inside the larger circle called *life*. (Petition to start calling it the *work-life fried egg*; you read it here first.) When work becomes the core part of your identity, fatherhood begins to feel like a distraction or career sabotage. This path is well trodden, but this generation of men are beginning to ask whether it's a fruitful one. We're surrounded by stories of perceived career "successes" that really mean sacrifice—mental health, marriages, relationships that all fall by the wayside as you attempt to climb the ladder. Fatherhood is shifting, but many in power cling to old worldviews that mean your "work family" is just as important, if not more, than your actual family. I've known managers who only saw their children over the weekend and expected others to follow their example. After my daughter was born, and I was still working at Google—widely perceived as being one of the most progressive, forward-thinking companies in the world—I was chastised for regularly leaving the office at five p.m. to be home for her bath time. Of course, once she was down, I'd be back online, dealing with the deluge of emails and instant messages making their way across the Atlantic and keeping my cortisol running high into the midnight hours. But no, I was clearly putting family first.

We spend our twenties making a name for ourselves. Fatherhood comes along and has us asking bigger questions about how work might fit into our lives, rather than us contorting ourselves around it. Back in 2015, when my daughter was only a year old, I met my good friend Nick for a pizza and a few beers in San Francisco. We'd known each other for close to ten years after working side by side at an ad agency in London. We discussed work, of course. He was about to take a top-secret job in a top-secret lab with another tech titan and was wondering if it was the right move. I was talking about some work-related drama or project that was incredibly important at the time but has since faded into the ether of "shit that didn't actually matter."

We talked about our families too. But conversations kept coming back to work. At one point in the evening, Nick turned to me and said, "In all the years we've known each other, I've always thought the most interesting things about you were what you did outside of work. You spent years running a music blog and club night, you had that famous Tumblr about people turning up to work dressed up like each other, you organized that concert in a church in Manchester. But then you got a job at Google. And now all you do is that."

I've spoken to Nick about this moment many times since. I'll no doubt talk to him again before you read this, to make sure he's still okay with me telling the story. Because he thinks he comes off as cruel in the retelling, but my perspective is entirely different. I am thankful for that moment, for feeling the indescribable pain of searing truth, one that instantly cuts to the core. In a weaker moment, it might have filled me with rage, causing a reaction I'd regret. But that day I was lucky to realize I'd been seen by a friend in a way I could never see myself. It was one of the first times I understood that what I'd been chasing—getting the dream job, climbing the ladder, and then...something else—maybe wasn't what I wanted. That I'd started following the same well-trodden road that ambitious young men had followed before me, without actually asking "Why?"

If that wasn't the path I wanted to be on, what was?

Attraction and the Law of Opposites

Theodore Roosevelt, Mark Twain, and C. S. Lewis were all mistakenly believed to have coined the phrase *comparison is the thief of joy*. We might not know who first spoke it, but I know I've lived it. I'd spent decades having my joy stolen comparing my career trajectory to those more successful than me. No matter how much I'd achieved, I'd spend my time going through the history of those who had done better than me. I'd work backward through their LinkedIn job experience, concocting a work time line from the selected highlights of their career, then measuring it against my own; a professional cover version, a business echo of the particular flavor of sadness that comes from judging your own life against the carefully curated photos of others on Instagram.

For the longest time, my definition of success was clear: Get a job at Google. Sometime around the turn of the millennium—when Google became a better way to find things on the internet than Ask Jeeves or Altavista, and stories started to surface about the type of work, and kind of perks, their employees were enjoying—I knew I wanted to work there. I spent time at various different jobs, never intentionally heading toward the Googleplex, but always having it as a north star, a dream scenario, should things go my way. I headed into the advertising industry in 2010, arriving through a small but increasingly important side hatch marked "digital." I marketed myself as "the geek you're not afraid of putting in front of your most important client." After a few years, that most important client became Obi, a marketing director at Google. She shared my disdain of Facebook—an app that many were beginning to hate—and wondered if I'd be interested in working on something new (a social network called Google+, which would become as hated as Facebook—if not in volume, then at least in negative sentiment). By the end of 2010—after six months of interviews and answering as many "how many windows in New York" questions as I'd been warned about—I got an offer. Contract signed. Box ticked.

I was Heath Ledger's Joker, the dog that finally caught the car. I'd gotten what I was after. Now what? With that long-held goal achieved, there was a void where drive had once been, a fuel tank marked "ambition" running empty just as it was pulling into the driveway. Nature abhors a vacuum, and something had to take its place. It was filled with a definition of success that wasn't my own. I got sucked up into caring about what I once hadn't: internal visibility, promotions, performance scores, industry awards; corporate junk food, filling my sense of success but ultimately unnourishing, eternally unfulfilling. I took the yardstick of what a large company had decreed as success and made it my own. I chased shiny things, eventually following the modern-day gold rush to Silicon Valley, thousands attracted to the West Coast once again, but instead of pickaxes and shovels they were armed with MacBooks and dreams of IPOs and unicorns.

San Francisco was once the home of counterculture, ground zero for turning on, tuning in, and dropping out. But that rebellious spirit had been honed into a capitalist laser, printing circuit boards, building microprocessors, and writing code in an industry that, by 2025, was driving one-third of the value of the US stock market. It had become yet another avenue to chase the American Dream, every individual working their hardest while collectively contributing to shareholder value and growing portfolio prices. The tech industry praised itself for its nonconformism. But as you looked around, the same was all you saw, an illusion of diversity only skin deep: everyone working for the same four companies, having attended the same eight schools, posting to the Instagram grid from the same four ice cream hotspots, lining up every weekend for brunch at the same dozen top-rated restaurants on Yelp.

The city's sense of ambition was as disturbingly homogenized as the style of its inhabitants. What did success look like here? The goal was simple: Don your finest Patagonia fleece and go get paid. If you were running your own company, you needed a venture capitalist or six to fund its growth. And if you worked for one of these companies, it was the place where you could make your mark. Called up to the big leagues. I arrived under similar pretenses. I had no idea where my career was heading, but if the direction I wanted to go was considered "up," then I'd arrived in the right place. Looking around me, I was surrounded by people with a similar set of beliefs. Colleagues who talked about their careers with words like *trajectory*, *velocity*, and *momentum*, words more familiar to builders of medieval catapults than the tech bros who spent their evenings in their inboxes. My ambition had taken me this far. But was it still pointing me in the right direction?

The Corruption of Ambition

Ambition and success are fine bedfellows. If success is planting your flag at the top of the mountain, ambition is what drives you to the summit. Success is the result—the job title, the salary package, the perfect body, whatever sits at the end of that perilous path—while ambition is the fuel that gets you out of bed every morning. Rising, grinding, crushing your to-do list (and competition) on your way there.

When success and ambition align, they act as powerful forces to push you toward a better future. But not always. Their relationship can just as easily push you into a downward spiral, as you furiously try to pull the plane up as the ground approaches fast. My path felt preordained for most of my twenties, and the lion's share of my thirties too. Things changed when I had kids, but not as I expected. It wasn't a stark, everything-changes-in-a-heartbeat shift—more a mild burn that eventually envelops everything it touches.

It's not unusual for new parents to ponder fundamental questions about their life direction. What does success even mean anymore? Society tells us that to be successful is to be wealthy. To be ambitious is to be hungry for the accumulation of wealth. If you were part of an alien race, observing from afar, and asked to rank Earth's inhabitants in order of success, you'd end up with something not a million miles away from *Forbes*'s World's Billionaires List. This annual collection of the world's richest people began in 1987, the same year that Michael Douglas's *Wall Street* trader Gordon Gekko would tell a young Charlie Sheen, "Greed, for lack of a better word, is good."

This is the corrupt perversion of ambition: the pursuit of wealth at all costs. We don't have to look hard to see how such a fundamental belief shapes our understanding of fatherhood. Walter White was stuck in a job he hated, working for students who didn't respect him, still holding on to resentment after selling his part of a company for thousands of dollars instead of billions. Spite can be a powerful motivator, and his journey in becoming Heisenberg was an attempt to reclaim his dignity, power, and the wealth he felt he'd been denied. What is *Breaking Bad* but a sixty-two-episode-long piece of revenge porn, born out of a misplaced sense of ambition? Break all the rules, destroy your enemies, and go out in a blaze of glory while promising everyone who will listen that you're doing it for your family—before finally admitting it was all for your ego. (I wonder how *Breaking Bad* will stand up to a rewatch when you hit fifty, the age that Walter White was supposed to be? Will everything seem clearer then?)

Since time immemorial, we've been spoon-fed tales of ambition through what we watch. In 1992, *Glengarry Glen Ross* explored how deeply intertwined success and survival were, as Alec Baldwin threatened poorly performing salesmen with the sack. Ed Harris wonders who this slick salesman standing at the front of the room might be, asking a simple question—"What's your name?"—leading Baldwin to tear into him with an ostentatious tirade on how the things he owns are all the proof of success he needs:

> *"Fuck you! That's my name! You know why, mister? You drove a Hyundai to get here. I drove an $80,000 red BMW that's parked right outside. THAT'S my name! And your name is you're wanting. You can't play in the man's game...go home and tell your wife your troubles. This watch costs more than your car. I made $970,000 in sales commissions last year. How much did you make? You see, pal, that's who I am, and you're nothing. You're a nice guy? I don't give a shit. Good father? Fuck you! Go home and play with your kids."*

Mad Men hinges entirely on the illusion of identity, and what it means to pretend—at work, at home, to your wife, your children, and your boss alike. Don Draper's existence depends on maintaining the mirage of success in the office, his ambition fueled by the need to escape the demons in his past: voices questioning who he really is under that suit and title. Who is Don without work? He knows the answer deep down and spends seven seasons of spectacular television running from it. And at home? His fatherhood is performative—gifts, vacations, the same charm he can turn on in the office—but is devoid of real emotional depth, and the cycle of intergenerational trauma continues, deepened through his dishonesty and destructive coping mechanisms.

If your personal definition of success is achieved, what comes next? What role does ambition play now? If you find your dream job, hit that bonus target, or make it to the level of seniority you've long felt you've been unfairly denied, then what? Without a new destination, the train will roll to a stop. So you jump back on the hedonic treadmill, point another marker onto the horizon, and take a new definition of success just like the old one: Everything will be fixed once we arrive here, a road that extends off into infinity, or until you die—whichever happens first.

If that's all we've been fed, it's no wonder we become disillusioned by the idea of what success can be. When I think about some of the dads sitting atop the *Forbes* list, the lives they're living don't feel like success to me. But when the world is only telling us one story, how can we ever imagine another?

Enough Is Enough

Alfred, a Swedish friend, once told me about *lagom*, a word that can be translated as "balance" or "moderation" but more accurately represents the idea of "just the right amount." He told me how this mentality influences a definition of success for many Swedes, with people happier, and more satisfied, as they work toward whatever "enough" means to them: a warm home with sufficient space to grow as a family; enough food on the table; a car that's practical, safe, and not flashy (ladies and gentlemen, I give you: the Volvo).

Enough means being happy with your fair share, instead of pushing for the biggest, the best, the most. As John Lithgow reminisces in the opening scenes of *Interstellar*: "Six billion people. Just imagine that, and every last one of them trying to have it all." Because there are diminishing returns when chasing the upper echelons of success. In 2010 Daniel Kahneman (yes, fellow behavioral science nerds, the *Thinking Fast and Slow* guy) found that money does bring happiness (or, in the language of their study, "emotional well-being rises with income") but added, "there is no further progress beyond an annual income of ~$75,000." Newer research disputed this finding, seeing well-being continue to climb after this supposed ceiling, albeit with diminishing returns. Either way, it seems the real question we should be asking isn't "How much can we get?" but instead "How much is enough?"

"Enough" moves with your zip code. If you end up in San Francisco, as we once did—chasing an apparition of success before realizing that shiny block of gold is a foil-covered rock—then a salary of $104,400 would classify you as living below the poverty line, a number that rises to $149,100 if you're raising two children. I know many will read this and think it incredible that a family of four bringing in $150,000 would be living below the poverty line. But having had firsthand experience of the Bay Area's eye-watering cost of living, I can attest to it. Numbeo, the global cost-of-living database, puts the average cost of raising a family in the city as $5,674.70 per month *before rent.* You read that right. In a city where the average three-bedroom family apartment costs $5,600 a month, where it'll set you back $2,900 a month to put your toddler in full-time daycare, and a meal for two at a midrange restaurant will leave you at least $150 out of pocket (and even more once you factor in the $25-an-hour sitter, the taxi, and a tip of at least 20 percent).

So take the exact number of "enough" with a light seasoning of local flavor. There are places where $50,000 a year would be more than sufficient. For others, it would hardly touch the sides. But the actual amount that Daniel Kahneman and Angus Deaton found in their original study was less important than what interviewees did *after* they had hit it. Because while sitting under your threshold would lead to an increase in hardship and what the researchers called "significant emotional pain," they noted that passing it was "neither the road to experienced happiness nor the road to the relief of unhappiness or stress."

In 2022, the journal *Nature Sustainability* published a study on "enough," spanning thirty-three countries and nearly eight thousand participants. A question was posed: What size lottery win would enable participants to live "their ideal life"? Most picked moderate sums of $1 million to $10 million—a foundation to live comfortably, but by no means enough to buy a gold-plated rocket to Mars. The United States stood out in stark contrast to the rest of the world, with participants desiring more money than anywhere else—even regularly citing stratospheric twelve-digit figures. Thirty-two percent of US participants said they'd only entertain offers upward of $100 billion in order to live their life.

Nowhere in the world was higher: 22 percent in South Korea, 19 percent in the UK, as low as 13 percent in France. It's one thing to have a cushion, and quite another to desire wealth so colossal that you'd be raising the next set of *Succession* siblings.

Why does the United States skew extreme? Part is an echo of popular culture and society writ large. Income is the ultimate scoreboard—your numeric proof of success, just like Alec Baldwin and his shiny red BMW. At the same time, there's also the eye-watering cost of living—skyrocketing rents, college fees that can mean six figures' worth of debt, and a medical system that ties your family's health and well-being to your ability to earn.

This means "enough" is something entirely different today than it was for the dads who came before us. Since my parents bought their first house, the average property price in the UK has increased 10x while average salaries have only increased 5x. Buying a home in the 1970s required 4.1x times the average annual income; in 2023, it was 8.8x. A 2023 report claimed it would take the average British adult almost a decade to save up for a down payment, 40 percent longer than in 2012. Part of your fundamental role and the social contract of fatherhood is putting a roof above the head of your family; it is now twice as tough, across every measurable metric, as it was for our parents.

My mum once told me a story about when I was a toddler. The year was 1985; her first son—yours truly—had just turned two years old, and the arrival of my twin sisters would rock our world imminently. We'd just moved into a new house: their first home, bought so long ago that the land registry databases show nothing when I search for its value, but my dad recalls it costing £13,000. The house was located on the main road of a north Manchester town, had rickety old wooden windows that would rattle violently as traffic rolled past, and let in every gale of wind during the all-too-regular storms. They put every penny they had toward the house, and soon after they moved in, a salesman came around offering some PVC windows, promising that they'd keep the house quieter and warmer and reduce their heating bills in the process. And to sweeten the deal, they wouldn't even need to pay up front—they could pay it back over the months to come. Unbeknownst to them, they signed up for the same predatory interest rates that daytime TV advertising would be plagued with in years to come.

They worked hard to get themselves out of that particular money-related pickle. It wasn't their first, and it wouldn't be the last. Thirty-five years later, those same parents came to visit their son in San Francisco. Their trip collided with an immovable object: a product launch for yet another Google app that has since come and gone, joining a graveyard fast running out of plots. I spent most of that time in the office, or on my laptop, shamefully sneaking away to work whenever I could, barely seeing them in the week they were there. I often think about that trip. I'd climbed to a point where anyone would decree my career a huge triumph. But if that was success, why is looking back on it so tinged with regret?

Irish writer and comedian Spike Milligan once said, "All I ask is the chance to prove that money can't make me happy." That I am able to sit here, think these thoughts, and spend hours writing and editing them (and, to an extent, that you have the time to read them) comes from a position of immense privilege. The fact that I'm able to look back on time spent working and living on another continent on a Thursday afternoon, and wonder what didn't work, is indication that I'm able to dedicate brain cycles to tackling issues at the higher tiers of Abraham Maslow's hierarchy of needs than my parents once had. Many find it hard to escape the existential issues deep in its foundations, focused on the primal survival of the family—how to keep the metaphorical wolves from the door, a roof over your head, food on the table. For those parents, *enough* means something entirely different than for those who spend their time, energy, and worry working their way to the summit. The idea of success is clear at lower levels: Earn enough to move from survive to thrive.

But beyond that, what if the stars align for you? If the right combination of factors hit—the right education, with the right network, with the right story in the right industry and just the right time, and with a shake of enough luck—what does your template for success become? A bigger house, a nicer car? My uncle once shared that he was never happier than when he was in his first real job as a salesman, hitting those early markers of success. The Rolling Stones might have said "You can't always get what you want." But when all you've done is tie your sense of success to the work you do, what happens if you're unlucky enough to make your way even close to the summit?

Scaling the Second Mountain

In 2019, *The Second Mountain* was published, written by *New York Times* columnist David Brooks. Say what you want about Brooks, but his book was able to codify something I'd spent years trying to understand myself. After the birth of his first child, he began to question his previously relentless focus on career success (or "scaling the first mountain," in the vernacular of the book):

> *The goals on that first mountain are the normal goals that our culture endorses—to be a success, to be well thought of, to get invited into the right social circles, and to experience personal happiness. It's all the normal stuff: nice home, nice family, nice vacations, good food, good friends, and so on. Then something happens. Some people get to the top of that first mountain, taste success, and find it…unsatisfying. "Is this all there is?" they wonder. They sense there must be a deeper journey they can take. Other people get knocked off that mountain by some failure. Something happens to their career, their family, or their reputation. Suddenly life doesn't look like a steady ascent up the mountain of success; it has a different and more disappointing shape.*

Getting to work at Google felt like the final box had been checked off my career to-do list. I was on the inside of the company that constantly topped the best places to work, getting well paid for it, with a clear path to work my way up. But—unbeknownst to me at the time—I'd reached the peak of my first mountain. I quickly started to see the paint flaking off the perfectly painted mural of my professional life. Just one example was the company-wide obsession with promotion. It was all everyone talked about, and the only meaningful measure of progress. But was it progress? Or was it an incremental number to an artificial "job level," to stroke your ego, add some digits to your bank account, and have to deal with more internal bullshit? Mo' money, mo' problems. Once I started seeing these things, I couldn't stop. The wizard behind the curtain was uncovered forever.

I'd become disillusioned with the company and what I'd been working toward for my whole adult life. What I had always desired wasn't what I wanted at all. I felt lost. We moved to San Francisco because I thought that was what I needed: a step up, a fresh challenge, a new set of problems. But I was papering over cracks. I saw what it took to get ahead, and it required giving up more than I was willing to offer.

I'd descended down the first mountain into what Brooks calls "the valley of bewilderment and suffering," where many stay. But some head into the valley and find something more: "A yearning to transcend the self and care for others, seeing familiar things with new eyes."

The fallacies of the first mountain had been laid bare. Was this the life I wanted to be living? When work takes so much from you and leaves your family to fight for scraps? It doesn't matter how good your parenting intentions are if your tank is running on empty whenever you're with them. I spent years focused on climbing a career ladder while attempting to be a better dad in the worst two hours of the day: getting them up and putting them to bed. The two most painful parenting pressure points, the toughest two hours on the job. Trying to get a toddler to sleep who won't settle, knowing you're due for another few hours in your inbox, attempting to clear the decks and finish the work you weren't able to do today because you were stuck in meetings talking about the work that you should have been doing. Those last emails before you can finally stop working—by closing the medium screen you've spent all day with, and reward yourself with an hour on the big screen while getting distracted by the small one in your pocket.

I'd spent years workshipping—offering myself up to the altar of work—and it wasn't working out. Like the inquisitive child questioning Santa, I wondered: "Where do you turn, once you stop believing?" It wasn't the first time I'd asked myself this question.

Let's hear it from the dads on...work and identity

I watched my dad pour everything into his job. He worked for the same company for over thirty years, from when we were born until he called it a day. He retired and was completely lost—he just didn't know what to do with himself. It was sad to see. I don't want that. I want to be someone outside of work—someone my kids actually know. If they grow up remembering me always at my desk, or stuck with my head in a laptop, then what's the point? **Andrew**

There was a stretch where every social event was just work in disguise—networking masked as friendship, drinks that were really just about comparing who was busier or more important. When I became a dad, it hit me how thin that all was. I realized that, outside of work, I didn't even know what I liked anymore. I'd forgotten about the music I loved, books half-finished on my shelves, mates I'd drifted from because they didn't "fit" the career-first narrative I was following. Since then I've been trying to claw those things back. I still have a job, of course, and I still care about it. But I don't want to only be "the guy from work." I want to be a dad who can tell his kids what he's passionate about that isn't tied to his nine-to-five. It feels like reclaiming parts of myself I buried along the way. **Paul**

I gave up on the full-time-career-ladder-life to go freelance a few years ago so I could spend more time with my family. It didn't feel like a hard choice at the time. I just wanted to be home as much as possible, more than any title or a guaranteed salary. Zero regrets. It's been a great ride. These days, I can feel my perspective changing. My kids are in school and daycare four days a week, I miss being part of a team, the freelance work has dried up, and our savings are only getting lower. I worry about going back to a full-time job and how it might impact my family time, but I may not have a choice. And that's okay with me; the last few years have been the best years I've ever lived. **Justin**

CHAPTER 6

A Higher Power

Spirituality is not religion. It is a path for us to generate happiness, understanding, and love, so we can live deeply each moment of our life. Having a spiritual dimension in our lives does not mean escaping life or dwelling in a place of bliss outside this world but discovering ways to handle life's difficulties and generate peace, joy, and happiness right where we are, on this beautiful planet.

—Thich Nhat Hanh, *The Art of Living*

Old rule: *Religion as an obligation.*
New rule: *Faith as an invitation.*

One question introduced, whence all others come: "Shall we have a baby?"

A seemingly simple query that begets so many others: "Can we afford it?" "What about your career?" "Do we have enough support?" "Is our apartment big enough?" "Should we move closer to our parents?" "What if we wait longer?" "What if we wait too long?" "Will we be good parents?" "Are we ready?"

After days, months, or years of debating, planning, and preparing, you have a child. You have willed an entirely new consciousness into the world. Suddenly, all your certainties feel a lot less certain—the answers you thought you were sure of are replaced by an entirely new set of questions, chief among them being, "How do we get this thing to stay asleep?"

You make it work. You get through those early months, a plethora of new experiences that eventually recede into the long fog, a compilation tape named *Raising a Baby*, where rose-tinted highlights can be replayed at any time, the toughest moments washed away in endorphin-dependent *Eternal Sunshine of the Spotless Mind*–style wipes. The questions you once asked will be forgotten. They'll be replaced with a walking, talking tiny human with questions of their own, which they'll hurl at you incessantly. Their sheer volume—in both meanings of the word, number, and decibel level—will rock you. No sooner than they've uttered their first word, they'll pair it with others, their very first clapback: "But why?" As their vocabulary grows, so will the complexity of their questions: "Why is the sky blue?" "Why do I have to brush my teeth?" "Where does rain come from?" "Why do you have to go to work?" Every so often—and *always* when you least expect it—you'll be floored with a "So where do babies come from?"

You'll yearn for those "easier" questions. Once their minds are open to the absurdity of this world we live in, their questions will only get more sophisticated and existential: "Why do bad things happen to good people?" "How did the universe start?" and "Where do we go when we die?" Questions that philosophers and theologians have wrestled with for millennia now asked over the dinner table between bites of fish fingers, definitive answers expected before peas go cold.

My mum passed away as I wrote this book, a year when questions around life and death reared their heads regularly. We were lucky that we could spend a short time together in the weeks before she left us. She was sick, sleeping on and off, but smiling as the house was filled with the comings and goings of her six grandchildren, whom she adored. I tried to explain to my recently turned five-year-old son what was happening. I told him that "soon Nannie will go to sleep, and she won't wake up." He replied with a somber nod. The next day, a little over twelve hours later, my mum walked into the living room. My son turned to me, his face amazed—as if he were a shepherd on Easter Sunday morning, and Jesus himself had risen up and walked out of the cave: "I thought you said she wasn't going to wake up?"

"It will be a while longer." I laughed. How could you not? So did my mum. It was the kind of exchange you can only ever have with a five-year-old. Earlier that week, he asked, "Has Nannie decided what animal she wants to come back as yet?" I had to explain—no, that's your Nani and Nana, who are Hindu and believe in reincarnation. Your Nannie and Grandad are Catholic and believe in Heaven. You could see the cogs turning in his head, grappling with different approaches to the afterlife as so many have before him.

In households where religion is integral, answers to some of the hardest questions can be provided via invoking one of the Three Big Gs: Google, Grandad, or God. But an ever-increasing number of people find themselves affiliated with no particular team and unable to sit on that three-legged stool. This group of what are termed "the religious nones" now make up the third-largest religious category worldwide—and while I wasn't born like this, I did find my way here.

All the Roads We Have to Walk Are Winding

1996 was the year. Manchester was the place. It was the center of my world, and—for a hot minute—felt like the center of the universe. I was twelve years old. Manchester United had established their dominance in English football. My hero Eric Cantona returned to football after an eight-month ban for kung-fu kicking an opposing fan after being told to "Fuck off back to France, you dirty French bastard." (He scored one goal and set up another on his first game back against archrivals Liverpool. Forever the best.) Manchester punched above its weight on the cultural map: While the Hacienda's best days might have been behind them, the Madchester scene it midwifed into the world swaggered on regardless;

Oasis were at the height of their powers, *(What's the Story) Morning Glory* reigning supreme as "Wonderwall" blared out of car and bedroom window alike. Teenage boys across the city recast themselves in the mold of Liam Gallagher—the fishtail parka, flicking two fingers to all and sundry, attitude and swagger, that iconic haircut—and I wanted nothing more than to join them. The only thing stopping me? My dad. His rules were clear and incontrovertible: "Until you're sixteen you'll get your hair cut every month, and you'll go to church every week."

Music was my religion of choice; Catholicism was the religion I was born into. My parents went to church every Sunday back in Ireland, and ~~god~~dammit we'd be doing the same here. I'd be in the pews every week, present and correct, dressed in my Sunday best, come heaven or high water. I'd stand next to my sisters, counting down the minutes until it would all be over, as we cycled through sitting, standing, and kneeling, over and over, perfectly synchronized (or else) with the rest of the congregation. We'd wind each other up, secretly pinching the back of a hand, trying to get someone in trouble (before smiling and silently mouthing *YOU JUST GOT IN TROUBLE* when it inevitably occurred). Closing time would arrive, and not a moment too soon. I'd slam shut my hymnbook and work my way to the exit—stopping briefly to light a candle in memory of those who were no longer with us, the one part I'd look forward to—before jumping into the car and heading home.

Religion wasn't limited to that one hour a week. We'd spend time at school preparing for the big milestones in the Catholic coming-of-age calendar—Confirmation, First Communion—while learning the history of Christianity (or a curated greatest hits) in class. We'd visit extended family in Ireland and see the extent to which they had invited religion into their homes. During our annual summer stays in Northern Ireland, six weeks at a time while my parents continued to work, my grandmother would come into the room every night to flick holy water on us as we slept. For those wondering: Yes, it will wake up a sleeping child, and yes, they'll get used to it after a few weeks. It wasn't an odd occurrence for the local priest to pop around for a cup of tea and a hello. A sleepover at one cousin's house meant you might get put on the spot and asked to lead a decade of the Rosary during their evening prayers. But religion was always there; as a young child, I have memories of reading an illustrated book of Bible stories with my mum, excited as we lost ourselves in a different tale every night before nodding off—Noah and his ark, Moses and the parting of the Red Sea, Daniel in the lion's den.

But as I worked through adolescence, I began to notice some...inconsistencies in these stories. One example, among many—how did Noah get all those animals onto one boat, then manage to keep them from eating one another? One question led to another. The answers I found didn't sit right. "It's called faith for a reason," I was told, in no uncertain terms, by a teacher. That didn't help. I started looking for answers elsewhere, a search that coincided with the rise in New Atheism, driven by writers like Richard Dawkins and Christopher Hitchens. I came to see organized religion as the contributing cause, not the solution, to pain and suffering in the world: a tool used by bad actors to impart their moral superiority over others. This point of view was surely compounded by growing up in such close proximity to a battle that had been raging my entire life, and would eventually see the loss of 3,500 lives in Ireland and the United Kingdom across three decades. Family members were dealing with the emotional shrapnel of physical explosions: some scars visible to the naked eye, others hidden away. Road trips were regularly interrupted as we were stopped at a police checkpoint to have our cars checked for explosives. On more than one occasion our time at the airport was extended because of a "random" suitcase search. This was Catholics against Protestants, but religion used a smokescreen for a proxy war between the English and the Irish, yet another chapter in the ongoing tale of the British Empire's chickens coming home to roost.

I began to feel uncomfortable every Sunday morning. I listened to the priest speak, questioning every line. I would fraudulently wait to accept the body of Christ, the small piece of unleavened bread that represented a ritual and sacrament I no longer believed in. I asked my parents if I could start staying at home on Sundays; this request was denied by the management. I patiently waited until I turned sixteen, until I'd be beyond my father's edict. And that proceeding Sunday my parents politely asked if I'd be joining them at Mass, which I politely declined. My Sunday mornings, and my hair, were finally my own. I turned my back on the religion of my youth—a teenage rebellion that was, unbeknownst to me at the time, becoming all the rage.

I tried on different hats as I got older. Strict atheism, in the vein of the writers I was reading, who were staunchly rejecting God, religion, and all that it stood for. I was, as we all are in early adulthood, stubborn and headstrong, closed off to opposing opinions. I began slowly softening to agnosticism—open-minded but still skeptical—where I'd spend most of my adult life. My story is familiar: an early introduction to religion, seeing if it fits, proceeding even when it doesn't; an unwillingness to continue this tradition while wrestling with worry about what your family might think.

I'm reminded of a conversation with my mum when we discussed the potential baptism—or not—of our soon-to-be-born first child. "I don't think it's right," I said, "to force this decision, and a set of beliefs, on a child who can't choose for herself."

Mum acquiesced. A few minutes later, she raised the topic of football.

"So, what team will the baby support?" she asked.

"Manchester United," I replied.

"Not Liverpool? Or Manchester City? Are you sure? Don't you think it's wrong to force a decision and set of beliefs on a child who can't choose for herself?"

Nicely done, Mum. That was over a decade ago. But something shifted in the years since. I'd begun to open my mind, considering how other cultures, outside the one I grew up with, considered religion and asked the big questions. While I would classify myself among the religiously unaffiliated, my wife would not. And I am growing accustomed to the charms of other faiths—by invitation rather than obligation.

My children are growing up learning and practicing the beliefs and traditions of Hinduism. We head to the UK annually to celebrate Navratri with my in-laws and their local community. My daughter will tie a rakhi around my son's wrist as a symbol of protection—a perfect gift from an older sister to a younger brother—for Raksha Bandhan, the annual celebration of siblings. These rituals are important to all of us and help my kids feel connected to a religion different from the one I was born into. Having children forces you to rethink your long-held beliefs—or your conviction-fueled lack of them. You may be among the quarter of married Americans from different faiths, working together to decide what your children will believe (or not). You may have spent decades outside of religion, only to feel yourself pulled back toward it on becoming a parent—whether you're a true believer or simply a better-school-seeker, choosing between the two education alternatives of "pay or pray."

I've followed my own course, arriving somewhere more open to not knowing and learning to become comfortable with that uncertainty. I have begun, as Mark Epstein suggested in *Going to Pieces Without Falling Apart,* to make my own spiritual path rather than following one. To search for the answer outside the framework I inherited. Among Native American traditions, the Lakota use *Wakȟáŋ Tȟáŋka*—translated to "The Great Mystery"—as a name for the sacred or divine. They believe that inherent in the idea of spirituality is, as my teacher offered all those years ago, accepting that we may never have the answers. I spent my youth desperate to solve the mystery—just as I would years later, tuning in to watch *Lost* every week—instead of accepting, as comedian Pete Holmes once quipped, that "trying to understand God is like a dog trying to understand the internet."

That this shift in mindset has occurred since I've become a father—during the years I've been regularly offered moments of awe and transcendent connection that are provided by these tiny humans entrusted to my care—is no accident. I've spent this time gradually assembling resonant writings, nonreligious rituals, and a personal belief system I've come to think of as an "emergent spirituality." I spent decades fruitlessly searching for facts, believing that was the only place where answers could be found. Recently I've realized that asking the right questions can be just as fulfilling, knowing certainty will always be out of reach.

Weaving a Spiritual Patchwork Quilt

Those raised Christian grew up under three complementary—but often conflicting—ideas of fatherhood: the paternal lineage personified by your father and grandfather; the white-collared men playing the role of "Father" at the church you attended every Sunday (whether by choice or dragged by force); and the other Father, the one whose name would always be capitalized alongside other words like *Heavenly*, *Beloved*, or, simply, the collective *Our*.

My definition of *father* has been influenced by all three, to vastly varying degrees. I am one of many parents who were raised with religion playing a significant role in their life before deciding to break this tradition with their own family—slapping a "Confirmation date: to be confirmed" sticker on your child and hoping the grandparents don't ask too many questions. The data confirms it—three in ten US adults are now "religiously unaffiliated," and while Christians continue to make up the majority of the US population, they're now 63 percent of it, down from 75 percent a decade ago, and—if current trends continue—predicted to fall below 50 percent of the population by 2070. These figures are echoed in the UK, a country where more people now believe in ghosts than God.

Conservative outlets like Fox News regularly cite these data points, pairing them with scaremongering headlines that "most Americans aren't happy that religion is declining" and talk of "Christians increasingly being persecuted worldwide." Some want to paint a picture of a Godless world sliding into chaos and collapse. But digging beyond the headlines uncovers a more nuanced picture. Thirteen percent of "religious nones" believed in God as described in the Bible while another 56 percent believed in "some other higher power," leaving only 29 percent who believed in neither. The number of US atheists feeling "a deep sense of wonder about the universe" has increased by 17 percent in the years 2007 to 2014. Only 41 percent of "nones" say they "see no need for religion in their life" while 49 percent describe spirituality as important to them. The number of Americans saying they are "spiritual, but not religious" increased from 19 percent to 27 percent in the five years running up to 2017, growth that was consistent across genders, races, and even political affiliations.

This data rings true with my own experience. Since becoming a father, I've begun to experience a glacial shift from being a purely logical, data-based decision-maker—forming beliefs exclusively through facts and peer-reviewed evidence—to something…different. If not another side of the coin entirely, then at least surfing the edge between. It's not uncommon to find myself feeling at the whims of something bigger, offering an observation of "it feels like the universe is trying to tell me something," a sentence that would have caused the *me-of-five-years-ago* to roll his eyes beyond belief. Part of it is the heart-opening experience of bringing another life into the world, but it can't solely be attributed to that one thing. It's down to an inquisitiveness I've fed with a mélange of sources, consumed over the last decade—books I've read, conversations I've had, podcasts I've listened to—that have brought me to a place where I consider myself spiritually curious, and contemplating things that some—including the aforementioned me-of-five-years-ago—might term "wooey." I've begun to notice coincidences that, if employed as a plot device on today's hot prestige TV drama, you'd call out as being on the nose. I've started relinquishing attempts to control future events, becoming comfortable knowing things will work out. And even if they don't, *then we gon' be alright.* I wait. I read. I listen, I watch, I talk. I think of these various things as part of my spiritual patchwork quilt: ever-evolving, intentionally chosen, crafted with care. Just like a patchwork quilt, it tells a story that is unique to the crafter, connecting to memories, friends, and family, that becomes more than the sum of parts.

Whenever I come across something that helps me open up in a new direction, I sew it on—another metaphorical patch in my collection. The quilt continues to grow. Sometimes it's a book: Robert Wright's *Why Buddhism Is True* (which served as a handy on-ramp for a religious skeptic like myself), *The Art of Living* by Thich Nhat Hanh, or *When Things Fall Apart* by Pema Chödrön. Other times it comes from poets old and new: Rumi, Rainer Maria Rilke, Ocean Vuong, Yung Pueblo. Krista Tippett and her podcast *On Being* introduced me to great spiritual thinkers like Richard Rohr, John O'Donohue, Mary Oliver, and many more. Albums like Kendrick Lamar's *Mr. Morale & the Big Steppers* push me to think about the role I play as a father and how my upbringing colors my outlook, while albums like *Promises* from Floating Points and Pharoah Sanders provide a dependable moment of awe. (You know that feeling you get when the sunlight filters through the window, and you see the particles glistening in the air, moving in slow motion? That's what this album sounds like.)

These sources have turned into habits, forming the texture and cadence of my days, weeks, and months. I'll listen to a Joseph Goldstein lecture through a single AirPod as I'm going to bed, his voice comfortably navigating complex ideas and sharing compelling tales. His cadence and tone are reminiscent of a Catholic priest delivering the homily during Mass—the short interlude between religious rites where the priest is given space to freestyle, delivering his own sermon, connecting current events to religious teachings. I spent 2021 reading Ryan Holiday's *The Daily Stoic*, reflecting each day on a daily passage from Seneca, Marcus Aurelius, or Epictetus. The parallels were clear to see as I sat down with a passage each day, their names and guidance as helpful to me as the ones from Matthew, Mark, Luke, and John were for my grandma, who read the Bible every night, just as they have been for millions of others throughout history. I'd found a good book, if not *the* Good Book. I've collected phrases, passages, and ways of thinking that have helped me during the most testing moments with my children (and this book is chock-full of them).

Over the last few years, while walking the streets of Barcelona, I have found myself regularly drawn toward churches, perplexed at the draw they had on me, the feeling of peace radiating from them, a place to slow down and to reflect. I became aware of how relaxed I felt walking into a church, having spent almost every Sunday of my childhood in one, never having realized in my youth how peaceful they could be. I visited those churches only when they were filled with disciples or, on the rare occasion, during a not-incredibly-exciting school trip. Coming into them now feels different. Maybe it's because I'm here by choice. They are sanctuaries, not just from the heat, but from the trials of the modern world. They are silent and powerful, even though that power has all too often been used to continue a culture of silence. There's something about their ability to evoke a sense of wonder, a connection to something bigger than us. I know they've been built with that purpose in mind, but you can still enjoy a magic trick even if you know how it's done. I write here about churches, but it could just as easily be any of these sacred spaces—be they synagogues, temples, or mosques—spread across the world. They provide a space to seek solace in our thoughts and beliefs. Whether you identify as religious or not, you have a set of beliefs you hold strongly, that you worship in your own way. In today's society, it's hard to know who is praying to what; in these buildings, you see it clearly. People sit in front of an embodiment of what they worship, a manifestation of it. They sit in silence. And they reflect.

In *From Strength to Strength*, Arthur C. Brooks writes, "If you are in a transitional state in your life and find your interest in transcendental growing—even if you have marginalized this part of life in the past—you are right on schedule. Don't resist." I was never on an active search for spirituality. I didn't feel something bereft at my core, a hole that needed to be filled. I considered it a dilemma already decoded. These sorts of mental gymnastics—"do I believe, don't I believe, what happens if I say I don't believe, what happens if I say I do"—make up another entry on the ever-growing list of "things our parents never needed to worry about." For generations almost eternal, parents could lean on religion as a blueprint for teaching their children the Art of Being Good, using these stories to explore morality, compassion, and resilience. I grew up with these beliefs. It's unfeasible that they don't inform the thought patterns I use today and the parent I've become. Our kids expect us to be—like the big man himself—omnipotent, omniscient, and omnipresent, to know the answer to all of their questions, all of the time. Religion offers pre-vetted answers to many of life's big questions, ones that we might not have figured out for ourselves yet, or may never. What parent wouldn't want a helping hand, a CliffsNotes for the existential queries that our children throw at us, delivered at the most inopportune moments?

Parenting requires a kind of faith—not necessarily the religious kind, but faith nonetheless: faith that you're up to this task, faith that your stumbles won't break them, faith that somehow, through all the questions you can't answer and the problems you can't solve, your children will find their way. As more of us raise our children adjacent to religion—or, at least, less strict in our application of it—we continue to search for great stories to fill those gaps. My children will spend as much time learning about Jesus at school as they do learning about Hindu deities like Ganesh and Hanuman at home. These rituals and beliefs play a prominent role in their lives. As I'm getting older and learning to let go, I'm becoming more comfortable with the religion I grew up with, and able to look at its teachings with a new perspective. While I'm not reading Bible stories to my children at night, there's a power in these tales, a reason they've stayed around for thousands of years. They captivate the minds of young readers (and listeners) while embedding important life lessons. The beautiful *Greek Myths* and *Egyptian Myths* books, retold by Jean Menzies and illustrated by Katie Ponder, come from this same place—wonderful stories, delivered beyond simple black and white, with moral and ethical wisdom to impart. The world needs more books like that, because there's only so much you can learn about humanity from a Gruffalo and a Big Bad Mouse.

What you put your faith in as a parent doesn't need to be a deity, a doctrine, or a denomination. It can be anything that gives you the conviction to shepherd another human being through this wild world. It could be the profound mystery of a universe conducting its cosmic dance for 13.8 billion years, pausing for a moment as you're reading a bedtime story to your child. Or the unwavering belief that love—imperfect, messy, but persistent—is enough of a north star to guide you through this journey. The key isn't what you believe in, but believing in something. As David Foster Wallace said in his 2005 commencement speech to the graduates of Kenyon College, spread far and wide as a short book titled *This Is Water*: "There is no such thing as not worshipping. Everybody worships. The only choice we get is what to worship. And the compelling reason for maybe choosing some sort of god or spiritual-type thing to worship—be it JC or Allah, be it YHWH or the Wiccan Mother Goddess, or the Four Noble Truths, or some inviolable set of ethical principles—is that pretty much anything else you worship will eat you alive."

Let's hear it from the dads on...religion and spirituality

We are Hindus, of the Upanishidic variety—our focus is on understanding the true nature of ourselves and the universe. Our eleven-year-old girls have been having a tough time seeing my dad on late-stage palliative care. It's been impossible to answer their questions about why their granddad of all people has such a rare disease, and why is it so unfair. I don't think I can answer any of these, and I don't know if answers will help. I don't think my beliefs come into it. The only thing I can do is to acknowledge what they are feeling, assure them their feelings are valid, and keep reminding them that I am pretty lucky and massively proud to have such compassionate kids as my daughters. **Kartik**

I grew up in church: really large nondenominational/evangelical churches. In high school, I started to move away from "I go because my parents make me" to finding my own meaning and value in a relationship with Jesus. So much so that I decided to go into ministry as a career. So now I work as a pastor. I have shifted away from some of the external baggage of white evangelicalism, but still am extremely compelled by Jesus and rely on God for strength. I've actually found a lot of value in a diverse church that focuses on the two great commands: love God, love your neighbor. As far as parenting, we've tried really hard to make faith an invitation instead of a requirement. Our two oldest came to us later in their life (nine and thirteen) so they already had a church background, although I get the impression their experience wasn't great. Neither of them are very communicative so it's hard to know exactly what they think about Jesus and the gospel, but they both decided on their own to get baptized and they really like attending church. **Troy**

My personal beliefs waver between apathetic, anti-religion, and agnostic. My main concern is that I don't want my kids to get all the baggage I got from religion. Shame, guilt, the whole lot. It's taken a long time to ditch that and I don't want them to get it because someone told them they're going to hell. I don't believe that and I don't want them being told that. We'll find a church, mostly for community. My wife misses it. But it's tough to find the right one. I am a spiritual person. But more in the Ram Dass and Alan Watts sense than the [Billy] Graham sense. All of Jesus's ideas are amazing. But people really miss the point and screw them up. I see all religions as trees in a forest. Same roots, different trunks, intertwining canopy. We can't really know anything. But I am in awe of the universe and oneness of it all. **Neil**

I sometimes struggle with teaching moral lessons to my kids because the reason I was given (the promise of heaven) has no relevance to them. It's been important work for me too: to think beyond the basic explanation I was given and look to the root of why we do things. To be honest, I keep coming back to the golden rule—to treat others as we wish to be treated. **Matthew**

CHAPTER 7

The Point of Parenting

No man can possibly know what life means, what the world means, until he has a child and loves it. The whole universe changes and nothing will ever again seem exactly as it seemed before.

—Lafcadio Hearn

Old rule: *Children limit possibilities.*
New rule: *Children expand horizons.*

Why are you here?

I'm not asking the big existential question, forcing you to wonder why you are alive on this rock, spinning around the sun at sixty-seven thousand miles per hour. That question is a little out of scope for this book. But why are you reading these words, right now? And the question behind the question: Why did you choose to have children?

You may have landed on Planet Parenthood by choice. You may have been a wayward asteroid, hurtling toward the maternity ward against your will. You may have arrived here entirely by chance—parenting via unplanned trajectory.

However you ended up in this wild world of raising children, you'll be asking yourself what life means now. The first time you held your newborn baby to your chest, breathing in tandem as you marveled at how your entire universe had shifted from broad and all-encompassing to a tight focus, your modus operandi now how to protect this new creature in your orbit. Parenting led me to more questions about who I am, and why I'm here, than during the three decades that preceded it. These questions haven't had easy answers, and the paths I've followed have led to some hard, messy, and altogether necessary work. In the dark night of the soul, listening to a screaming child who won't settle, I've questioned my sense of self to its very core: Why exactly did I sign up for this anguish? What I excavated in these caves was enlightening and terrifying in equal measure.

"Why am I here?" may not be a question as old as time, but it's older than any of us. We can trace it through the works of Camus, Nietzsche, and Kierkegaard, back to the streets of Athens as Aristotle and Plato questioned the nature of being. "The unexamined life is not worth living," their great teacher Socrates suggested. And just as we question the point of life, we also question the point of parenting. Because it sure as shit ain't the fast track to euphoria. As well as hammering your disposable income and making a good night's sleep a thing of the past, repeated meta-analyses from across the world have found that having children decreases your well-being and makes you less happy in your marriage (a decline that continues until your children leave home). A 2023 Pew Research study saw 62 percent of parents admitting that raising children is harder than they expected. And praise be that you're a man! Women see their bodies undergo a transformation before, during, and after childbirth, with repercussions that remain long afterward.

You won't be happy, but maybe that's okay? A 2013 study confirmed that satisfying your immediate needs will lead to increased happiness but is "largely irrelevant" to living a meaningful life. And that same study found that "a more meaningful life" also means signing yourself up for higher levels of worry, stress, and anxiety across your lifetime. And what is raising children if not a lifetime supply of worry, stress, and anxiety?

So why would anyone in their right mind decide to take on eighteen years of this? Well, while the day-to-day happiness of a parent is markedly less than that of a nonparent, research consistently shows that having children has its upsides. That same Pew Research study found that while 41 percent of parents found raising children "tiring all of the time," twice as many said it was "one of the most rewarding parts of their life." And research shows a link between parenting and a sense of purpose: A 2018 study found that parents reported significantly higher levels of meaning in life compared to nonparents, even when controlling for other variables—particularly pronounced in fathers actively engaged in their children's lives. In a 2014 paper titled "The Pains and Pleasures of Parenting," researchers discovered that parents spent more time thinking about the meaning of life than nonparents, reported more meaningful moments in their daily lives, and ranked time spent with their children as the most rewarding—comparable to levels for activities like volunteering and prayer in nonparents.

Raising children offers constant glimpses toward a higher sense of purpose, elevating life beyond daily humdrum. That feeling as you watch your child overcome an obstacle—literal or metaphorical, a chair they climb or a social situation they navigate—using the tools and techniques you've imparted, or that they've simply picked up, is hard to beat. At the same time, there's a danger here, a cliff edge where our kids are the only place we find meaning. We've all witnessed the friend whose entire sense of self fades into the background as the role of "parent" becomes all-encompassing, as they disappear into the part like a modern-day Daniel Day-Lewis. There is meaning to be found, everywhere you look, as a parent—but we do our children a great disservice when we pin our entire reason for existing upon them.

Becoming a parent means arriving in the middle of your life while spending your days watching another life begin. (Grab the tissues—we're deep in "Circle of Life" territory here.) Parenting transforms a vague silhouette of legacy into a walking, talking, tiny human being. What else will we leave behind, if not our children? It is a forcing function in man's search for meaning: It is biblical to become the giver of life, and a gateway drug to more existential questions: Who am I, now that I'm a father? If you're asking these questions, you're not alone—in fact, you're following in the footsteps of some of history's greatest thinkers.

Ye Olde Pros and Cons

On April 7, 1838, Charles Darwin opened his notebook, turned to a fresh page, and began to muse on marriage. He was considering asking Emma Wedgwood, his cousin, to become his bride. (Quiet, those smirking in the back—kissing cousins were all the rage back then; Darwin was in a historical clique with men as renowned as Albert Einstein, Edgar Allan Poe, and Jesse James.) Quill in hand, Darwin wondered whether his life would be better spent alone or with his wife-to-be. One of history's greatest thinkers attempted to answer this unquantifiable question with—you guessed it—a list of pros and cons.

Darwin could clearly see positives to a life shared with a loving companion: "It is intolerable," he wrote, "to think of spending one's whole life like a neuter bee, working, working, and nothing after all. Imagine living all one's day solitarily in a smoky dirty London house. Only picture yourself a nice soft wife on a sofa with good fire, & books & music perhaps." But to settle down was to give up a great deal of control over his life. Darwin noted all the things he would need to wave goodbye to: "Freedom to go where one liked. Conversation of clever men at clubs. Not forced to visit relatives & to bend in every trifle. Perhaps quarrelling. Loss of time. Cannot read in the Evenings. Fatness & idleness. Anxiety & responsibility. Less money for books."

Francis Bacon came down harder on the institution of marriage in his essay "Of Marriage and Single Life," suggesting only the unmarried can achieve greatness: "He that has wife and children has given hostages to fortune; for they are impediments to great enterprises, either of virtue or mischief. Certainly, the best works, and of greatest merit for the public, have proceeded from unmarried or childless men." Writer and critic Cyril Connolly agreed, memorably stating: "There is no more sombre enemy of good art than the pram in the hall."

Society no longer deems parenthood as the default path. People are increasingly choosing to take the road less arduous: In the United States, the number of nonparents who never want children doubled over the last two decades, rising from 14 percent in 2002 to 29 percent in 2023. The language we use around this route is fraught with sensitivities; the idea of choice factors strongly. Is this person "child-free," having made a conscious decision not to have children? Or are they "childless," their agency taken from them, wanting more than anything to become parents but with insurmountable barriers—physical, mental, societal, or financial—in their way?

With so many accepting a life without children, watching their friends become parents, and witnessing the sheer exhaustion that family life brings, it's only fair to wonder if Francis Bacon was on to something. Once a child enters your life, will they forever be in competition for the time and energy that could go toward other endeavors? Might we have more left in the tank if our energy, time, and attention weren't being constantly siphoned away by our kids?

It's impossible for me to offer an unbiased opinion. I have too much skin in the game. My decision to marry and to have children brought me to where I presently stand: a life I'm grateful for every day, even on the hardest of them. My second child put me through the wringer in a way that fundamentally transformed how I see the world and the role I choose to inhabit in it. Religious texts, spiritual practices, and mindfulness exercises all espouse a similar belief: If you can view life's hardest moments as the ones that grant you the greatest experience, then even the most challenging situation is an opportunity for growth.

Writer Michael Chabon once shared a piece of advice he received from a writer he admired: "Don't have children. That's it. Do not. You can write great books, or you can have kids. It's up to you." Chabon railed against the advice; a decision he did not regret:

> *If I had followed the great man's advice and never burdened myself with the gift of my children, or if I had never written any novels at all, in the long run the result would have been the same as the result will be for me here, having made the choice I made: I will die; and the world in its violence and serenity will roll on, through the endless indifference of space, and it will take only 100 of its circuits around the sun to turn the six of us, who loved each other, to dust, and consign to oblivion all but a scant few of the thousands upon thousands of novels and short stories written and published during our lifetimes. If none of my books turns out to be among that bright remnant because I allowed my children to steal my time, narrow my compass, and curtail my freedom, I'm all right with that. Once they're written, my books, unlike my children, hold no wonder for me; no mystery resides in them. Unlike my children, my books are cruelly unforgiving of my weaknesses, failings, and flaws of character. Most of all, my books, unlike my children, do not love me back.*

Chabon wrote *The Amazing Adventures of Kavalier & Clay* after becoming a dad, which I'd argue belongs "among that bright remnant" that will outlive us all. He is just one of many who rail against the conventional narrative framing fatherhood as limiting and finding the reality far more nuanced. Becoming a father serves as a catalyst, forcing men to reexamine priorities and discover purpose in unexpected places. Rather than merely restricting opportunities, fatherhood opens new avenues, caves that have remained unexplored in a life dominated by career ambitions. I've lost count of the dads I've spoken with who came back to work after the birth of their child and reported the feeling of returning into the same physical space but from an entirely new emotional one, and the realization that what mattered mere weeks ago was now drained of meaning.

This shift in perspective can lead to what psychoanalyst Erik Erikson called *generativity*—the concern for establishing and guiding the next generation. While the focus of generativity will be initially toward one's immediate children, this impulse frequently expands beyond the family unit, especially in smaller communities. This can be observed today in the increasing numbers of fathers who, after having children, become more engaged in community service, environmental activism, or educational initiatives. The experience of nurturing awakens a desire to contribute to the world their children will inherit.

Artist and writer Austin Kleon wrote, "Rather than being 'the enemy of art' your children can inspire you to go new places. Hanging around a four-year-old can get you unstuck." Karl Ove Knausgaard's escapades as a full-time father were spread across six books totaling thirty-six hundred pages, provocatively titled *My Struggle*. For Knausgaard, fatherhood delivered an exothermic reaction to his creative output rather than draining its vitality away. His earlier books had been moderately successful, but it was his writing on the minutiae of fatherhood that turned him into a global sensation. Chronicling the harsh realities of fatherhood proved transformative, with observations on being the primary carer becoming the ne plus ultra of dad lit; his ornate explanations of the mundanity of parenthood inspired readers across the world to seek out the extraordinary beauty of life's most ordinary moments.

But back to Darwin, and his list. He eventually decided to marry and become a father. He must have found something in it, as he ended up having ten children. We all know his greatest work, *On the Origin of Species*, was inspired by his voyage on the HMS *Beagle* and his observations in the Galapagos Islands. But it took a further twenty-one years to publish the work. Scholars have suggested that it was becoming a father—and particularly the death of his eldest daughter Annie in 1851—that influenced his decision to finally share his theory that directly challenged the religious orthodoxy of the time. Darwin knew his work flew in the face of the foundation upon which many Victorian families were built, even at home. His wife, Emma, was deeply religious, and Darwin was acutely aware of how his conclusions might impact her faith.

What Darwin experienced in becoming a father, and losing a daughter, would never have come from riding a boat around the Galapagos Islands for his lifetime, no matter how idyllic that sounds. Becoming a father invites us to ask life's biggest questions, and to do so when we have less time, energy, and functioning brain cells to answer them. For everything that pram in the hall takes from us, what it gives, beyond all else, is a role to play—a sense of purpose in becoming a better role model for these children you have sired and providing them with what you may have found lacking in your own childhood. But in order to do it, you're going to have to rethink your relationship with one of the scarcest resources in the life of a parent: time.

Let's hear it from the dads on... the most joyous part of fatherhood

As they get older (my kids are nearly ten) the joy I used to get from stupidity and messing around is starting to be replaced by the joy of engagement. The times when you visibly see the spark of imagination kick in and the genuine excitement in learning and discovering something new for themselves. Watching them work these things out for themselves and put the random pieces of the world together is awesome to see. Even better when it results in long rambling conversations without the distraction of a screen. **Dan**

My son's genuine excitement to see me brings me the most joy. We spent a lot of time together during lockdown but even now, I'll leave to go work out or take out the trash, and no matter how long I'm gone—whether it's two minutes or two hours—his face lights up when he sees me. It's the best. I know it won't always be like this, so I try to remember to be present and just let that joy wash over me. **Justin**

At the moment I'm feeling pretty present, which is meaning I'm finding joy in regular moments of pain, where (usually) I'd invariably want to move things on. So the emerging arch schemes of procrastination are starting to deliver great joy. Last night, my kid's delaying tactic was to keep starting the book again. It was so brazen and ridiculous I was just pissing myself in my head. Needed to get him to sleep, but was bringing total joy. Because I was in the moment with him, not thinking about some other bullshit. It's a privilege to have the time and space to feel like this and I hope I keep it going. **Nic**

CHAPTER 8

All You Need Is Time

Time is what we want most, but what we use worst.

—William Penn

Old rule: *Maximize every minute.*
New rule: *Lose track of time.*

A few years back I was coaching Joe, a father of four. He told me how overwhelmed he felt, both at work and at home. He was a lawyer, on track to become a partner, but drowning in responsibilities and a weight of expectations—from his boss, his wife, his siblings, his parents (getting older every day), and his four children. We were talking from two sides of the Atlantic, a cold front approaching his house in Midwest America. I noticed his eyes dart away from the screen before quickly coming back to meet my eye as he sighed.

"What did you just look at?" I asked.

"It's getting colder here now. Winter is definitely coming. And every day I work from my desk and feel overwhelmed with all the wood that needs to be cut. It will take me an entire weekend to do it."

I asked if he enjoyed cutting wood. "Sometimes it can be meditative. But there is so much I'd rather be doing. For the past six months, I've had an outdoor climbing frame lying there, still in its protective wrapping, waiting to be assembled and installed. I don't have the time to do it. And I don't have the space either, until all that wood is chopped and stored away."

"How much do you charge your clients per hour?" I asked.

"Four hundred dollars."

"What's the hourly rate of a lumberjack there?"

"About twenty dollars an hour. And he'll be faster than I ever could be."

I made a suggestion—between now and the next time we spoke, could he find a local logger and get a quote? We jumped on a call a week later. I was greeted by a beaming smile: The lumberjack had already been there, the wood was chopped and stored away. It was all done for less than what he charges a client for thirty minutes of his time.

"I'm going to spend this weekend building the playground for my kids," he told me. "I can't wait."

The Three Eras of Scarcity

We're going to talk about money here, which comes with an essential caveat: These choices aren't available to everyone. More and more parents are spending their time focused on the more foundational layers of providing food, shelter, and security. But a lawyer is offered an opportunity that a lumberjack is not: to trade his money for time. You might not fight cases for a living, but there are places where you have this opportunity and don't take it. Why?

Loss aversion is a cognitive bias inherent in all of us, in which a situation is perceived as more painful if it is framed as a loss rather than a win. Research has found that we experience losses as if they were twice as large as the equivalent gain. This is easy to calculate when you're thinking about money—most would experience winning $100 and losing $200 as having a similar emotional weight, just one positive and one negative. But it becomes murkier when we try to value our time. When someone offers to provide a service to you for a fixed fee, your brain immediately latches onto the loss of that money. But what about the gain? Hours to spend however you like—playing Lego with your daughter, teaching your son to ride a bike, or simply, heaven forbid, sitting with your feet up and a good book. The money feels tangible, immediate, painful to part with. The time feels abstract, theoretical, hard to quantify. But ask yourself: If someone offered you five hours to do whatever you want, in exchange for $100 this weekend—and they'd take a hated task off your to-do list at the same time—would it be worth it? The same trade, framed differently, becomes absurd. Yet this is the mental calculation we make—and get wrong—every single day.

There are mental models related to money that many of us have inherited, handed down by generations of fathers before us, preventing us from moving forward. They cannot be eradicated, only replaced. And one model I've thought more about since becoming a parent is on the eras of scarcity we experience across our lives—life stages when access to one key attribute will be the primary contributor to your overall quality of life, sense of satisfaction, and ability to find joy:

Era 1: Scarcity of Money. This will surface sometime before reaching adulthood, when the stomach-gnawing "need" to have something is interrupted by the inability to pay it. It's the first time you experience the internal turmoil of an immovable force (your desire for something new) meeting an unstoppable object (the amount of money in your piggy bank). The era of money scarcity is something you (ideally) move out of as you advance in your career. Some get out earlier than others. Many dads are still working to free themselves from it. Parenting here is an existential battle to do what often feels like keeping your head above water and clearly maps to the lower levels of Maslow's hierarchy of needs around physiological and safety needs.

Era 2: Scarcity of Time. You've got the money. You've leveled up. You may be happy here. You may increasingly want more. Money is more readily available. But you know what isn't? Time. You don't have enough of it to do the nice things you could with the money you have. Now you've got grown-up money, you can buy any video game you've ever wanted. But you won't have the time to play them. You won't have the time to do anything: to see your friends, to cook those ambitious recipes you've been meticulously saving, to learn how to play that instrument that's been gathering dust for months. Because—irony klaxon—the job you took, the one that pulled you out of the money scarcity era and gave you the things you were craving, left you with everything you wanted but without the time to enjoy it. Damn you, cursed monkey paw!

Era 3: Scarcity of Health. The kids have flown the nest. Retirement is looming, with its many possibilities: Check all those countries off your bucket list, finally see the pyramids, maybe you'll even have time to take up surfing. But you won't, of course. Because your back has been giving you grief for a decade, and you wouldn't want to aggravate it. Never mind taking up a sport that ends up hurting you more than it helps. Boxing? Don't you think tai chi is more "your thing" now? You have the money, and you have the time, but you don't have the body you once did, and the ability to enjoy the wonders of the world are diminished. And who knows when the linear health scale we use turns to the more definitive binary one—you're here, and then you're not. The final era, and unless they've figured out how to raise the dead by the time you kick the bucket or that zombie apocalypse finally arrives, it's the only one you're unlikely to move out of.

Unlike the generational eras—Boomer, X, Millennial, Z, and now Alpha—the eras of scarcity have no fixed ranges for age, salary, or measurable metric. These are more vibes-based, their barriers more porous. Also unlike the generational eras, era mobility is a core tenet—you are expected to move between them, and it won't always be in the right direction. You may have found yourself out of the money scarcity era, only to fall back into it because of redundancies at work or increased costs of living.

There is a library's worth of definitions on privilege, but one could be thought of as having "never been born into, or been able to move out of, the era of money scarcity." Some are born with beyond enough. Others, who watched their parents work enough to move from one to the other, or maybe did that work themselves, will still carry remnants of the scarcity mindset.

Trading time for money doesn't always need to be prohibitively expensive. In my late twenties, I started wearing shirts to work more often. They required regular ironing, and I was terrible at it—I'd take around ten minutes to iron a single shirt badly. Walking to the train station one morning, I noticed the local dry cleaners was charging £1.50 (US $1.98) to iron a shirt. I realized if I did it myself, I was valuing my time at £9 (US $11.90) an hour, and to "earn" that hourly rate doing something I hated, through gritted teeth. As soon as I'd made that calculation, I stopped ironing shirts forever. (Side note: To this day, we still don't own an iron at home, which has led to some funny moments, like my daughter seeing a man walking down the road with an ironing board and saying, "Look, Papi, he's going surfing.")

Understanding these eras isn't just an intellectual exercise—it's about recognizing where you are right now, and what opportunities that presents. If you've managed to climb out of money scarcity, you're faced with a choice that our fathers rarely had: Continue accumulating wealth while time slips away, or leverage that financial security to buy back time with your children. We're not alone in trying to solve this puzzle. An entire industry has sprung up around our desperation to find more hours in the day—promising a future where technology will be our saving grace, where the right combination of productivity apps, time management tools, and life hacks will somehow unlock the secret to being everywhere at once. The siren song of Silicon Valley whispers in our ears: "Tap here to make it all easier."

No, There's Not an App for That

As soon as you become a parent, you realize that time is the one thing we can't control. Let's look at a typical morning, before and after children:

Before: Wake up, hit the snooze button, head to the kitchen, and make yourself a pour-over coffee. Look at your phone for fifteen minutes. Hit the shower, luxuriate in it, let the warm water roll over your skin as you think about the day to come. You're both feeling frisky? Maybe a quickie? Why not! Then pull on some clothes and walk out the door with a smile on your face. Take your preferred method of wheels to work, engage your noise-canceling headphones, and shut the world out.

After: Be woken up at an entirely random time. Potentially due to one child screaming at the other. Or the sound of a boxful of toys falling from where it's supposed to be to where it's not. What time is it? It doesn't matter. They're up now. So that means you're up too. And this morning, like every morning, requires getting them to school on time. Making sure their bags are packed in exactly the right way for this day of the week—uniforms are all present and correct, PE and swimming kits are ready, and flotsam and jetsam needed for a successful day is securely zipped up in their backpacks. Don't forget extra clothes for the little ones, should any unforeseen (and entirely predictable) issues arise. And don't forget to pack water. You always forget water. No, not in that cup. In the cup they like. "Daaaaaaaaaad!?!" And snacks. Don't mess up and give them a snack they don't like. Or even worse, a snack that might send their classmate Toby into anaphylactic shock if he so much as sees it. You drop them off at the school gate, ideally on time, before navigating the grueling traffic to actually start your own workday.

Technology was supposed to solve all of this. We were promised jet packs, flying cars, and new frontiers of productivity. Instead, all we got was an endless barrage of notifications and the guilt of what seems like an impossibly overestimated screen time. It can often feel like you've done an entire day of work before nine a.m. That's before the after-school clubs, the extracurriculars, and the kids' parties: sugar-fueled hyperactivity, screaming for an outlet. And we're just talking weekdays. During the weekends you've got them 24/7, so you better have something planned, and you aren't thinking you'll get any time for yourself. If you're a dad co-parenting in the same house, you're tag-teaming: divide and conquer, or be conquered. Communication is key. For those co-parenting after a separation, or even going it alone, your time is even more scarce—trying to align a patchwork quilt of iCloud calendars in an attempt to make it all work, like an astrologer awaiting the fateful aligning of the planets.

Schools don't make life any easier. For parents of babies and toddlers, you dream ahead and foolishly believe that dropping them off for seven hours a day somewhere might create a new window for getting things done. But no—you'll be batting back messages and emails from three different school apps—none of them working as promised—multiple WhatsApp groups, and a barrage of emails to your inbox, informing you of the fifteen new things that need your attention since you dropped your kid off at school and got to your desk. While writing this chapter, my school emailed to inform me they've created a new Google Site to "share some of the activities happening in the classroom." It's yet another digital destination with an entirely different login and set of password requirements, some version of "the first two letters from your child's surname, the last four letters from their middle name, four random digits from their date of birth, a capitalized first letter from the city they were born in, their favorite color from two years ago, and your favorite characters from the shrug emoticon: ¯_(ツ)_/¯"

And during that small window, when you almost feel like you're winning? That's precisely the moment the school will call to tell you that your son just vomited everywhere, or they'll email to inform you of yet another outbreak of head lice.

Families are finding ways to integrate technology into the operating system of their family. One friend told me about two separate Slack instances he runs with his wife—one for their business, another for their family life—fifteen channels in total, and an Asana board to go with it. They're both project managers, if you hadn't guessed. Raising a family is work, so why not use work tools to go with it? Is it strange to think about "collaborating" with your significant other or with older children? The language of productivity is the oxygen supply of these apps: "Where great teamwork starts," promises Slack. Asana is a place to "manage projects and focus on what's important." Only with Jira can you "move fast, and stay aligned."

These sound like things that could be as useful at home as they are in the office. But is life improved when working styles encroach on our home turf? Soon we'll be scheduling daily stand-ups over breakfast, defining SMART parenting goals, and working through annual budgets. I'm not looking forward to the quarterly performance reviews. I've been pushing for a promotion. The outlook isn't great.

We keep things simple in our house. A shared page of iOS reminders that acts as a shopping list. A shared family Google Calendar that reduces 90 percent of appointment-based stress. "If it isn't in the calendar, it doesn't exist" has become my mantra (and I'm not alone, based on conversations with other dads). One dad shared how well their family digital calendar was working until his daughters took to planning their week on a paper calendar on the fridge. Sync issues, rearing their head in real life.

Sometimes apps can help. But others can lull you into a false sense of security, a new source of stress designed as a mirage of control. When my son was a baby, I was logging his sleeping patterns on an app called Huckleberry. What I thought was helping actually became a source of anxiety rather than a balm for it. I was in a moment when there was very little control available, and I was trying to force structure onto it (another way of coping with a mental health breakdown, I see in retrospect). And there was something icky about the constant upsell from the app—telling me that I was only a tap (and authorized Apple Pay payment) away from speaking with a sleep expert, subtly implying that "You're doing okay, but you'd be doing better if you went for this $29.99 in-app purchase."

Just as I was ready to write off technology's ability to meaningfully help parents navigate the era of time scarcity, something interesting happened. The last few years have seen a rise in large language models like ChatGPT and Claude, opening up new parenting possibilities. Kids love to ask questions, and they expect Dad to know all the answers. Now here was something I could lean on when I hit my limit. And it could do so much more! One summer, during a long road trip through France, I found myself using ChatGPT to generate personalized quizzes about the TV show *Phineas and Ferb* for my kids—their then favorite, with the AI model prompted to avoid spoilers and ask questions only about the episodes they'd already seen. More magic happened when we started playing with AI image generation. My son's offhand comment about "Shark Vader" turned into a bout of creating increasingly ridiculous Sith Lords, every image generated coming with its own backstory. This experiment showed technology could amplify our imagination rather than drain our attention, using tools that feel less like digital babysitters and more like creative parenting collaborators, helping us spend time together with moments of joy and play. They give us new ways to use our time. But there's only one way to put more time in our days.

The Power of Saying No

If technology can't save us from the time famine, what will? It won't come from what you agree to do. Only from the things you don't. Because every time you say yes, for whatever reason, you're agreeing to give up part of your future.

We say yes for the wrong reasons: a reluctance to be labeled as contrary, a perceived obligation to friends and family, an attempt to avoid the discomfort of dealing with a perceived backlash. We feel pressure in the moment to acquiesce; we seek protection from the awkwardness of delivering a no. We kick the can down the road, locking ourselves into a future we might have avoided. For parents, these decisions take on an extra level of intensity. Signing up for a new project at work means missing bath time at home. Taking on a new client means increased pressure on your partner to pick up the slack. Something's gotta give. Your world—and the people within it—must bend to accommodate your yeses.

But a good *no* can change that. Think back to the first *no* you can remember. After your own name, closely followed by *mama* and *dada*, it will have been one of the first words you learned. Research has shown that babies begin to understand it around age six to nine months, although they won't stop what they're doing in response to the word until they hit twelve to eighteen months. A strong, stern *no* commands attention. It's loaded with power. It can stop a child in their tracks. It might even save their life. It provides a moment of respite among the chaos. You've probably used it—more than once—with your kids today. And if you haven't? Don't worry, there's still time.

As children get older, they start to use *no* for themselves. It's an odd occurrence, watching them weaponize those two letters back toward you to assert their independence, demonstrate their character, and rebalance what they see as an unfair power dynamic. And what do we do in response? We overrule them; teach them their *no* isn't as important as ours. As we get older, our understanding of the word hardens. We begin to see it as a profanity. *No* closes doors. Prohibits experiences. Saps energy. Limits possibilities. It's so negative! But while negativity is an attitude, *no* is an intentional choice. A considered *no* is a powerful act, a radical statement in favor of self-care, a demonstration of self-respect. It takes conviction in your beliefs, confidence in the person you are, and certainty in the path you're on. Aside from ten minutes of peace in the bathroom—with no one banging on the door or sliding notes underneath—few things in life are more satisfying than a good *no*.

One good rule of thumb is to ask yourself, *If I had to do this today, would I agree to it?* Commitments will eventually arrive, no matter how far ahead you punt them into the future. The things you say no to will shape your life, your career, and your family. They will define your past, present, and future. For a word so simple, so short, so fundamental, we don't use *no* anywhere near enough in our lives. Nineteenth-century American humorist Josh Billings wrote, "Half of the troubles of this life can be traced to saying yes too quickly and not saying no soon enough." In other words: Say yes to no.

The Four-Inbox Strategy

"This is all well and good," you might be thinking. "But it's not as simple as just saying no to everything." I get it—you want to be a more involved dad, not one who grunts and shouts "No" to every request that comes his way. You need surgical tools, not a blunt hammer. Here's one way I've taken to looking at things over the past decade. Think about an inbox. No, not the one on your phone, the one that follows you everywhere you go, flashing notifications that mentally hijack, reminding you to resume the terrifying game of email *Space Invaders* that knowledge workers play on their laptops every day. Think of the old-school inboxes that once sat inside offices, your name written on a plastic tray. Imagine four of those trays, each representing a different approach to the daily deluge of jobs and responsibilities that come your way.

I. Tray One: Things Only I Can Do

This is, as Gay Hendricks puts it in *The Big Leap*, your "Zone of Genius." These are the things you do that light you up, that you do better than anyone else, that move you closer to the person you want to become. It might be strategic thinking for your business, creative projects that light you up where you lose track of time completely, or bedtime stories that only Dad can tell right. These are the moments that define who you are and who you're trying to become. By the time this book comes out, my daughter might not be asking for the silly voices in her bedtime story, so I'm relishing it while I can. This tray should get most of your attention.

II. Tray Two: Things I Need to Get Better At

These are the skills that, once mastered, will help you excel at the work in Tray One. Maybe it's learning to write more consistently, improving your public speaking, or figuring out how to have difficult conversations with a teenager. Investments here pay dividends—every hour spent improving these skills multiplies your effectiveness in Tray One. This is a tray that's easy to ignore—it's easier to maintain the status quo, to keep doing what you're good at. But these skills are muscles you need to build every day.

III. Tray Three: Things I Don't Love That Others Can Do Better

There's something about being a dad that makes you feel like you should be able to do everything yourself. But I've learned that asking for help isn't weakness—it's wisdom. The local student who walks our dog three times a week, giving me back precious hours with my kids. This is where leverage lives. (Unless you love walking the dog, then move along.) These people might be found in your local communities, and for other tasks you can lean on platforms like TaskRabbit, Upwork, or Fiverr for qualified experts who can take on whatever you are looking to delegate. From bookkeeping to lawn maintenance, website design to house cleaning—there's someone who specializes in exactly what you need to offload.

IV. Tray Four: Things I Shouldn't Do

These are the tasks that drain your energy, add no value, and keep you from what matters. The endless social media scroll. The meeting that could have been an email. The social gathering with no one you truly like. The volunteer commitment you took on out of guilt. This tray exists for one reason: to help you identify what needs to go.

These trays should be considered porous, and you'll find that tasks naturally move between them. What feels like a Tray One task might actually belong in Tray Three. That Tray Two skill that never seems to escape your to-do list? Maybe it's actually a Tray Four task in disguise. The goal isn't to empty all the trays—it's to ensure you're spending your limited time on what matters to you.

Between learning where to step away, saying no more often, and bringing a more methodical approach to what we choose to do (rather than just assuming we should do everything), today's modern father can choose mindful presence over mindless productivity, spend more time with the people that truly matter, and learn to thrive in the era of time scarcity. You might even find time—shock horror—to finally begin looking after yourself.

Let's hear it from the dads on…trying to make it all fit

I've personally always had the philosophy of checking in with myself and asking if I was to die next year, would I regret the path I was on...and if I feel really way off, I make some serious life decisions. It occurred to me last week that my disgruntlement with work may be actually because I am actually content and happy with my lot and this need to strive is now not needed. Having a child has so radically altered my perception of what life is about. I have to be open to the idea that maybe, just maybe, work is not the defining quality of my life and I should orient around being with my family and friends as much as possible. **Ivor**

My phone used to be permanently attached to my hand. Work emails at dinner, client calls during bedtime stories, the whole catastrophe. Then my five-year-old daughter asked me why my phone was more important than her. That was my wake-up call. I instituted "phone-free zones"—no devices during meals, bedtime routines, or weekend family activities. My business didn't collapse. In fact, my clients respect the boundaries more than I expected. And my daughter? Of course she was happier, she'd stopped competing with a screen for my attention. **David**

I'm lucky that my wife and I have always tried to balance our lifestyle so we can enjoy it as much as possible now, rather than working as hard as possible for a long-term payoff that may never come. What that looks like in practice isn't massively special—but we chose about ten years ago to move out of our nearest city, and next month will be moving even farther into the countryside. About five years ago I took a local job so we no longer had to commute every day; now we both work from home most of the time. This has given us more free time, so we can be together as a family as much as possible. **Jon**

CHAPTER 9

Health Is Wealth

He who has health has hope. He who has hope has everything.

—Arabian proverb

Old rule: *Dad bod decline is inevitable. Accept it.*
New rule: *Your health is a gift to your family.*

I wish I could remember where I first heard it. It's been seared into my mind ever since. "There will be a time when you pick your child up for the final time," it foreshadows, "and you won't even realize it." The concept compels you to parent in the present, warning against the ephemeral nature of raising young kids. For parents whose children have already flown the nest, it serves as a poignant reminder of a time that once was. Or a challenge to attempt next time they see their adult children face-to-face.

This thought remains front of mind, nudging me to be here for my children, both physically and mentally. My eldest is well into her double digits. All of those cycles around the sun, rotations increasing in speed at a terrifying pace. The final time I lift her up may pass me by. (By the time you read this, it may well have happened.) But I can tell you, with absolute certainty, the last time I will lift her into the top bunk of her bed:

’Twas the night of Wednesday, April 26, 2023. The night I put my back out for weeks.

“Pain is inevitable. Suffering is optional.” So said Haruki Murakami in his 2007 memoir *What I Talk About When I Talk About Running*. My relationship with my lower back is a long, complicated one, with more tears than a Christmas Day rerun of *It’s a Wonderful Life*; I could spend an entire book going into gory detail, but let’s see if we can nail it in a paragraph: By the time I was thirty I’d already had three operations around my coccyx (that’s “the top of your arse,” in medical nomenclature). I see my physio so often she has become a close friend and confidant. I’ve done everything she—and the rest of the internet—have told me would work: daily stretches, a regular yoga practice, Pilates, and finally learning to lift things in a manner appropriate for a man in his forties. I own a shelfload of books on back pain—mostly useless, except for *Healing Back Pain: The Mind-Body Connection*, the book that finally opened my eyes to the idea that “the battle going on in your mind results in a real physical disorder that may affect muscles, nerves, tendons, or ligaments.”

If this was to be believed, and the battle was occurring in my mind, what might those electrical impulses be trying to tell me? I write this as I ascend toward the middle of my forties, a time when my relationship with pain has started to shift. My body had been trying to tell me something for years but has spent that time screaming into the void. It’s only recently I’ve started to listen—rather than be resigned to the inevitability of aging, I’ve begun to see this pain as a positive signal. It’s my body’s way of reminding me I’m pushing it too far. Ever put your palm flat onto a hot surface? Didn’t leave it there long, did ya? The pain was a sign your body couldn’t take the heat, and this flag—flying through your nervous system at 270 miles per hour—was all that was required to pull that hand away fast, ensuring that cold water and a hand towel wrapped in ice would effectively manage it rather than needing a trip to the emergency room.

It took me a while to get here. It’s taken us, collectively as a gender, even longer. Men are diabolical at prioritizing our health—and it’s literally killing us. Men die four to seven years earlier than women in most countries, and even in countries where healthcare is widely available—and for free!—we're still not using it. We're less likely to get screened for cancer, and if we do get a positive diagnosis, survival rates are lower because we find out about it too late. Heart disease is the number one killer of men—regularly ignored because we dismiss chest pain as "nothing to worry about." Men are more likely than women to have undiagnosed high blood pressure and diabetes, both of which increase the risk of stroke, heart failure, and kidney disease in later life.

We do everything within our power to avoid seeing a doctor. Half of men haven't seen a medical professional for six months, and four out of ten haven't been within striking distance of a reflex hammer for over a year. We're twice as likely to leave two years between doctor's visits as the women in our lives. Why? Because we're invincible, clearly. We don't need no stinkin' doctors. A 2022 study of one thousand American men found that two-thirds believed they were "healthier than the average man," a mathematical impossibility that echoes the infamous 1986 study in which 80 percent of respondents believed they were better than the average driver. It also found that one-third of men believed they "didn't need a regular health screening," and 55 percent of men admitted they don't get an annual checkup. That sentence will lead you to one of two thoughts—either shaking your head and muttering, "We really need to get better at taking care of ourselves," or wondering, as I did while writing this: What exactly does a "regular health screening" mean? How regularly should we be doing this? What should we be getting screened for?

I know I'm not alone in dismissing pain in order to avoid the doctor at all costs. I use my dodgy knees to kick the metaphorical can down the road, requiring any pain or ailment to trouble my system for at least forty-eight hours before I'll consider seeing a medical professional. When you dig beneath the surface, avoidance runs deeper than mere inconvenience. We put our heads in the sand, bad back be damned, and why?

There's the primal fear of bad news, as if closing your eyes and pretending monsters don't exist will keep them at bay—a childish logic that follows us into adulthood. There's the persistent voice, sounding suspiciously like the male role models we watch on TV and at the cinema, whispering that real men tough it out. Like Murakami suggested, pain is fine, but you should be ashamed of suffering. Pain is a foe to conquer rather than an ally to communicate with; discomfort a badge of honor, not a warning sign. Perhaps the most dangerous belief is our unshakable optimism that whatever's wrong will simply fix itself, as we treat ourselves the same way we'd fix a wayward piece of technology: Turn it off, wait for a while, turn it on again. The body, we tell ourselves, knows what it's doing. It'll sort itself out. Until it inevitably doesn't, and we're faced with a problem that's grown from manageable to critical, all the time we were clicking *Remind me later* to get rid of the annoying pop-up notifications warning us of our impending doom.

Becoming a dad means you're not just doing this for yourself—there's a duty to be there for your kids. But in order to be your best for others, you need to be your best in the first place. You've no doubt heard the popular refrain that parents share with one another: "Put your own oxygen mask on first." I first heard this from my therapist back in 2019, and I've seen it repeated in Reddit threads, Instagram self-help carousels, and TED Talks in the years since. It implores us to take care of ourselves, in order to take better care of our children. But there is a telling flaw in the oxygen mask principle—the only time we are told to use them is when our plane is hurtling toward the earth and our demise is imminent. Waiting for a crisis is entirely the wrong mental model.

There is a glimmer of hope. Becoming a parent brings us into the proximity of medicine in a way most men won't have experienced since their childhood. Trips to see doctors and midwives as you prepare for the birth of your child and blurry memories of ultrasound gel, heartbeat monitors, and anxious waiting rooms mark a profound shift—perhaps the first time you entered a medical setting without being dragged against your will, unexpectedly engrossed in conversations on fetal development, maternal nutrition, and birth preparations with an enthusiasm foreign to our usual doctor-dodging selves. Something transformative happens inside those harshly lit rooms: The focus on a new life—one you're partly responsible for creating—can subtly recalibrate your relationship with physical health. You're not just there for yourself. You're there for them—your unborn child, your partner. In that sideways glance, men may find a back door into their own well-being.

Men's involvement in prenatal appointments and classes vary by societal expectation, cultural background, and personal comfort levels. In some countries, a father's presence throughout pregnancy care is assumed. In others, it remains uncommon. But taken globally, things are trending in the right direction. Public health services are beginning to recognize this unique window of opportunity: In Puerto Rico, researchers spent 2017 conducting a groundbreaking program engaging with expectant fathers during their partners' prenatal visits, offering health screenings and wellness education specifically for men. The results were striking—men who had avoided medical settings for years were suddenly checking their blood pressure, discussing nutrition, and even scheduling follow-up appointments for themselves. In 2022, a hospital in the suburbs of Paris piloted a prenatal consultation for dads-to-be that offered blood pressure checks, vaccines, and targeted lab tests—and more than half of the men contacted attended. These examples demonstrate that impending fatherhood creates a rare moment when men's protective instincts toward their families can be channeled into looking after themselves.

The genius of this approach is its indirection. We might stubbornly resist caring for ourselves, but caring for our children? That's nonnegotiable. These programs don't ask men to suddenly value self-care; they simply align health with what we already deeply understand: our historical role as protector and provider. It's not about vanity, or even longevity. It's about being there for those we love, who will count on us for decades to come.

Searching for a Signal

When you begin to listen to your body, pain becomes something if not welcomed, then appreciated. My body shoots a flare through the sky, screaming to be noticed by my amygdala and reminding me, once again, of everything I already know I should be doing: drink more water (and less alcohol), stretch every day, get my heart rate up a few times a week, see the doctor and dentist regularly. Finding time to do any of these is hard, especially in the depths of raising children. But the cruel irony is that these habits are more essential than ever, because nothing prepares you for the brutal physicality of raising kids.

All new parents sing their own cover version of our team's collective theme song: *We're exhausted.* Before having kids, I vaguely recall other parents or older relatives telling me—in those heady days when life was freer and easier—that they were tired. I'm sure I nodded empathetically, assuming it was just late nights and early mornings wiping these parents out. I was tired too—but my sleep deprivation routines were for different reasons, and entirely self-inflicted.

What I wish those parents had told me back then is this: "Yes, the nights are tough. But it's the days that will truly put your body through it." While I was writing this book, my wife took the kids away to see their grandparents, and it was a revelation how much easier life was when they weren't around. When I didn't have to clean every room of the house, yet again, every time I walked into it; the mental shock that physical spaces can remain, days since I last stepped into them, in precisely the same condition as before. There are times when my children are in the house, the doors to their rooms are closed, and I wonder: If I leave them like that, maybe the mess doesn't exist—a thought experiment I think of as *Schrödinger's Bedroom.* Parenting is the reluctant acceptance of becoming a full-time live-in cleaner, chef, teacher, taxi driver, coach, and counselor. You are consigned to the Sisyphean ordeal of occupying a house where you'll spend close to two decades on your hands and knees, picking play-time detritus out of the carpet, while a small cyclone (or two) works its way through the adjoining rooms: a Tasmanian-devil-in-training, destroying faster than you can rebuild, leaving a trail of puzzle pieces and dirty socks in their wake, and behind every corner is yet another Lego brick somehow both invisible and magnetically attracted to the soles of your feet.

No wonder we're tired. If you're not reaching down, you're lifting up: hoisting them out of the bath; raising them into the air in screaming delight; heaving the stroller out of the car with one hand while hefting a bag full of baby gear in the other, hoping they balance each other out. It's visceral—with every push and pull, the physicality of parenting lays a constant barrage on your body. It's a period of your life when, for a good few years, your morning can begin with a child jumping onto your bed and launching themself onto your delicates. And those days don't get any better.

"You got off easy," I hear a sea of women thinking as they read this. And yes, you are all correct. I'm not going to pretend, for even one minute, that what happens to the body of a new dad is even comparable to what a new mother encounters in the nine months before, and the years after, having a child. But while our pains are less, our inability to do something about them is what destroys us. Crisis is the only thing that kicks us into gear. We have mastered the art of the excuse. "No time" is a popular one, as we carve our days into tiny fragments of work, family, self, and sleep, convincing ourselves that not a single minute remains for our well-being. The truth is more uncomfortable: We make time for what we prioritize, and we aren't prioritizing our health. The same man who claims he can't find thirty minutes to see the doctor somehow finds two hours for a football match, to try out a new PlayStation game, or to binge "just one more" episode of TV before heading to bed hours later than he should've. (That "same man" is me, in case of any doubt.) "Too tired" to prioritize physical health is another well-worn path. Fatherhood fatigue is real—I feel it in my bones—but it becomes circular logic, a doom spiral. We're too exhausted to exercise, so we remain unfit, making us more tired, ensuring that exercise remains impossible. The cycle continues while our energy reserves dwindle further.

I spent years in this loop, each day promising tomorrow would be different. Finally, I found a way out.

Back to Basics: Sustainable Habits, Tiny Challenges

Without the right interventions, our bodies will only continue to get weaker. As much as we relished telling kids on the playground that "my dad could beat your dad in a fight," society normalizes the decline of paternal strength and attractiveness as a given. The running joke of "dad bod" permeates conversation while the Overton window on what constitutes it shifts dangerously. (Don't believe me? Google *Jason Momoa dad bod*. I apologize in advance for anyone whose day is ruined by this photo.) Dads are given permission to increase their waistlines as their muscle mass goes in the opposite direction. A fitness regime is a predictable casualty of fatherhood. When you begin caring for an entirely new body—supercute, incredibly defenseless, comes with complete dependence, available while supplies last—your own figure becomes less of a pressing concern.

Raising children is a marathon, not a sprint. And like any good marathon, it's all about training and pacing yourself (or so I've been reliably informed). Over the last few years, I've started listening to my body and working on my physical well-being: staying active, getting strong, ensuring that I can keep lifting my kids. Becoming a parent means new highs and lows in life—some today, others tomorrow. Every year will bring something new, for decades to come—one day I'll watch my children get married, have children of their own, and see that next generation learn to navigate the world just as my own children did. I don't know about you, but I want to be able to enjoy these moments, long into old age.

Since becoming a father, I've found myself reframing what physical health means. It's no longer selfish, mere vanity, or due to mortal dread, but it's a desire to be here, and be fighting fit for as long as I can, so I can experience as much as possible of what poet Mary Oliver called my "one wild and precious life." My health is a gift to my family, in the present and in the future. Years ago I coached a dad who told me about why fitness played such a huge part in his life: "I want to be as active and engaged with my grandchildren as I am with my own kids." To him, an hour in the gym wasn't an hour squandered, or taken away from his family—it was a down payment on a better life, to bear fruit after decades, not days. I look at my father-in-law, the man who first told me "health is wealth," who crawls around on the floor with his grandchildren well into his seventies, and I think, *I want some of that.*

So how do we get there, especially for parents whose time and energy are such a precious resource? Here are five things that have worked for me:

1. Focus on the basics. There's no denying that your health would be in a better place if you had an ice-cold plunge pool, a Peloton bike, and a personal nutritionist preparing your meals with scientifically optimized macros. But some hard facts: What's "boring" really works. Are you getting the right amount of sleep every day? (New parents, feel free to roll your eyes here.) Are you eating your five portions of fruit and veg, and drinking enough water that it feels like the bathroom is becoming your second home-inside-a-home? Or are you falling down yet another rabbit hole of supposed perfect solutions? I've spent hours watching workout videos of impossibly ripped men who have cracked the code of physical perfection—if I'd invested half that time with a set of dumbbells, I'd have arms like the Rock.

2. Find sustainable habits. Tolstoy once wrote, "True life is lived only where these tiny, tiny, infinitesimally small changes occur." One mistake many dads make when they begin to prioritize health is to do it in an extravagant fashion: committing to a thirty-day juice cleanse, signing up for a marathon after having only ever run for an arriving bus, buying high-end fitness equipment only to watch it transform into a very expensive clothing rack. What works? Start small. Find something that you enjoy doing and that you can consistently make time for. I started practicing yoga in 2019—I told myself I'd commit to once a month. Small stakes, to see if my body could handle it. Once I started hitting that commitment and noticing how much more flexible I was becoming, it became a no-brainer to start going every other week, and now I'm there every Sunday morning. My daughter started kids' boxing classes, and a friend of hers joined. At pickup, they'd tease both dads, telling us that they could now beat us in a fight, and wondering when we were going to start. Eventually we relented and started a small group class between four friends, and we now go twice a week. Every Tuesday and Thursday morning, I don't wake up and wonder, "Shall I go boxing today?" I get up, realize I've paid for ten sessions up front, and head toward the fight club, rain or shine, to get punched in the face by my nearest and dearest. This weekly cadence has become a necessary structure: nonnegotiable calendar blocks where I have given myself permission to leave the house and push my body to the point of exhaustion—by choice, not by child.

3. Hold yourself accountable. The lone-wolf myth of male self-improvement is a beautiful fiction. The truth? We need others to witness our journey. I doubt I'd have kept boxing for as long as I have were it not for the friends I do it with, the trainers that cheer me on while noting my beer belly evaporating in gallons of sweat, and some meager form of what might be termed "muscle definition" making its presence felt on my arms. This extends beyond the gym—apps like Strava encourage users to give "kudos" to friends who have completed runs and rides, and inside communities new norms are created, where group encouragement can pick up the slack when individual motivation fails. In the Dadscord, our online fatherhood community filled with hundreds of dads all learning to navigate the rocky terrain of New Fatherhood together, we've created a #fitness-and-health channel where we track progress, celebrate wins, and normalize the battle against dad bod. Men who would never discuss their weight at a barbecue will excitedly post screenshots of weight tracking apps, delighted that clothes they'd earmarked for donation fit once more.

4. Set tiny challenges. I can already hear you cry: "Tiny challenges? Don't you think I've already got enough challenges with these kids?" But stick with me. When I started practicing yoga, I became shockingly aware of my body's inflexibility. The teacher would suggest a simple position—like starting the class with legs crossed—and I would look around, realizing my legs didn't bend like everyone else's. A childhood memory rushed toward me—playing Teenage Mutant Ninja Turtles with the kids down the street, and their turtle toys were better than mine: They could move in more directions, using their elbows and knees, their Raphael possessing extra points of articulation that my Donatello did not, able to battle Shredder in positions that my rigid Turtle could only dream of. I spent those early yoga sessions frustrated that my body would never flex like theirs. But weeks became months, months became years, and changes were noticeable.

I began to measure progress not against others, but against myself. And I came to realize that small challenges could push me further. Toward the end of most sessions, a teacher will invite the class to practice their "inversions," in which a majority of my class would, like an incomprehensible shamanistic ritual or intricate best-friend handshake, interlock their hands and arms on the floor before hoisting their feet into the air. I tried, but it was impossible—my arms weren't strong enough, my legs didn't lift like that, and on the off chance I could make it happen, I'd tumble down immediately like a collapsing Jenga tower. But I kept at it. One day I saw my daughter doing a headstand in the back garden and something clicked. I saw the way she went up, and my body began to believe it could move in the same way. I went out, placed the crown of my head on the grass, and raised my feet into the sky. Challenge complete.

In the year of writing this book, I set myself another challenge. At our boxing class, a particularly sadistic teacher included pull-ups in an exercise circuit, of which I could do big fat zero. He placed what looked like half a beach ball at the base of the unit and told me to jump up and down on it while holding the bar. Here I was, well into my forties, being told I was only allowed to bowl on the lane with inflatable bumpers. The humiliation burned, but I kept at it. I set myself the challenge: one pull-up before the book was delivered. Just one. I installed a bar at home and started simply hanging—sixty seconds, three times a day. I moved to assisted pull-ups with resistance bands. Progress was glacial but measurable. Every few weeks, the resistance bands would decrease in size. Last week, as I approached the final edits of this chapter, I gripped the bar, engaged my core, and hauled myself up until my chin cleared the metal. One clean pull-up. A tiny victory that nobody saw, but had me smiling like an idiot for the rest of the day.

5. Technology is your friend. I'm writing this book in 2025, and generative AI models like ChatGPT and Claude are transforming the world in unimaginable ways. Right now, it's a trivial task to upload my last few years of medical history, blood tests, data from my connected weighing scale, and nutritional intake from the tracking apps I've been using, and ask AI to become my personal fitness coach and nutritionist. It's helped craft a pull-up training schedule to take me from zero to not-quite-hero, and it can adapt the schedule on the fly based on what I'm struggling with and what is coming easy. It can offer daily modifications based on pain and issues—suggesting I switch my grip further overhand to help with painful calluses, for example. It can meal prep for me, making sure I maintain a calorie deficit and hit my protein goals while cooking something that the kids won't launch into the air as soon as I place it in front of them. I can take a picture of the fridge and ask it to suggest something healthy for dinner, based on the half-eaten pack of hummus and random assortment of vegetables that will soon begin to rot in the drawer below. And I do this knowing all the time that these are the worst models we'll use (they're getting smarter on what feels like a weekly basis) and having absolutely no clue how much better they'll be by the time you read this. (If you are, however, reading this from inside the Matrix after we've all been enslaved by an evil AI, I offer my apologies and promise to fix this in a future version of the book. That's if society hasn't crumbled entirely.)

Let's hear it from the dads on...keeping fit

After our second child was born, I found an outlet trail running two to three times a week. Working with your partner to make sure each of you gets a little time to exercise can help to lift everyone's mood. It helped me become much more present as a dad. Something else I have started to do is a little yoga, ten to twenty minutes in our living room. The kids see me doing it enough that they will join in even if for only a couple minutes (toddler attention spans, right?). Start small and build from there—it's not necessary to jump into some Olympic-style training, then get overwhelmed and give up. If you begin with some easy goals and build upon it, I think that goes a long way to maintaining some fitness over the long term. **Ivor**

I have found that for me it has been easier to stay in great shape than before I had kids because I have a more reliable schedule. But it is way harder to get out of the house, and my free time is very limited. So I bought a basic set of barbell weights and do a one-hour routine three times a week. All my lifts start at the floor. Lots of squats, deadlifts, and overhead presses. I'm in great shape, better than before I had kids. I don't get out much, so lifting is a way that my mind can escape and get out of the craziness of raising kids. I stopped about 90 percent of my drinking. I started tracking my macros and use 1.6 grams of protein per kilo as the baseline to measure my diet. It's all quite a low commitment in money and time, and brings me great joy. **Samuel**

My wife and I have one daughter under two, and a boy on the way, but I've been able to keep up my climbing routines and training. I would say that I am in excellent shape, but it isn't due to some supernatural self discipline. Not at all. In fact, it's actually because I am in love with the activity of climbing, and am motivated by the hard work, training, and incremental improvements that accompany the sport. I have had many friends at various times compliment me for my fitness, but I always dodge, or at least redirect, the compliment by pointing out that it's the love of the sport that brings the fitness along with it. I don't consider myself a fitness buff in any sense. Rather, I'm a lover of activity. So, to anyone who needs to hear it, find a sport or activity that's FUN. Don't judge where you are relative to someone else. Enjoy where YOU are at. If you enjoy it, you'll do it more. The better you get, the more motivated you will be to keep doing it. **Caleb**

Too often I hear other dads talk about "baby comes first" and that's true. But you as a protector and provider are equally important. If you are run-down, you are less capable of providing the quality of physical and emotional support that's required from your little one. It's not selfish to set aside thirty minutes a day for yourself. You are important. Your needs are important. Be a dad with vitality. Your kids will notice and love you for it. Plus, it's a great example to set for your kids in the long term if they see a parent dedicating time and energy toward a fruit-bearing endeavor. Good luck, and get to it, gentlemen! **Eric**

CHAPTER 10

The Mental Toll of Raising Children

As other fathers have done to their sons, my father—through the look in his eyes, the tone of his voice, the quality of his touch—passed the depression he did not know he had on to me just as surely as his father had passed it on to him—a chain of pain, linking parent to child across generations, a toxic legacy.

—Terry Real, *I Don't Want to Talk About It*

Old rule: *Push it down.*
New rule: *Bring it up.*

In 2018, Mind, the UK-based mental health charity, approached Ogilvy, the global advertising agency, with a problem. One in four men will deal with a mental health episode at some point in their lives, a number that, according to the World Health Organization, is consistent globally. It is almost certain that someone you know will struggle—if they haven't already—with their mental health. Mind wanted to change the framing around male mental health, to remove stigmas that stubbornly persist, helping millions affected by mental health problems—the men who suffer, and the people who love them.

For those in the advertising industry, where I once plied my trade, these are the projects you dream about. All that time you've spent shilling cleaning spray, getting teens to nag their parents for new sneakers, convincing folks to upgrade their phone, buy a better car, or switch to a new app rather than continuing using whatever they're already happy with. You get jaded—fueling the capitalist machine, persuading people to buy more stuff they don't need. And then, every so often, a brief like this lands on your desk.

Ogilvy approached this endeavor not by focusing on the men fighting the fight, but on their best friends—delivering a compelling big idea to help them sit up and take note: "Be in your mate's corner." They made a TV commercial, a website, posters—the usual ad suspects—that went up across the country. So far, so normal. But then—in one of those ideas that usually ends up languishing on page 43 of the client presentation, sandwiched between social media stunts or some futile attempt to "make it go viral"—a wise strategist or copywriter (or maybe a magical combination of both) suggested a concept brutal in its simplicity, laser focused with its insight: a beer mat asking *Is there a mate missing around this table?* If their curiosity was piqued by the front—*Yeah, has anyone heard from Danny?*—flipping the beer mat over would nudge them into action mode. "If your mate's been acting differently," it suggested, "it could be a sign of a mental health problem."

Anyone with an ounce of creativity in their body knows this feeling—delighted envy, smiling through gritted teeth—of seeing the work of another and closing their eyes, followed by their fists, seething: "I wish I'd made this." That's how I felt, seeing this recontextualization of the humble beer mat, something primarily ignored, its raison d'etre to prevent liquid stains on a wooden table. One moment, having a drink with friends, and then, in a heartbeat: The invisible is recognized, an impression of a dotted outline discernible, an absence recorded. That friend—the one who always used to be here, who we haven't seen in a while—what's happening with him? The beer mat suggested three simple steps: *Reach out, be yourself, do what you love together.*

It's difficult to measure the impact of a single piece of advertising. Even harder in the real world, and certainly when the required outcome is more complicated than "Install Now" or "Buy Here." So it's impossible to measure the effectiveness of this gentle nudge, this reminder for men to look out for a friend. But the impact wasn't zero. Even if you didn't see the beer mat in the pub, you might have seen it on the website formerly known as Twitter, where the tweet where I first encountered this beer mat still stands, seven years, 62,525 retweets, and 181,668 likes later.

Sitting around a pub table, it's easy to picture the friend who isn't there. But what happens when weekends in bars become a thing of the past? When a change in lifestyle means you're now home more than ever? The first year after the birth of a child is when new parents are particularly at risk for first and recurrent episodes of mental illness. Younger and first-time dads are most susceptible, and those with a partner experiencing depression can have a 50 percent chance of following suit. And it doesn't just come for us at the starting line. One study found that by the time their children reach age twelve, 21 percent of dads will have experienced a depressive episode. A follow-up study found that children are 43 percent more likely to develop depression later in life if they grew up in a household with a depressed father. I've seen these numbers firsthand. They've shown up in my inbox and on comment threads. They've been discussed in dads' circles I've attended. Like any evolved predator, paternal postpartum depression has its defenses—a chameleon-like ability to disguise itself as standard new-parent stress: constantly tired, lacking the energy to leave the house, having no time to do anything—take a shower, cook dinner, answer the phone—because it's all too much.

When undiagnosed, unacknowledged, and untreated, mental health episodes lead to grave outcomes. Depression is linked with more hostile and violent parenting, issues with children's physical and mental health, poorer academic performance, and a higher risk of developing chronic conditions, including depression and anxiety, as adults. For postpartum depression, research remains heavily skewed toward the female experience, where we have seen incidents of self-harm on the rise and diagnoses of suicidality for new mothers tripling since the pandemic. When we layer on what we already know about male suicide—that it's the leading cause of death for young men, that a man is four times as likely to kill himself as a woman is, and that 62 percent of male suicides occur on the first known attempt—it becomes clear why fathers dealing with mental health problems are up to forty-seven times as likely to show suicide warning signs in the months after a baby arrives. This sickness has been killing dads for decades. We're only just starting to connect the dots.

When you layer this data over the increased time that dads spend at home, and its correlation with depression, a painful picture begins to emerge. How many of these deaths have we already witnessed? Frances Bean Cobain was twenty months old when her father, Kurt, took his own life. INXS front man Michael Hutchence's daughter Tiger Lily? Sixteen months old. Joy Division's lead singer Ian Curtis died leaving behind a daughter who had only just turned one. Donny Hathaway, Chris Cornell, Chester Bennington—all musicians and fathers who took their own lives. The names, places, and ages change, but the song remains the same.

I've Been Down Here Before

I carried that beer mat through my depression and out the other side.

I was working remotely in 2019—a rare pre-pandemic work-from-homer. My son was born in April of that year. I'd leave Barcelona for meetings and to run client workshops, but I was home the rest of the time—a new city where I didn't have a lot of support, in a place invisible from old friends who might have noticed my withdrawal from society, becoming increasingly irritable, unsatisfied with the life adjustment, leaning on crutches like alcohol and drugs to help escape the pain and mask reality. Living like that is hard, but those symptoms mask a deeper, more troubling existence: The only thing more exhausting than depression is pretending to everyone else that you're okay.

"Where's *my* Jenny?," the question I asked back in Chapter Three, was one of the first pieces of writing I shared publicly. I was trying to make sense of what seemed like an impenetrable conundrum—to understand why, for so many generations, men have failed to support each other during one of the most challenging phases of their lives. When I was battling my own demons, I wondered, "Where are all the people lining up to help me?" But pointing the finger gets us nowhere, and it artfully dodges the actual truth: I was the one who didn't want to talk. I wanted to be left the fuck alone. I was a Thom Yorke lyric made manifest: *I'm not here, this isn't happening.* If my phone started ringing, then ring it would until it rang out. (It didn't ring, of course; it's been constantly set to silent since 2016. What am I, some kind of monster?)

When you search Google for images about depression—you're always at it, you can admit it, we're all friends here—you're guaranteed to see the same hackneyed depictions: a rain cloud following someone around, a man with his head in his hands. My recollection of this time was less of a black cloud, but ping-ponging between alternate states: the first where every action—a walk with the dog, a call with a friend, a quick nip to the shops—was akin to a punishing walk through knee-deep sludge toward nowhere; the other, a complete nothingness—devoid of emotion, numb to life, a vacuum of space where joy used to be. Looking into your newborn child's eyes and feeling nothing as he cracks his first smile? I don't recommend it. It was the emotional equivalent of watching paint dry. It was horrible. For all of us.

Looking back on this time isn't easy. Writing about it leaves me emotionally exhausted. For dads who lived through a similar experience, reading about it can feel like a workout. (Feel free to take a break, get some fresh air, go touch some grass.) What pushes me to write every week, rain or shine, is knowing that other dads out there will find solace in a shared experience, and that they're not going through this alone. A few months after I started the newsletter, a good friend left a comment: "I also suffered from depression after my son was born, even though I never admitted it to anyone, including myself. Convincing myself that I was only tired and everyone goes through it. All sorts of hostile feelings of resentment and jealousy and feeling tired and sick of it all. Trying to bury it and rise above it only meant it lasted that much longer. Thank you for writing about this."

I invoke the specter of suicide in this chapter not for shock value but as a cautionary tale on where this road may lead. In the years of writing the newsletter, I've penned well over a dozen essays on mental health. (Google *fatherhood mental health checkpoint* and you can read them all.) The intention is that they collectively form a digital honeypot: an attempt to game Google's opaque algorithms in the hope that dads out there struggling might find their way to them and begin to pull on the red thread as a way out of their personal labyrinth. And I raise it with great hesitation, knowing that many reading this will feel a searing pain in seeing the words *dad* and *suicide* in such close proximity. It might have been a friend. An uncle. It might have been your own father. Far too many of us have grown up without men in our lives who should still be here. That's why it's essential that we get better at spotting the signs, calling them out, and caring for one another.

On December 13, 2000, NBC aired "Noël," the tenth episode of *The West Wing*'s second season. It sees Josh Lyman, White House deputy chief of staff, dealing with the fallout from an assassination attempt on the president. His boss, Leo McGarry (a recovering alcoholic), pushes him to see a therapist after a failed suicide attempt, and he is diagnosed with post-traumatic stress disorder (PTSD). Toward the end of the episode, Leo tells Josh a story:

> *This guy's walking down the street when he falls in a hole.*
>
> *The walls are so steep he can't get out.*
>
> *A doctor passes by and the guy shouts up, "Hey you. Can you help me out?" The doctor writes a prescription, throws it down in the hole, and moves on.*
>
> *Then a priest comes along and the guy shouts up, "Father, I'm down in this hole, can you help me out?" The priest writes out a prayer, throws it down in the hole, and moves on.*

Then a friend walks by. "Hey, Joe, it's me. Can you help me out?" And the friend jumps in the hole. Our guy says, "Are you stupid? Now we're both down here."

The friend says, "Yeah, but I've been down here before and I know the way out."

Less than six months after this episode aired, writer and showrunner Aaron Sorkin was arrested at Hollywood Burbank Airport. Security staff found a plethora of drugs in his carry-on luggage, including crack cocaine. Sorkin checked himself into rehab, later admitting that the first two seasons of the show were written entirely while he was holed up in a hotel room, with a Do Not Disturb sign on the door and a crack pipe close to hand. It's not a huge leap to see these words as something that Sorkin was seeking himself, manifesting his own Jenny into Leo's dialogue.

Since coming out the other side, I've been more intentional about reaching out to friends who have become new fathers. Sometimes I'll share a version of what you've read above. Other times, it's just a text: "Hey. I had a tough time and I'm here if you ever want to talk about it. It's okay to not be okay." I'll regularly call new dads who have opened up and told me they're finding it tough. When I tell them what I went through, some will have the same realization I did when I first opened up to other dads: "So I'm not alone. I'm not just 'being soft.' This isn't all in my head." Today's dads are being asked to navigate territory our fathers never entered. We lack the guides and necessary equipment. We're expected to be vulnerable caregivers in a culture that still rewards stoic providers. We're treating mental health as an afterthought, then acting surprised when the shit hits the fan and explodes everywhere.

From the depths of this hole, I'd think of that beer mat's simple advice and feel its crushing weight. How do you reach out when your instinct is to disappear? How do you *be yourself* when you no longer recognize who you are? How do you do what you love when nothing brings joy? That impossibility contains depression's dirty secret: While we picture it as an individual battle, it's a collective failing—a gap in the fabric of society that fathers keep falling through, and a damning indictment of the individualistic society that we live in. When I read about another dad lost to suicide, I don't see individual tragedy. I see hospital check-ins that screen mothers for PPD while fathers sit quietly in waiting rooms, flicking through their phones; workplaces that expect new dads to function at full capacity days after their world has been fundamentally altered forever; tumbleweeds passing through group chats while dads quietly scream for support.

I spent months in that place. I know the effect that paternal postpartum depression can have. How it can rip families apart. How it makes dads resent their children—maybe forever, during the most magical months of their lives—because they aren't getting the help they need. I always lean glass half full and feel lucky that this happened with my second child, when I had the sense that something wasn't right and had enough curiosity to keep pulling on that thread. But there are thousands of undiagnosed dads, silently suffering, unsure of why they feel the way they feel. Taking it out on themselves. Their partners. Their family. Their friends. And—worst of all—on their children.

Now What?

We often perceive mental health struggles in terms of binary—we are okay, or we are not. Men underestimate their need for help, suffering silently until they hit some imaginary threshold before they reach out for help. By then, just like with a delayed diagnosis for our physical health, we're months behind schedule. If you have a friend who recently became a dad and you think he might be going through a hard time, think of the beer mat: "Reach out, be yourself, do what you love together."

If you recognize yourself in this chapter and want help, start small:

- Talk to one person—anyone—about how you're actually feeling. Not the sanitized version, but the truth, the whole truth, and nothing but the truth. Reaching out isn't a sign of weakness. It's the bravest, boldest thing you can do, flipping the finger at the generations of fathers, past and present, who refuse to open up.

- Earlier in the book, I talked about the Edinburgh Postnatal Depression Scale, and how useful it was in helping to screen new mothers for postpartum depression. While it's not perfect for fathers—as men exhibit different symptoms—I've reviewed multiple papers and worked with medical experts to develop an online questionnaire you can take that will give you an idea of whether you might be exhibiting symptoms of paternal postpartum depression and should seek medical help. This is completely anonymous and should take less than five minutes. I've put a link to access this self-assessment in the appendix.

- If you've had thoughts about harming yourself or someone in your family, help is available. If you are in immediate danger, call 911 in the United States, 999 in the UK, or 112 in the EU. Many countries provide free 24/7 crisis support: In the United States and Canada you can call or text 988 to get help; in the UK and Ireland, contact the Samaritans on 116 123.

- And keep reading. Because I've been down this hole before. And I know the way out.

Let's hear it from the dads on…mental health battles

My daughter (our first child) is now thirteen months old and I have recently had to take some leave from work, as my depression and anxiety became unbearable. So much of what you wrote about resonates. I didn't feel the instant connection to her when she was born, which devastated me, and that led to me disengaging and instead focusing on other things (work, house projects, etc.). I have seen a therapist regularly since 2018 and continue to now. Overall, despite not feeling like there is light at the end of this tunnel, I am so grateful for those who open up and share their experience. I have only one friend in my life that I can talk to openly about this. He hasn't gone through the same with his two children, but he definitely understands, can empathize, and is a great friend. Thank you for helping me not feel alone and so ashamed. **Nate**

I was diagnosed with paternal postpartum depression about six months after my son was born; having been in denial about it for a while, I just found myself crying a lot. Up until reading your story, I struggled to find anyone dealing with the same thing—or at least willing to talk about it. All the dads I met through our baby group seemed fine and loving fatherhood; my few friends who have children couldn't stop effusing about how much they loved it. It just pulls you further and further into the hole. I came out of therapy back in June, but have just had to restart it again. It's so good to know that others go through the same thing, as it's so easy to fall into the mindset that there is something fundamentally wrong with me. **Alex**

I suffered in the exact same way. It took two years to the date of her birth to begin to come out of my depression. Today, she is seven years old; she and I have an amazing relationship. I couldn't imagine my life without her. Dads who are suffering, this will pass, this will get better. Hang in there, the positive will shine through, there is light at the end of this tunnel. **Mark**

PART III

UPGRADE YOUR OPERATING SYSTEM

Knowing where fatherhood was, and where we now find ourselves, means we are armed with the knowledge to step into a new version of it. But crossing that threshold will require nothing less than a fundamental rewiring in how we parent, and a tool kit of techniques to make it a reality.

CHAPTER 11

Reframe the Present

Instructions for living a life: Pay attention. Be astonished. Tell about it.

—Mary Oliver

Old rule: *Control their behavior.*
New rule: *Understand your own.*

I'm occasionally asked, "What's one piece of advice you would give new parents?"

It's an easy answer. The same nugget I wish I'd been given ten years ago: "Buy a small notebook, keep it handy, and write down things you notice about them." It doesn't need to be every day, once a week, or with any kind of regular cadence. Simply start scratching in pencil the things that itch your brain. They may be significant milestones, but they'll just as easily be minor, almost imperceptible, events that you alone observed. Maybe it was how they smiled to themself on that first crawl. Or the time they played for hours with a cardboard box, instead of the sustainably sourced and outrageously expensive wooden blocks that came inside it. As they grow older and start talking, you'll be able to capture the funny little phrases they said, their adorable mispronunciations and malapropisms. Over the years, you'll end up with a book filled with almost-forgotten memories, and verbatim quotes to be remembered forever. "Future You" will one day offer thanks to "Today You" for forever enshrining these fleeting moments.

I didn't do it. I wish I had. I got there eventually, I suppose. The weekly newsletter might become the best record of the early years of my kids' lives, the only journaling habit that has managed to stick. When I started sending the newsletter, I had no claim calling myself a writer—I'd spent my career writing decks and docs for internal stakeholders, not external audiences. I was fluent in business bullshit. If I was going to write, I wanted to do it right. I focused on the craft. I read stories: from comedians, philosophers, and poets; books from fishermen, wannabe chefs, dying doctors, and psychedelic explorers; personal stories regaled with vivid prose and deep vulnerability. And I read books that taught me how to write. These books wormed their way into my brain as I began "noticing in public" to a growing audience of dads. The finest of all these books, and the one I have recommended consistently since—where I slowly savored every page and paragraph, that felt more like reading the philosophy of writing rather than its rules—was *Several Short Sentences About Writing* by Verlyn Klinkenborg. I spent weeks methodically tagging favorite passages with neon pink and blue stickies, pencil notes forged in margins like I was seventeen and back in English literature class once again. This is not a book about writing. This is a book about writing as a tool to rethink living itself. Klinkenborg, author, academic, and former editor of *The New York Times*, wrote in praise of paying attention and the power of noticing:

> *Noticing means thinking with all your senses.*
> *it requires a suspension of yearning*
> *And a pause in the desire of pouring something out of yourself.*
> *Noticing is about letting yourself out into the world,*
> *rather than siphoning it into you*
> *In order to transmute it into words.*

This book about writing permitted me to slow down in every aspect of my life, teaching that the only way to transform thoughts into meaning was to stop, look up, and pay attention. This book upgraded my mind's operating system—changing the way I perceive the world and the interactions I make as I move through it. It did, without question, make me a better writer. But becoming a better dad was an unintended side effect. Because your ability to notice is impaired if you're mentally somewhere else—body at home, mind at work, or face stuck in a glowing rectangle. Noticing rewards your ability to observe the connective tissue of family life and experience ephemeral moments that might otherwise go unnoticed. Our days raising children are filled with countless curiosities to be followed, and the rewards are vast. As Klinkenborg writes: "It's catching your sleeve on the thorn of the thing you notice, and paying attention as you free yourself."

Emotion Does Not Equal Response

But noticing is more than chronicling the external events you see and hear. What might start as seeing everything around you will inevitably lead to turning attention back on itself—noticing the forces that influence your thoughts and the actions you take. Life moves fast; it's all too easy to throw ourselves down the icy parenting track on a toboggan made from old boards and duct tape. Perhaps babies should come with a warning, the same way cigarettes do: Raising children leads to emotional whiplash. In any given day, you'll sharply steer between any and all of the twenty-seven distinct emotions that Berkeley researchers identified as part of the human condition. You've got the tier-one feelings, the *Inside Out* stars: joy, sadness, anger, fear. You've got the others that crept in for the sequel: anxiety, envy, embarrassment (the incredible French je ne sais quoi of ennui didn't make the Berkeley list, but they had boredom in there, which is her non-French close cousin).

Becoming a father is a crash course in emotional recognition. Quick: Is this baby happy? Why did his face just turn sad? He's cranky, he must need sleep. Or maybe he's hungry again. You use every sense in your toolbox, including regularly sticking your nose into their arse in public to see if you can locate the root cause. He's mad at something, and just like a time bomb ticking away in your hands, you need to cut the right wire before it blows up in your face. Babies inevitably get older. Become toddlers. Further feelings join the fray. They're up on two legs, navigating the world with their emotions at the wheel, everyone else holding on for dear life. The toddler tantrum is a force to be reckoned with, but every storm provides a chance to teach them how to navigate through it. When they're younger, naming emotions can be enough. *Inside Out* offers parents a useful shortcut to getting kids to talk about their feelings—we've had many a tear-stained conversation about the angry red man who sets on fire, especially as my son seems to noticeably heat up by a few degrees when he loses his shit. As they get older, their emotions get more complex, interdependent, a wiry web that will keep going into adulthood. Our job is to help them grab a handle on the reins rather than have the horse bolt off course.

But, for many men, this work can feel entirely alien. Your ability to do it for your children is inexorably linked to your ability to do it for yourself. And it wasn't something that came easy to me. Before I was a father, the simple act of noticing, naming, and sitting with an emotion felt akin to transporting a caveman into modern-day New York City, showing him an iPhone, and asking him to tell you about his favorite apps. Many of today's fathers were young boys who grew up in a different era of fatherhood: a home, a society, and a world where men were not expected—or permitted—to discuss their feelings, but only act on them. Fathers told sons "boys don't cry" and attempted to stop the tears the only way they knew: with the threat of physical or emotional violence, offering a terrifying alternative: "Stop it, or I'll give you something to cry about."

When I first started seeing Mia, my therapist, whom I'd work with for two years after my son was born, I was proud of my long-distance relationship with anger. We didn't know each other that well, he went to a different school, it all seemed to be working out for both of us. "I hardly ever get angry," I told her. "Maybe the last time was over a year ago?" For all my life, I'd kept it at bay. There remain a few clear and occasional instances of me losing my temper: attempting to kick my twin sisters as a young boy, when they closed the door at the perfect time and I put my foot right through it; a fight with a friend in the changing room after gym class; my final year of university when I couldn't get some computer science coursework to compile, battling bugs I couldn't fix, and slamming my laptop shut, tipping my feeble IKEA table over, and storming out of the house.

Mia wondered why I would suppress an emotion that seemed to occur naturally in everyone else. She pulled the blinkers down, offering a path toward a different perspective: "What happens when you're in a situation that would normally make others angry?" I wasn't sure how to answer. I pictured myself in such a place and noticed a tightness in my stomach. I wasn't sure what the feeling was, but I knew what it was telling me to do—stand up, walk away, and do what I've always done. It's how I react to conflict: I remove myself from the vicinity of it. When she asked me to name the emotion, I would struggle. "I'm overwhelmed," I'd offer. "That's not an emotion," she'd counter every time I mislabeled a state as a feeling. It was like being asked to call out the colors on the rope that was pulling me into the depths of the ocean.

One of therapy's biggest unlocks seems simple in hindsight. Mia asked me why I wouldn't allow myself to get angry with my kids, even when they were exhibiting behaviors that clearly called for it. She told me to close my eyes and picture myself in such a moment, asking why I wouldn't, or couldn't, allow myself to get mad. I began to name something I'd never found the words for, something always present: "I'm afraid I will hit them." She told me: "Anger is not the same as violence." Those seven words, an idea seemingly obvious to many—that emotion does not equal action—still seems to me, years later, like a magic trick: like she pulled apart the hemispheres of my brain and unwound two wires that had been crossed decades earlier.

Emotions come thick and fast for a parent. The insight commonly offered to expectant dads is that "the highs will be higher, and the lows will be lower." Even if your highs may have been chemically driven in your youth, they won't get close to how parenting can blindside you with feelings. One day, I was reading my six-year-old son *Dogs Don't Do Ballet*, and we came to the point where—spoiler alert for children's picture book—the dog steps up at the ballet show and performs all the moves: *"Plié! Jeté! Arabesque! Pirouette!"*

"Those words sound French," my son noted. I was surprised. He speaks Catalan and Spanish at school, but French was a new one on me. I wondered how he knew. He talked about his friend whose mother is French but who doesn't speak it at school. He just felt they were French. My mind was blown. How did he figure that out? This isn't my first rodeo—I've a laundry list of similar moments with his elder sister, who dazzled us from her early days. As children get older and spend more time with friends and teachers, they begin to produce what my computer science mind would call "unpredictable outputs." Their brains work in a way that is a step beyond what you thought they were capable of.

I don't know how long this book will be on the shelves, but there's a fair chance that by the time you read this, bedtimes will look very different in our house. In the newsletter, I once wrote a list of books I'll miss reading to my kids (I'll leave a link in the appendix). By the time you read this, even more of my favorites will be passed to nephews and nieces. (But you'll only pry *This Is Not My Hat* from my cold, dead hands.) Your experience of bedtimes is—in a leitmotif that will resonate throughout your years of fatherhood—entirely dependent on your mindset going into them. Are you entering the bedroom and willing it to be over already? We've all been there: an inbox of unanswered emails beckoning you from the other side of "however long this will take." But is that the exception or the rule? Because a good bedtime? We all know how that feels. Like a sharp pair of scissors gliding through wrapping paper. When the stars align, everything falls into place—a drama-free soak in the bath, out and dry, standing proud to have their teeth brushed rather than squirming around like Houdini attempting to free himself of chains. When you get them into their pajamas and tucked in with F1 pit-stop-like efficiency. The semi-honest yawns you fake as you're reading their book are taken as intended, echoing contagiously from their mouths and sending them slowly toward slumber, into which they fall and, hopefully, will remain until the morning.

Sometimes the best part of my day—and theirs too—arrives at its end. It's a chance to recap the day as your child decides bedtime is the ideal opportunity to tell you—in a Dickensian level of detail—what happened since you dropped them off at school, after giving up diddly-squat when you asked, "How was your day today?" when collecting them. Putting them down to bed offers a chance to peer into that brain they're building, to see what they're processing from the past twenty-four hours, to notice the new things they've discovered about how the world works, and to answer the inevitable questions that will be coming your way.

Your ability to be the parent you aspire to be hinges on your ability to manage the everyday emotional flashpoints in the house, and to stay present in these situations, interrogate your feelings, and find space between emotion and action. Renowned therapist and psychologist Rollo May once wrote, "Human freedom involves our capacity to pause between the stimulus and response and, in that pause, to choose the response toward which we wish to throw our weight." This can be tough, especially in the midst of what regularly feels like a world collapsing for a young mind (and occasionally for an older one too). Anything you can use to your advantage is essential. Opening the empathy valve and learning to label my emotions has helped me become more fluent in the language of my own thoughts and feelings. Sure, that means I fall apart at movies more often now (damn you, Moana, and your fierce feminist drive to ride those waves alone), but it also means I can demonstrate how to show anger appropriately: if and when the situation warrants it, when I consciously choose my kids have crossed a line and it becomes a proportional response.

This work isn't easy. It requires nothing less than a fundamental rewiring of your emotional CPU, and a fight-or-flight response that may have been dictating your decisions for decades. I've found two sets of techniques to make this rewiring take hold: one consisting of short-term and fairly simple reframes, and another that's going to require you to open up Pandora's box and go deeper.

I. Reframes and Hacks

You've spent this chapter reading about some reframes; longtime newsletter readers will be familiar with many more. Buried deep in a Reddit thread I found a similar, golden-gilded elegant hack to fatherhood that is now seared in the minds of so many dads I know.

It's simple: If your child is having a meltdown, say to yourself, "They're not *giving you* a hard time, they're *having* a hard time." With this short phrase, you're gifted an instant shot of empathy to the heart as you burst back to life like Mia Wallace in *Pulp Fiction*. Another: In a moment of crisis, find comfort in these four words: *This too shall pass*, nudging you toward the importance of impermanence. If it nudges you as far as Gandalf the White, you've been pushed too far; it was "You shall not pass!" he bellowed in the Mines of Moria.

Another powerful mental reframe is the Last Time Meditation. I first wrote about this in 2021 and have lost count of the number of dads who have thanked me for sharing it in the years since. One told me recently: "I've thought about this at least once a day ever since I read it five years ago." You don't need to know anything about meditation to do it—in fact, the word is a red herring here. It couldn't be easier. As William B. Irvine, who coined the term, explained it:

> *When you're doing something, you should reflect on the possibility that this might be the last time you do it. Again, you don't dwell on this possibility, it's just a flickering thought. Doing this can dramatically change your perspective on the events of your daily life. Mowing*

my lawn can be a burden, particularly on a hot day, but I can lighten that burden by remembering that there will be a last time that I am physically able to mow a lawn, and that after that time has passed, I will likely look back on these as the good old days.

The Last Time Meditation works. I promise you. I do it all the time. I did it for years when drying my daughter's hair. It's incredibly long—she's a few years off becoming a teenager, and it's only seen a pair of hairdresser scissors once (and our kitchen scissors occasionally, when she got a hair tie caught in it). She hated getting it dried—and I hated drying it too, because she'd complain, refuse to sit still, and get frustrated as I attempted to comb out the knots. We would both end up annoyed with each other. Years ago, I'd stop, ponder on the last time, and observe a feeling of sadness, knowing that very soon she'd be drying her own hair. And here we are, a few years later: She dries her own hair, and I look back on it nostalgically. Its power is its versatility: Walking back from school in a storm? Imagine it's the last time you'll feel raindrops hitting your face. Heading back to your desk after a nightmare meeting with your boss? One day it'll be the last time, and you'll walk out of the office and on to whatever comes next. Changing your baby's diaper? Realize, with gratitude, that one day you won't be doing this, while aware—sorry to inform you—you'll still be wiping their crack for a while to come.

II. Toward Deeper Changes

Noticing. Reframing bedtimes. Getting curious about the last time. These small-scale hacks are essential to get you through what can feel like a battlefield, and to do it leaving no child behind. But they are only what psychologists call *first-order changes*: adjustments that help you cope better within the confines of an existing system. Think of them as seat belts in a car—if you end up in a crash, you've got something to lessen the impact and avoid the worst consequences. First-order changes are valuable and necessary. They help you navigate parenting with more grace and less reactivity and can be the difference between losing your temper when your child has a meltdown in the grocery store and taking a breath and activating the empathy valve.

But there's a deeper level of transformation available: *second-order changes*. These don't just help you cope with stress; they fundamentally alter your relationship to it. While reframes help you recover from emotional overwhelm more quickly, second-order changes can prevent those reactions from arising at all, and the parenting applications are profound. Rather than merely surviving challenging parenting trials, you develop the capacity to remain present and engaged, and your kids notice the difference. They will feel the solidity of your presence rather than the precariousness of your coping mechanisms.

The better you get at managing your own mental state, the better you'll be at helping your children to do the same. Do you want to be the parent who dives toward the perceived shelter of safety, or the one who lands on the grenade so your children develop better mechanisms for dealing with their own extreme emotions? In *The Whole-Brain Child*—a parenting book all-timer, and one I go back to every few years—readers are offered a mental model to help children navigate difficult moments and shift their mindset. Roughly paraphrasing—because go buy the book already—the central metaphor used throughout is to treat a child's developing brain like a house under construction. The authors, Daniel J. Siegel and Tina Payne Bryson, overlay the common "left versus right" neurology narrative with the additional dimensions of "upstairs and downstairs": a downstairs brain that aligns with and controls our fight-or-flight response and emotional triggers, and an upstairs brain that deals with higher-order reasoning, which is "responsible for producing many of the characteristics we hope to see in our kids: sound decision-making and planning, control over emotions and body, self-understanding, empathy and morality."

Siegel and Bryson implore parents to take every opportunity we have to lead our children up the staircase, aiding them in the necessary remodeling work so they can become more emotionally resilient and fully functioning adults—avoiding a life "trapped in the basement" as they grow older. And the book draws a clear link between your ability to use these tools on yourself and your ability to provide them for your children:

> *By integrating your implicit and explicit memories and by shining the light of awareness on difficult moments from your past, you can gain insight into how your past is impacting your relationship with your children. You can remain watchful for how your issues are affecting your own mood as well as how your kids feel. When you feel incompetent, frustrated, or overly reactive, you can look at what's behind those feelings and explore whether they are connected to something in your past. Then you can bring your former experiences into the present and weave them into the larger story of your life. When you do that, you can be free to be the kind of parent you want to be. You can make sense of your own life, which will help your kids do the same with theirs.*

This type of thinking offers the struggling parent an escape hatch: the ability to pull yourself out of an emotional doom spiral. It allows you to view your child's tantrums and defiance not as behavioral problems but as developmental opportunities: "My child isn't being difficult—they're asserting their independence and learning emotional regulation in an environment where they feel safe to do so." And it does it while inviting you to explore the emotional baggage that you carry unwittingly to each and every moment.

This deeper work is about progress, not perfection. It is an everyday process; on some days it will come easily and with grace, and on others it absolutely will not. The reality is that rewiring our brain takes time. Setbacks are part of the journey. But the act of simply noticing the contents of your mind, and understanding the patterns that emerge, starts you on a route toward molding those rivers of thinking in new directions, kick-starting a deluge of transformation. Listening objectively to your internal narrator can be the difference between continual self-criticism and breaking free of a narrative holding you back. I will still, upon self-flagellating for some minor infraction, break the negative thought cycle by considering that "If a friend spoke to you in that way, you wouldn't be friends with them." Or to catch an outlandishly negative moment of self-sabotage, identify it as the voice of someone else, and move on. Observing our thoughts, without judgment, is a critical component of self-compassion: Noticing is an active choice in becoming kinder to yourself. So if you're ready to move beyond short-term hacks and create scientifically backed, long-lasting neural changes, there's plenty of food for thought in the next few chapters.

Let's hear it from the dads on...how you handle stress

Learning how to care for myself, much less another human, has personally been a journey. I've tried it all, and have held on to what has worked, integrating them into some kind of daily practice/habit. I found that the simple things turn out to be the most effective when done consistently over time. Things like taking vitamins that support my mental functioning and health, drinking lots of water throughout the day, getting fresh air multiple times a day—walking my dog has taken on new meaning! Also talking to friends and/or family, a book, a joint, some incense burning, hot shower and deep breaths. In the end, I just try to do things that support my mental and physical health daily, and when I have a particularly tough day, I just turn up the dial on those things. **Kervs**

In the early days of fatherhood, I tried to control the uncontrollable and found that was an impossible task. This led to more frustration, losing my temper at tiny things, just generally being unpleasant to be around. It took me some time (my little girl is sixteen months now) to realize that sometimes I just need to take a step back and breathe. Think about the situation, the outcomes, and do the best you can. I still get stressed, but I try to spot the triggers, be it that rising feeling in my stomach or rush of blood to the head, and go straight into my breathing...it makes such a difference. **Chris**

I've had anxiety and depression in various guises most of my life. Over the time it has manifested itself in drinking, smoking, drugs, overeating, and destructive behaviors. All related to traumas, insecurity, and low self-worth, and then in recent years my dad got very sick with Alzheimer's and he died just before Christmas. I watched in real time as he disintegrated. I helped care for him and comfort my mother. We live two hours' drive away, and I've got a now five-year-old boy, so there was a time we juggled a lot. I experienced a lot with no release valve. As with most modern men you get on with being practical and stoic. Then you feel numb when the trauma smashes you sideways. My healing was with breathwork, journaling, cold water exposure, and reading up on consciousness and the transient nature of life and death; these all kept me going for a while. It's exhausting and debilitating. But the healing process always helps lighten the load; the trauma sits in your body, in your nervous system, ready to pounce at the slightest hint of stress. **Pete**

CHAPTER 12

Rewire Your Brain

Civilization changes a person on the outside. Meditation softens a person from within.

—Henepola Gunaratana

Old rule: *Tough it out.*
New rule: *Tune it in.*

I want you to think about something that's bothering you. It could be a problematic client at work, testing your patience. Or a colleague who's contributing to a constant low-level hum of stress. It may be a toddler who won't eat consistently or isn't sleeping well. It might be a dog that won't listen to you. (Maybe that one is just me?) It might be something bigger, the existential questions that keep us awake at night. What if you had taken that other job? What if you moved to that other city, state, or country like you said you would? Are you sending your kids to the right school? Are you teaching them the right way to live? Are you a good dad? Are you even a good person?

Now take that thing that's bothering you. Feel it. And then, imagine in an instant, it was gone. Wouldn't that be something?

I want to talk to you about meditation. And in order to do that, I need to address whatever you felt as you read that word. You may be an experienced meditator. You may have tried before but "failed" to become one, if such a thing were possible. But I'd wager that, until now, you haven't looked at it through the lens of fatherhood and considered the impact a daily practice might have on your home life: helping you be a better partner, parent, and all-around happier human being. So let's talk about how it changes the way the brain works at a basic machine code level, and talk through some examples of how it has totally rewired mine.

I know you already know about meditation. It's not new. It goes back, way back, to India, where documented records can be traced back to around 1500 BCE. This was when some of the earliest written words carried the concept of "the training of the mind." Hinduism, Buddhism, and Taoism spread meditation through the Eastern world. The practice of meditation itself didn't start to take hold in the West until the eighteenth century, when texts like the Bhagavad Gita and the Buddhist Sutras were translated to English for the first time. In the middle of the twentieth century, the first gurus started to come from India to the United States, introducing a new audience to an ancient practice: through teachers like Paramahansa Yogananda, who once wrote, "Learn to be calm and you will always be happy"; Swami Satchidananda, who opened Woodstock in 1969 (offering the crowd of over 460,000 Americans a prayer of peace and love rather than a guitar solo); and Maharishi Mahesh Yogi, who rose to prominence as spiritual advisor to the Beatles.

The history has been well told. The benefits are just as familiar. But—for fellow admirers of peer-reviewed studies—there's no snake oil getting sold here, and a compelling body of scientific research backs it all up. There have been hundreds of papers published extolling the virtues of meditation: It reduces anxiety and stress; decreases negative self-beliefs while improving emotion regulation; improves attention; positively influences memory, attention, and cognitive flexibility while reducing age-related cognitive decline; helps inform better choices and overrule cognitive biases; helps you live longer and age slower; reduces pain, insomnia, blood pressure, heart rate, and the likelihood of heart attacks; and increases happiness by encouraging us to "live in the moment." Not bad for something you can do anywhere, anytime, for free. How is this possible?

Welcome to Your Monkey Mind

The default mode network (DMN) is the area of your brain that controls what you think about when you're not actively doing something. Think of it as "standby mode" for your brain, the screen saver that engages when the more active part of your brain has nipped off for a break. It's related to various mental functions that fall primarily into four areas: thinking about oneself, thinking about others, remembering the past, and envisioning the future.

The DMN is the voice inside your mind, constantly reminding you of that stupid thing you said in a meeting last week—or the even more stupid thing you said decades ago in high school. It chastises you for losing your temper with your kids, it worries about what other people think about you, it freaks you out by reminding you you're not yet where "you should be" in life. Are you prone to revisiting events that didn't go to plan, and interrogating who and what caused it and why? The psychological term for this is *rumination*, and it has been shown to be powered by the DMN, driving unhappiness, anxiety, and even depression.

An unruly DMN robs us of joy. And try as we might to not dwell on bad memories, we can't simply will them away, like shooing away flies from a picnic. We need tools. Meditation is one of the few proven ways to increase the brain's neuroplasticity, which dictates our ability to forge new mental pathways, rewiring the brain in a way visible by fMRI scanners. An ongoing practice can create an observable quietening of the DMN. While science has proven this only recently, contemplative religions have been aware of it long before innovations in medicine made them visible on a screen. The Buddha called this "the quietening of the monkey mind," which vividly paints a picture of the internal chaos: a troop of primates leaping around, screeching, chattering, getting up to all sorts of hijinks when we'd really prefer them not to. Meditation teaches us to calm these wild monkeys and overrule the DMN.

So, once again: Think about something that bothers you. I have many—one that comes up consistently is what I'll call "all the fucking mess" that living with children can produce: the inescapable flotsam and jetsam that lies in their wake, toys and books scattered like abandoned tents and empty beer cans on the Monday morning after Coachella, all kinds of shit, in every room, every time I walk into it. I can feel myself getting annoyed when—yet again—my children manage to desecrate a clean room faster than I could clean up the previous one.

Meditation is more than a way to destress and pull yourself back from the metaphorical ledge every day. That's a mistake I made myself: I'd started at Google and was feeling a lot of pressure in a new job, the impostor syndrome dial turned up to eleven. I turned to a well-known mindfulness app in an attempt to help me keep things under control. I'd schedule ten minutes a day, go to a quiet space somewhere, and sit and listen. And it helped—for ten minutes a day. It was a moment of calm shoehorned into my calendar, my head coming up for a breath of relief before being pulled back into an ocean of chaos. It was a way to unclench my jaw so I could get home in one piece. It would be years before I committed to the practice and began to understand exactly what meditation was capable of.

Consider, for a moment: You are standing on a boat. Waves approach incessantly, an endless sea of tribulations. You know they're coming. They're inevitable. A big swell approaches, so you batten down the hatches, steering straight into them. You feel them crash upon you, take the strain, endure the struggle. But there is another way. You can take a moment. Take a breath. Reorient yourself, learning how to position the boat so the surge can peacefully pass underneath. Or, to quote Jon Kabat-Zinn and keep rolling with the ocean metaphor: "You can't stop the waves, but you can learn to surf."

Think of the last time you reacted in a way you'd rather not have. A trigger event occurs. Emotions arise: frustration, envy, fear. In an instant, you become that thought and begin to lose control. But with meditation, it's like that TV trope where a character's soul temporarily leaves their body before looking at their physical form and thinking, *What the hell am I doing?* You are able to take a step back from emotions that flood your nervous system and preempt the fight-or-flight response. This is a skill that, once you develop it, will enable you to see yourself and the world from an entirely new perspective. You don't cast these feelings away; you witness them, honor them, then act in accordance with what you actually want to do, not just what your programming is dictating. You can still get angry sometimes. But not as often as you might think you need to.

I know what some of you are thinking: "Meditation? Really? Between four a.m. wet-the-bed wake-ups, endless emails from work, and trying to get them off to school with the right things in their bag every day, I'm supposed to find time to sit in silence?" Trust me, I get it. If I were to be gifted ten minutes of silence with a toddler, the top five ways I'd spend it would all involve being as horizontal as geometrically possible. When meditation first crossed my radar, I filed it squarely under "things for people with more time than me," right next to making sourdough bread from scratch. Even ten minutes seemed laughable when I couldn't take a shit without someone slipping a handwritten "When will you be finished?" note under the door. But things changed once I stopped treating it as a pressure release valve for work and started seeing it as a tool for second-order change. I reframed meditation from the idea of emptying my mind (entirely impossible) or achieving the blissful state of enlightenment (not the point) to a practical skill: the ability to notice my thoughts without being hijacked by them.

Back to the messy room. Before I started meditating regularly, I'd get fired up every time I walked into a living room full of toys. Waking up to a messy kitchen was enough to put me in a bad mood if not for the whole day, then at least for the morning. But today? I'm learning to care a lot less. Of course, it can still test me when my son lifts the entire yellow Lego Large Creative Brick Box and dumps its contents onto the floor, before calmly walking away to find the source of his next Godzilla-like destructive moment. But that becomes a chance for me to practice what I've been working on during my hours spent "on the cushion." Today—most todays but not every today—I can walk into the most disorderly space and feel a calm that once seemed impossible. Meditation enabled me to understand where that tension was coming from. (Therapy played its part too, especially in helping me realize why a messy room was constantly triggering.) It gave me the ability to locate the feeling in my body, and to know it would pass. It gave me the insight to understand that, with two kids, rooms are always going to get messy, and stressing about it wouldn't help me, or them. It taught me all I needed to know in order to let go. And it's just one of the ways I'm happier every day as a result.

David Lynch said, "The thing about meditation is you become more and more you." Over the years, meditation has helped me feel more like me than I ever have and has aided me in becoming a better dad in all manner of ways:

I. Happiness is here, if you want it

I have learned to live more "in the moment" than ever before. The amount of time I spent ruminating on past events or worrying about future problems is a sliver of what it once was. I know that happiness won't be found in a new house, a big promotion, or a nicer car, so I'm free to enjoy things as they are, instead of chasing what might come to be. What you have today is all you once hoped for. Take a second. Soak it in.

II. Change is out of your control. How you deal with it is not

Deeply understanding the idea of impermanence has given me comfort amid a world that screams with uncertainty. Discomfort arises primarily when we hold tightly to what must change.

III. Stimulus doesn't have to lead to an uncontrollable response

You are not your emotions. They're layers of programming built up from past experiences and relationships. These shortcuts can be useful. But ask yourself: Is this thing I'm feeling helping me? Or is it doing the opposite?

IV. Patience isn't a virtue, it's a muscle

The more you train it, the more powerful it'll become, and the more of it you'll have to give to your kids. Speaking of which…

V. Imagine the power of learning these tools as a child

That's what you can do for your little ones right now. I have the knowledge and vocabulary to talk to my kids about how their emotions can feel overwhelming. To help my son learn to care less about what other kids think about him. To help my daughter make the "monkey mind" stay quiet. I'm hopeful that understanding these concepts at an early age will aid them immeasurably as they grow older.

VI. Letting go is a radical act, for yourself and others

A big part of the Buddhist teaching around meditation, and intrinsically connected to the concept of impermanence, is the idea of letting go of what doesn't serve you. This matters just as much in our personal lives as our professional ones. If we can learn to let go of attachments to people, objects, and beliefs, forgetting the times we've been wronged in the past, we will be free to enjoy the moment as it is.

VII. Take it with you, wherever you go

Meditation is not just about the minutes spent with eyes closed, focusing on the breath and trying to clear your mind. The learnings and insights travel far beyond the cushion, and with regular practice you'll start applying them to interactions across your life.

How to Start

Do you like the sound of this? Want to get some of it for yourself? It's easy. Let's give it a try right now.

Meditation can be done anywhere, as long as you won't be disturbed for a few minutes. Don't worry about background noise, and don't feel you need to sit cross-legged on a cushion—for dads with tight hamstrings, that might actually do more harm than good. Wherever you are—your desk chair, on the side of your bed, sitting in the driver's seat before school pickup—set your phone timer for one minute.

You can leave your eyes open or closed, whatever is most comfortable. Notice where you are carrying tension in your body. Now, take three slow, deliberate breaths—the kind that make your shoulders drop an inch on the exhale. Relax your jaw. And just notice your breathing. That's it. Feel the air coming in slightly cooler than it goes out. (I like to picture cold blue air coming in through my nose, and warm red air going out. Some people count the breaths in and out.) When—not if, but when—your mind wanders: onto that looming deadline for a presentation, or what you're going to cook for dinner—notice this happening, without judgment, and gently bring your attention back to your breath.

It'll feel like herding cats at first. Your mind will oscillate between different thoughts—your to-do list, that weird thing your boss said yesterday, whether your kid is falling behind because they can only read Dr. Seuss and your friend's son just devoured all seven Harry Potter books. Don't worry. That's normal. The practice isn't about stopping thoughts—it's about watching clouds pass overhead and calling out their shapes rather than getting stressed about the oncoming storm.

This is a first step toward observing, naming, and eventually predicting waves of emotions. To go deeper, you can read one of hundreds of books on the subject (I'll leave a list of my favorites at the end of the book) or download one of the apps you've seen advertised in your feeds since becoming a parent. These apps are a great place to dip your toe in—many are completely free, while others come with monthlong trials and introductory courses that will help you make it a regular habit. We've become so rightly suspicious of the overzealous claims of advertising: "Do this for free for thirty days and change your life!" But all you're being tricked into here is a path toward equanimity—the ability to stay calm and composed in situations, especially difficult ones. If you can get into the habit of a daily practice—some research says two minutes a day is enough—the compound effects of meditation can change your worldview forever. The benefits are not immediately apparent—no one finds enlightenment after a week—but as an effect that grows exponentially over time.

Many introductory courses inform you that making meditation a habit means you must do it at the same time every day. For parents, finding the same ten minutes isn't always possible. But you can almost always find them somewhere. I tend to do it either in the morning (if I'm up before the kids), during a short window in the daytime when they're at school and I'm not on a call, or in the evening once they've gone to sleep. I've done it on a park bench with a pair of AirPods, lying next to my son in bed as he's falling asleep, or sitting in the car before heading into the house. For the last few months, my son has asked, "Can we do meditation?" at bedtime, and I'll play it through the iPhone speaker while he listens along.

For me, there's one app that managed to instill a daily practice where others failed. The reason I've found Sam Harris's *Waking Up* to work so well for me—and other dads who have told me the same over the years—is its ability to completely rewire your brain functions by combining the latest research in neuroscience with ancient Vedic traditions, blending in modern developments in psychotherapy and philosophy. If you've tried one of the other apps before and it hasn't stuck, consider giving *Waking Up* a go. It provides an accessible on-ramp to the framing of consciousness, where thoughts come from and their power over us, and the nature of nonduality, leading you inevitably and inexorably to a place where you reevaluate how your brain perceives all it encounters.

Meditation offers a gradual path to modernizing your mode of thinking—consistent practice creating lasting neural change, fundamentally shifting how you respond to your children and the rest of the world. But some seek more direct paths toward second-order changes. The most dedicated meditators speak of breakthroughs that come after thousands of hours of practice—profound shifts in perception where the boundaries between self and world dissolve, where the DMN temporarily quietens, where we glimpse our lives with fresh eyes, unburdened by the stories we've been telling ourselves for decades.

Throughout human history, we've found various on-ramps to expand our awareness, and a growing body of research points toward ways that we can discover similar insights without years of practice—temporarily lifting the veil that separates you from a more compassionate, present version of yourself. These experiences are not an escape from parenting responsibilities but a potential shortcut to the destination many of us hope to reach: a mind that's more aware, flexible, and at peace with itself. A mind that might just make you a better father.

Let's hear it from the dads on...the power of meditation

I'm currently on a 202-day streak. I say that not to brag but to say that just keeping it simple has been the key. My goal, with my current busy season of life, is just five minutes a day. Often that ends up as more, but that simple goal makes it really easy to keep consistent. **Neil**

I started because it let me drop anchor in a wildly turbulent period of my life. What began as something that let me keep my cool when my newborn was screaming in the car gave way to a much deeper sense of fulfilment and presence in the joys of being a dad and was the foundation that gave me the strength to weather a major mental health episode when my daughter was eighteen months old. **Seb**

My old man's solution to stress was Stella Artois and silence. I was following the same path until a panic attack forced me to find another way. Meditation didn't just save my mental health—it saved my relationship with my twin daughters. Now when they're fighting or melting down, I can meet their chaos with calm instead of adding my own fire to theirs. That small space between trigger and response is where I became the father I always wanted to be. **Chris**

Meditation helps me see what is true about the world. And it does so in a way that is deeply personal—the insight that the Buddha's teachings can essentially be boiled down to "see for yourself." Just as I try to come into a relationship with everything in my life by seeing for myself, so too it is with parenting. This has been tremendously stabilizing. The second insight is, in some ways, that there are no answers—only questions, and to be deeply okay with that. This is akin to an insight passed on to me by a teacher—that walking the path is the feeling of jumping out of a plane and realizing (1) you have no parachute and (2) there is no ground. And that's parenting in a nutshell. **Matt**

CHAPTER 13

Reconsider Reality

The mind is like a parachute; it works best when it's open.

—Frank Zappa

Old rule: *Drugs are bad.*
New rule: *Open your mind.*

The ego is a wily beast. You can spend your entire life oblivious of the power it holds over you, how it makes you perceive the world—coloring everything you see, contorting everything you hear, the mental machination it forces your brain into. The ego is Oz's Wizard, a shadowy figure behind the screen, a puppeteer pulling the strings, controlling each and every one of your decisions.

This is a book about fatherhood as a transformation. As you turn its pages, I hope these tales resonate in a way that confirms or rejects long-held beliefs and provides a sense of momentum. But for others, there's a feeling that this door you're pushing against won't budge. All too often, that resistance is the ego at the wheel—the primary obstruction between the person you are today and the one you want to be: the nagging voice in your head telling you to rethink that major life decision because it isn't going to work out for you, echoing the narrative that "that might have worked for them, but it won't work for me." It constantly critiques, reminding you at critical moments of past failures, making you hit the brakes, second-guess yourself, and remain in no-man's-land. Feeling inadequate, paranoid, anxious, or filled with shame, guilt, and self-doubt? That's your ego taking control.

It isn't all bad—the ego provides confidence and self-belief in challenging situations. One day, in the not-so-distant past, it told you, "Yes, go talk to that person, what's the worst that could happen?" (or, if you're a dad of a newer vintage, "Yes, swipe right on that person, you've got a hope in hell"), starting a conversation that put you on a path to becoming a father. But the ego loves to overstep its bounds, thriving in chaos, a hypercritical voice constantly reminding you of how much better things would be if only you weren't such a gigantic fuckup. How much more patient you would be with your children. How much easier everyone else seems to be finding this parenting lark. It's the engine that powers the overriding guilt that you're spending too much time at work and not enough time with your children, who seem to grow older every time your laptop closes.

Ego is the Latin word for *I*. Ergo, ego places us at the center of the universe, the bottomless well of main-character energy, powering a personal narrative that makes us the hero—or villain—in the only story that matters: our own. If only it would get out of the way, we could live happier, healthier, and more fulfilled lives as parents, partners, and human beings. But its roots run deep, making it impossible to imagine life outside of its all-encompassing tendrils.

The ego makes a great servant, but it's a terrible master. There are many ways to wrestle it under your control—mindfulness, meditation, breathwork, hypnotherapy, fasting, and faith, to name just a few. For those who catch a glimpse of the peace of mind on the other side, and can find a way to carry that through into their daily life, worlds can be radically transformed. The idea of "dissolving the ego" by tapping into what psychologists call "nonordinary states of consciousness" offers the space and perspective necessary to silence your mind's most destructive tendencies. These tools work. But there's another way that is becoming more popular, more prevalent, and more socially accepted in the work of ego dissolution: the therapeutic use of psychedelics.

If you're reading this book, I'm going to assume you're well-informed, and relatively open-minded. So rather than go full Michael Pollan, we'll take a whistle-stop tour through the history of psychedelics. Roughly speaking, they're a group of plants and synthetic compounds grouped under the broad classification of *entheogens*, derived from the Greek word *entheos*, meaning "the god within." Recorded history of their usage can be traced back nine thousand years to Algerian cave paintings showing shamanic figures dancing with mushrooms sprouting out of their bodies. Native tribes across the world have long used them in indigenous rituals, with some scholars arguing they played a formative part in early religions. As research was formalized in the 1950s and 1960s, they were found to be nonaddictive and suitable treatments for a wide range of social and psychological conditions. But Timothy Leary, who did as much to further the cause of psychedelics as he did to damage it, fired up politicians and defenders of the status quo by telling America's youth to "turn on, tune in, drop out." Psychedelics became entangled in a growing counterculture movement in the United States, contributing to a pro-peace movement in a country vying to control public perception of the Vietnam War. They were outlawed in 1968 and the burgeoning field of psychedelic research was slammed shut, where it remained for decades.

For those uninitiated: A psychedelic experience is a little like falling in love, or watching your child come into this world. It's a life event that can only be experienced, one that is only lessened by offering a verbose play-by-play recap. In *How to Change Your Mind*—required reading for anyone interested in this space—Michael Pollan talked about the possibilities offered:

> *It was a little like being shown a door in a familiar room—the room of your own mind—that you had somehow never noticed before and*

being told by people you trusted (scientists!) that a whole other way of thinking—of being!—lay waiting on the other side. All you had to do was turn the knob and enter. Who wouldn't be curious?

The written word is powerful but still woefully inadequate to communicate the depths of a significant psychedelic experience. William Richards, psychologist and psychedelics expert at Johns Hopkins, summed it up as follows: "There are words we need that don't yet exist. We've got five crayons when we need fifty thousand different shades." Metaphors—while still insufficient—can prove useful. One that Pollan offered is from psychedelic researcher Mendel Kaelen and begins by thinking of your mind as a snow-covered hill. Every habit, behavior, thought pattern, and mode of operation is a route downhill. They're perfectly sized for your own sled, and so they should be—you ride these routes every day. The only way our brain can get through the overwhelming chaos of eighteen hours awake is to continually search for the most efficient and easiest routes, those free from danger, and throw itself down them. Every time, the route gets more defined, the snow cuts deeper, and with each trip what was soft powder transforms into hard ice. These routes, which once provided convenience, now constrict thought, choice, and free will, an inescapable groove disguised as a fun toboggan ride. Psychedelics, in this metaphor, provide fresh snowfall. They offer your brain the opportunity to explore novel and hitherto invisible paths.

Every decade brings new leaps in understanding how our brains work. Czech psychiatrist Stanislav Grof suggested that psychedelics could be for the study of the mind "what the microscope is for biology or the telescope is for astronomy." Under the hood, modern imaging has shown us that psychedelics reduce the noise and disrupt the integrity of the DMN as effectively as five thousand hours of meditation or one near-death experience. (Take your pick.) Rewiring the DMN short-circuits how we think, and psychedelics offer a chance to stand at the crest of your snow-covered hill, zoom out to view all the paths your mind had taken in the past, and understand both the how and the historical why you use them, objectively seeing how your childhood and major life experiences contribute to how you perceive and navigate the world today. The idea of what researchers have termed REBUS (relaxed beliefs under psychedelics) offers freedom to release long-held dogmas and to allow new systems to be forged in their place.

Parenting in the Shroom Boom

I never thought I'd be the type of person to sit and read research papers for pleasure, but a by-product of writing this book has been an increasing amount of time spent with them. Of all the positive studies I encounter for personal growth and transformation, the psychedelic research is consistently the most compelling. Traditional approaches to mental health, as well as the burgeoning well-being industry, will be completely transformed by what they're calling "the shroom boom." In combination with therapy, psychedelics are changing how patients work through depression, anxiety, PTSD, substance use disorder, and more. Research has shown comparable results to traditional antidepressants while leading to increased emotional connection, unlike traditional SSRIs (selective serotonin reuptake inhibitors) that can cause a general emotional blunting. They've been shown to help cancer patients manage overwhelming emotions in end-of-life anxiety and depression. Seventy-one percent of people who took psilocybin for major depressive disorder showed a greater than 50 percent reduction in their symptoms, and half of the participants entered remission. In an oft-cited report on mystical experiences, 64 percent of hallucinogen-naive participants said their first psilocybin experience increased their sense of well-being or life satisfaction moderately or very much, and 67 percent rated it among the five most spiritually significant experiences of their lives. Ezra Klein, writing about this topic in 2021, suggested that "even if further research finds psilocybin only 50% as effective as these experiments suggest, it will still be a breakthrough."

Psychedelics fundamentally alter how we think about concepts like death, grief, consciousness, healing, and forgiveness. I've spent over twenty years experimenting with macrodosing (taking large amounts of psychedelics) and microdosing (taking small, subperceptible amounts), including periods where I grew my own. The contribution that these plant-based medicines have had on the parent I am today can't be understated and are impossible to pry apart—like mycelium roots, invisible to the eye, they are connected together, one and the same. I can guarantee you, with 100 percent certainty, that you would not be reading this book today without their guidance. And though my children don't yet know the role that psychedelics played in helping me become the father I am, their lives are immeasurably better because of the therapeutic breakthroughs I have made with them. Parents looking to be more present, manage extreme emotions, reduce cravings and dependencies, or break cycles of trauma would do well to consider the formidable force of these fungi.

A few things for parents considering stepping through what Aldous Huxley called these "doors of perception." Of utmost importance is to carefully consider where you are, both physically and mentally, right now and at this life stage. The concept of "set and setting," popularized by Timothy Leary in the 1960s, refers to the two sets of factors that will influence any psychedelics experience: the mental load that is brought to the experience—thoughts, moods, expectations, and previous life experiences (the "set") and the physical and social environment of the participant's experience (the "setting"). These will play an oversized role in the nature of any trip and are why many first-time users seek out an experienced guide or explore doing this with a group as part of a "psilocybin retreat." (Public data on Google searches indicates a 450 percent increase in the number of people seeking out these types of experiences between the years 2020 and 2025.) Also important is intention: What do you hope to achieve from the experience, what do you consider to be the path forward that needs to be unlocked, and what do you yearn to leave behind but your ego holds on to stubbornly? Setting an intention has become part of the popular lexicon, thanks to its role in mindfulness practices like yoga and meditation, and forms a fundamental part of a good trip and successful integration into your daily life.

Another essential aspect encompasses both your personal attitude toward what we can loosely term "drugs" and the legality of plant-based medicine in your country or state. The legal status of psilocybin shifts from country to country, state to state, and even city to city—for three years in the United States, they were banned in San Francisco, but any resident could drive across the Bay Bridge and pick them up legally in Oakland, a city situated a twenty-minute drive away. And legal or not, each person will have their own reaction to the idea of drugs: Some will have spent a lifetime D.A.R.E.-ing to resist them and "just saying no" while others will have spent their pre-parenting years experimenting, using them as accelerants toward memorable nights out, and briefly losing that hardwired connection to the world. You may have taken drugs in your past—and had a very good time with them!—but since having kids have left that life behind. But once you're a parent, you can't carry on pulling all-night ragers on the regular—not only because it's socially irresponsible, but because what kind of sadist would wantonly put themself through the Monday morning school run after pulling a five a.m. finish over the weekend?

For years, I've discussed this topic with close friends and dads across the world. We are—broadly speaking—the first generation of parents with a firsthand experience of drugs. Sure, your dad might have smoked a joint or two when he was young. He may have dabbled with more regularity. But those parents were the exception, not the rule. When I first wrote about this topic online, my inbox was filled with outraged dads, disappointed that I was promoting drug use, asking to be removed from mailing lists and canceling paid subscriptions. Some will read this and think it careless, or a huge risk, to even consider something like this after having children. There's a chance this chapter might undo everything that came before it, because there remains a huge stigma around drug usage, and you don't have to go far to find stories of families whose lives have been ripped apart by harmful substances. But there's a gulf between the types of addictive substances that are damaging to people and society at large and plant-based medicines that have been proven to be nonaddictive and offer unparalleled opportunities for rapid, meaningful, and long-lasting transformation. The tide is turning, and a new wave of self-development is rapidly approaching. Depending on where you live, it might have already reached your shore.

Those who have taken psychedelics throughout their life will talk about the mushrooms "calling" them. You're going through a period of change in your life, asking big questions, and coming up short on answers. You've read the right books, had conversations with close friends. But there's a ledge you're approaching, a leap into the unknown required. You might get there yourself, with time. But psychedelics can guide you toward the gate, deftly remove the padlock, help you battle the demons blocking the way, and enable a letting go, a moving forward. Author Tim Ferris—who has dedicated a significant chunk of his time and millions of dollars of his own money to furthering the cause of psychedelic-assisted growth—called them "performance-enhancing drugs for personal development." It's as pithy and powerful a testimonial as you're likely to find. But they're no panacea to all of life's problems: "Just eat these mushrooms and you'll be a better dad tomorrow." You still need to do the work.

I've worked through personal issues during psychedelic trips that would've taken years of personal work or thousands of dollars in therapy. It's not a case of either/or. These are complementary approaches. Psychedelics, taken therapeutically, have brought me face-to-face with significant traumas that remained hidden under the surface for decades, and have—on multiple occasions—liberated me from emotional dead weight I'd been carrying around for my entire life: issues I hadn't realized I'd pushed down and locked away, that were resurfacing in how I showed up as a father and how I connected with—and reacted to—my children. You can live an entire life ignoring this baggage. Or you can deal with it, head-on.

A psychedelic experience is akin to sorting that drawer in the kitchen and its assortment of detritus built up from decades of emotional hoarding. It occasionally surfaces in your mind as something to be dealt with, but it's all too easy to imagine it doesn't exist. Because it's never the right time to deal with it. Because nobody ever taught you how. Because your ego gets in the way, protecting itself, preventing you from letting go. Because you've learned from a young age—from every institution in your life—that these things aren't supposed to be talked about, but to be ignored. But there will come a time when you decide it's finally time to clean house, to drag that drawer open, audit its contents, and ask yourself: What is useful here? What do I want to keep? What is that half pair of scissors doing for me, apart from being a constant stabbing hazard? What have I been unwittingly holding on to that serves me no longer? What is here that I've inherited from my own parents, and their parents before them, that I don't want to pass on to my children? What are those negative patterns of thinking that I can finally see—free from the normal operation of my DMN—and let go of forever?

This chapter won't be for everyone, and that's the point. Psychedelics are one option among many; if this chapter doesn't fit your beliefs, health, or life stage, just turn the page. You'll find plenty of other levers in this book; my aim is to widen your toolbox rather than prescribe a single path. If you're curious, speak with a qualified clinician or licensed therapist, and—if you proceed—work with an experienced, reputable guide, where possible. And always follow the law where you live—nothing here should be read as encouragement to break it. I've written about this topic with reluctance, but as this book is an honest account of everything that has helped me become a better father, I'd be remiss if I didn't talk about psychedelics because I was worried about how others would respond. One of the core responsibilities of the conscious parent is to carefully sift through our life experiences—separating them into what is useful and can be carefully passed on to our children, and those that are hurting us and will potentially do so for generations to come. Psychedelic parenting can change the paradigm of how we think about these substances—from helping us get fucked up in early adulthood to enabling us to fix the fucked-up things from our past, breaking cycles of intergenerational trauma and preventing our children from having to deal with it in years to come.

The idea of psychedelic parenting may initially sound like a contradiction, or even irresponsible. But the evidence suggests that a properly structured psychedelic experience can catalyze the same kind of second-order changes that meditation fosters—helping fathers reconsider reality itself, break free from destructive thought patterns, and discover new depths of empathy and presence with their children. It can play a colossal role as part of the modern parent's tool kit, enabling us to live tranquil, joyful lives, with our ego finally working with—and not against—us.

Let's hear it from the dads on...psychedelic parenting

My first psilocybin journey happened a year after my son was born. I was drowning in anxiety, constantly worrying if I was doing everything right. During that experience, I saw how my father's need for control had shaped my own parenting fears. Three hours taught me what years of therapy hadn't—that my job wasn't to be perfect, but to be present. Now when my son makes a mess or has a meltdown, I can step back and remember we're both just learning how to be human together. **Neal**

Growing up with an alcoholic father, I swore I'd never use any substances once I became a parent. The irony is that a guided psilocybin session helped me face the trauma from my childhood and break the cycle I was unconsciously continuing with my own kids. I wasn't drinking, but I was emotionally unavailable in many of the same ways. What I thought would be a spiritual experience ended up being intensely practical—I literally saw patterns of behavior that had been invisible to me before. Two years later, my relationship with my kids has completely transformed. Sometimes the thing we fear is what we need the most. **Thomas**

It takes courage to "come out of the closet" about intentional psychedelic use, especially as a parent, and in a culture that stigmatizes much that it does not understand. It is not without irony: Sometimes, the best way to stop abusing drugs—or to allow the self-serving ego to take a back seat—is by taking yet another "drug," this one from the ancients. **Alex**

CHAPTER 14

Rewild Your Attention

The art of knowing is knowing what to ignore.

—Rumi

Old rule: *Focus on noise.*
New rule: *Find the signal.*

Cool computer-science-studying kids like me know all about garbage in, garbage out (GIGO), a simple concept that encourages using only the best inputs—data that's sanitized, verified, and as error-free as it can be—to run through algorithms and get your desired output. In the early days of computing, Charles Babbage was asked, "If you input wrong figures, will the right answers come out?" To which he curtly replied, "I am not able rightly to apprehend the kind of confusion that could provoke such a question." (Now he'd simply reply "RTFM + STFU.")

Cost per mille (CPM) is the oxygen of the digital economy—how much money an advertiser will pay a digital platform for every thousand views they provide. In 2023, advertising still delivered about three-quarters of Google's entire revenue, and an even starker 97.5 percent of Meta's. Digital platforms prioritize engagement over all else, because engagement brings eyeballs, and eyeballs mean dollars. In a world where attention equals money, given the choice, why wouldn't these companies figure out the best way of capturing ours? This was laid bare in 2021 with the *Facebook Papers*, a deluge of documents leaked by Facebook whistleblower Frances Haugen, connecting the dots between enragement and engagement. When asked to test a version of Facebook that was "nicer," researchers warned Facebook executives that "lowering outrage content" would cut into "core engagement metrics" and impact revenue. For years, Facebook stoked the fire with techniques like giving the angry-reaction emoji five times the weight of a simple "like," supercharging divisive content and misinformation on their platform.

These companies utilize "growth hacks" that trigger our own cognitive biases as we respond physiologically to news based on how negative it is. Manufactured outrage has become the primary currency of digital spaces: If you can make people angry, they're more likely to comment, to share in their own closed messaging groups, and to drive more of those sweet advertising dollars into the pockets of the platforms. It's not just social media: In the United States, cable news saw a 25 percent rise in revenue during 2017, Donald Trump's first year in office, and MSNBC—arguably the most outraged channel during this period—saw their revenue rise a whopping 62 percent. Ratings peaked when political controversies were front and center and presenters could wrestle you away from whatever you were doing and have you freak out about the news.

The great screen time debate rears its head even before your newborn child pushes theirs into this world. I'd wager you've already spent longer thinking about screens than your parents did during your entire childhood. Because the world today is different—I might not have walked to school through miles of snow in my bare feet, but I did have to get by on a lowly two hours of kids' TV every Saturday morning. Today, thousands of cartoons are only a tap away. Digital displays are ubiquitous—in our homes and in our pockets—and they provide parents with both a necessary breather and a worrying vision for the future.

My parents used to let me sit in front of the Super Nintendo until all hours, happy to have a quiet kid who could keep himself occupied. There were occasional warnings, sure: "Don't sit too close to the TV, your eyes will turn square." I'd have to stop sometime after the sun went down, placing the controller on top of the TV, before heading to bed and dreaming of mustachioed plumbers. Parents today are more wary of technology's role in raising kids. We agonize over the right age when our kids can start watching TV, holding strong opinions that get thrown out the window as soon as we realize the magical ability Cocomelon has in enabling a wild child to sit still and eat for ten minutes.

But the current debate about what our children should watch, and for how long, is a smokescreen for the real problem. As parents, we do ourselves a disservice when we fixate on our kids' screens rather than turning the mirror back on ourselves. Because what you focus on will influence your worldview like little else. The stories you read will change how you think, what you care about, and what you tell your kids when you're tucking them in at night. And what your kids see you watching and reading, even when you don't notice, will influence them too. So it's worth asking how we spend our most precious resource: attention.

Get Rewilding

In the years I've been publishing the weekly newsletter, I've spent ten to fifteen hours a week reading, writing, and editing that I could have done anything else with. Tens of thousands of dads across the world read it regularly because they know I value their attention as much as my own—and I respect that every moment they spend reading it is one not spent with their kids, their partner, their job, or a personal project or hobby they've been noodling on. The hours you have spent reading this book—which I hope have flown by at a pleasurable whip rather than feeling like you've been dragged by your hair through the bushes against your will—is time you could have spent on something else. Hours that, as parents in the age of time scarcity, we're thinly spreading across the toast of life.

But I continue to write it, and dads continue to read it, because we know it's time well spent. Writing has helped me to be more conscious about how I spend my time and to help others do the same: through forging better habits, using our children as an excuse to take up new hobbies, or watching shows together to help us have deeper conversations with our kids. I've had emails from people telling me, "Your newsletter gives me permission to just sit and think about the kind of dad I want to be, even for a few minutes every week, that I didn't have before."

Your attention is exactly that: *yours.* Yours to choose what you want to spend it on, and not something to be hijacked through relentless notifications and app design dark patterns by an Allbird-wearing, Patagonia-fleeced, Mount-Tamalpais-weekend-hiking product manager in the Bay Area. Aza Raskin, the designer who created the infinite scroll, enabling digital time lines to continue indefinitely, has expressed regret for the technology he brought into the world, and reports estimate that it leads to two hundred thousand human lifetimes wasted every day. What we focus our attention on can be as impactful as the people we spend our time with; as Goethe once observed: "Tell me with whom you consort and I will tell you who you are; if I know how you spend your time, then I know what might become of you." The first step toward reclaiming this resource is to notice and become aware of the patterns you might have fallen into and break out of them. Blogger Tom Critchlow coined a beautiful term for this: "rewilding your attention," and technology writer Clive Thompson unpacked what this phrase meant to him: "If you want to have wilder, curiouser thoughts, you have to avoid the industrial monocropping of big-tech feeds. You want an intellectual forest, overgrown with mushrooms and towering weeds and a massive dead log where a family of raccoons has taken up residence."

Yung Pueblo, the poet and writer, found this metaphor fertile too: "The mind is a garden; what we decide to grow there will determine our prosperity." Voltaire wrote that "one must cultivate one's own garden." Austin Kleon, a modern-day sage on the art of creative inspiration, shared Ann Patchett's powerful idea of the creative compost heap: "I am a compost heap, and everything I interact with, every experience I've had, gets shoveled onto the heap where it eventually mulches down, is digested and excreted by worms, and rots. It's from that rich, dark humus, the combination of what you encountered, what you know and what you've forgotten, that ideas start to grow."

A Field Guide to Rewilding Your Attention

If screens feel addictive, it's because they're designed to be. But telling the story of the tyrannical pull of these ubiquitous glowing rectangles requires more than a chapter in a parenting book. Shelves are littered with screeds on the damage they're doing to our children; podcast hosts have chalked up hundreds of hours decrying the end of childhood as we know it; Senate hearings have convened to drag tech CEOs away from their free lunches to answer for the impact their apps have had on the lives of society's children. It's on us to break out of the traps that these screens lure us into—and to teach our kids how to do the same—by asking them to do what we do, not just what we say. If you're wondering how to move away from mindless consuming, and instead begin to pile things onto your creative compost heap, here are five things you might try.

I. Notice your feelings

When feelings of despair, anger, or irritation arise when looking at your phone or another screen, do two things. First, think about whether you can use these emotions to affect real change. Tim Krieder, who coined the term *outrage porn* in 2009, said, "Outrage is healthy to the extent that it causes us to act against injustice." Second, interrogate whether these feelings are serving you in a positive way. If you're feeling neither of these…

II. Use guardrails to moderate your usage

Look at using the Screen Time functionality on your iPhone (or Digital Wellbeing on Android) to limit time spent on certain apps or on your device altogether. For a while I had a thirty-minute-a-day social "limit" and was attempting a "no phone before midday" policy. But it was a prison that was all too easy to break out of, as if the metal bars on the windows were made of dried spaghetti. For the time I've been writing this book, I managed to get my screen time consistently under two hours a day, thanks to an app that takes all the icons off my home screen and turns my smartphone into a "dumb phone." Will I keep this up until this book is published? I can only hope so.

III. Break bad habits

When dieting, one of the smartest hacks is to swap out the bad things you have in the cupboards for healthier alternatives—LaCroix on the beer shelf, nuts in the cookie jar, protein bars where you once stashed the chocolate. Why should your media diet be any different? Think about where you are when you reach for your phone. I like to start the morning (after the school run chaos) with a few minutes in my favorite chair with a cup of coffee. I realized that at this time, every day, I'd instinctively reach for my phone while I held the cup in the other hand. So I put a stack of lightweight, snackable books right next to me. I did the same thing in the bathroom—this may have made the biggest dent in my screen time. I've started to take a moment to notice three things while waiting for the crossing sign to turn green, a time when I used to needlessly check my notifications. Notice when you reach for your phone and think how you might begin to replace one action with another. The ex-smokers among you will have noticed the parallels here. And what does that tell you about the relationships we have with our devices?

IV. Consider a digital detox

Just like any addict trying to kick a habit, you may need to go cold turkey. Try a simple one-week reset: Monday—charge your phone outside the bedroom and use an alarm clock; Tuesday—delete your most tempting app for twenty-four hours; Wednesday—turn off all but truly human notifications and batch the rest; Thursday—add friction (switch to grayscale, move dopamine-rewarding apps into a folder on the last screen);

Friday—protect one sixty-to-ninety-minute single-task window with Do Not Disturb; Saturday—spend three hours out of the house with the phone on airplane mode; Sunday—leave the phone at home and go do something for a few hours without it. Do it solo or with your family, treat it as an experiment, and check your screen time app before and after. If it helps, keep the one or two changes that moved the needle.

V. Make it easier to resurface things you like

What you consume is just one piece of the puzzle. The next is how you bring it back at the right time. The internet is filled with systems and services to help you retain and recall what you once read. For years, I've been using a service called Readwise, and every day I get an email with five of my own highlights from the more than five hundred books I've read on my Kindle over the last decade. I can search through them all with a flurry of fingertips; many of the passages you've read here were retrieved from there.

VI. Ruthlessly prune your sources, then replace them with better ones

Unfollow accounts. If you don't want to come off as rude to people you know, mute them (they'll never know). Send group message threads to the archive, or better still, leave the group entirely. Stop visiting websites that pull you in with clickbait headlines. Turn off app notifications—or delete the worst offenders from your phone. Unsubscribe to emails that aren't getting you closer to being the person you want to be. Delete podcasts with two white guys talking over each other for hours, confirming what you already believe, and replace them with something that might fundamentally change your perspective forever.

What you spend your attention on will influence your daily mood, your yearly progress, and your entire worldview. It will define how happy you are with your life, and how you judge your success—or lack of it. But a new set of voices will only get you so far: Further reprogramming requires a more fundamental rethink.

Let's hear it from the dads on…reclaiming your time

I used to complain about my kid's screen time. Then one day he said, "Dad, you're worse than me." It stung because it was true. Since then, I've tried to hold myself to the same standards I expect from him. If I want him to look up and notice the world, I need to be willing to do the same. **Greg**

I replaced my end-of-day phone scroll with a phone-free stroll. Once the kids are in bed I set out for a short wander around the streets, sometimes with a friend as we talk, other times with only my thoughts for company. What used to be an hour of me doomscrolling, glued to a screen, has turned into an essential decompression ritual, a way to wind down after a hard day that doesn't require me firing alcohol in my body. It gives me something I used to get from the daily commute home, painfully missing since our company went fully remote. **Eric**

For years my Sunday mornings started with me half-asleep on the sofa, scrolling through whatever the algorithm threw at me. Then one weekend my son asked if we could go to the park instead. Now it's become our ritual—we grab a football, maybe a coffee for me and a pastry for him, and we're out the door. It sounds simple, but that swap completely shifted the rhythm of my week. I realized the choice isn't between doing nothing with my phone or doing something; it's between filling my attention with noise or with moments that actually matter. Those mornings in the park have become the highlight of my week, and they all started with me finally putting the phone down. **Brian**

CHAPTER 15

Redefine Success

The life which men praise and regard as successful is but one kind. Why should we exaggerate any one kind at the expense of the others?

—Henry David Thoreau

Old rule: *Success is measured by salary.*
New rule: *Success is measured by quality of life.*

In 2016, I made what was to be a make-or-break career move. I left a team I'd loved in Google's London office, primarily because of a falling-out with a manager who had a very different definition of what "working father" meant than I did. Nothing in London felt like the right fit, so my attention went over the Atlantic, where internal opportunities were plentiful. I ended up in a conversation with a team in California; it looked like a perfect fit for both of us. It was a huge change—leaving our life in London, taking our almost two-year-old daughter to the far side of the United States, to a city where we only knew a handful of people. But it was an opportunity that was unlikely to come up again. We'd likely regret it if we didn't.

We pressed go. The journey was arduous—an immigration process that was a nightmare, even back in 2016, the year before things would get a whole lot worse. I went first, to lay the groundwork—get my feet under the table in a new job in a new team, and find a place for our family to call home. I'm forever indebted to my wife's cousins, who offered their spare bedroom as a halfway house. Their daughter, born only a few days after my own, was a constant reminder of what I'd left back home.

The move was a stressful one. Being apart from my family exacerbated it. But on top of this, the cherry on the proverbial cake, was what was happening at work: My new job was a nightmare. The team I'd joined was imploding, in danger of being closed down after a new CFO had started taking the axe to teams that were deemed to not align with her plan to put "more wood behind fewer arrows." The writing was on the wall on a job I'd just moved my whole family to America for. Luckily, said writing was also visible to a VP I'd previously worked with, who jumped in and offered me a role on his team. It was going to go great: "You'll be working for Ethan, you guys will get on like a house on fire."

I threw myself into it, working harder than ever, experiencing the overwhelming force and contagious self-belief required to feed the American Dream. My thoughts became consumed with promotion cycles and director-level salary bands. What had been easier to resist from London—though not impossible—was felt in full effect in the United States. By the time I'd moved stateside, I'd been at the company for seven years. I'd developed a reputation for delivering effective, award-winning work—even if I wasn't always the easiest person to manage. I'd been in my newly relocated role for a few months, reporting to Ethan, a manager who provided equal parts autonomy and air cover. Things were going well, until about six months in, when he started acting frosty with me. We went from a relationship where he trusted me to get work done with minimal oversight to one where every decision was micromanaged; he was calling me out in front of senior leadership and going through all my work with a fine-toothed comb. I asked around within the team, "Anyone know what's going on with Ethan? Feels like things were going so well, and suddenly they're not."

"We were going to ask you the same thing" became the common refrain.

This continued for a few months. I was on a highly visible project that required presenting to senior executives regularly, including the chief marketing officer (CMO) and all her direct reports. From every signal I was receiving—apart from those Ethan was sending—things couldn't have been going better. So I was relieved when, one morning after a check-in with our VP, Ethan pulled me into a room for a "quick chat" on our way back to our desks.

"I know what you're doing here," he told me.

"Wonderful," I replied. "Because I'm lost and would love to know."

"I know you're trying to take my job."

I let out a laugh. Not one of derision, but of relief. *Did I think this was funny*, Ethan wondered? "No, but it's all starting to make sense." I did a quick calculation in my head, based on knowing his job level, mine, and the pay delta between them. "You're on about fifteen to twenty percent more money than I am a year. And I see you here every morning when I arrive. You're the last one to go in the evening. You're answering messages on your phone 24/7; whenever the VP has a problem, you have to drop everything and go fix it. I see all those things you have to do, and I don't think it's worth that extra salary. I don't want your job. Actually, I don't want our director's job, I don't want our VP's job, and now, thinking about it for the first time, I wouldn't want to be the CMO either."

On paper, I was doing better than ever. I was being paid a third more than my previous London salary. The monthly take-home would have made my twenty-one-year-old self blush. But at the end of each month, we didn't have, as my mum used to say, "two pennies to rub together for heat." (Those old Irish sayings come in heavy. It's like Frank McCourt grew up in the house with us.) Life in San Francisco was bleeding us dry. We found ourselves regularly dipping into savings just to stay afloat. Friends casually mentioned meetings with financial advisors who told them they'd need around $5 million invested in order to "retire comfortably" in the Bay Area. Our apartment sat across from the recently rechristened Priscilla Chan and Mark Zuckerberg San Francisco General Hospital—a daily reminder that if I could only work harder, buy the right companies, and steal the best features from other apps at just the right time, then maybe I too could have a hospital renamed in my honor.

We were living the Silicon Valley paradox—pixel rich but penny poor. Not exactly living like paupers, but coming to the realization that the life we wanted to live, and how we wanted to raise our kids, was going to be hard—if not impossible—here without a significant promotion or IPO-enabled windfall. Our outgoing costs were sky-high and would continue to grow; this was just with one child, and we were already trying for another. I was working myself to death, going AWOL during visits from my family, trying to be a good parent with whatever time, energy, and attention I had left over from work. If this was supposed to be success, why did it feel so bad?

At the time, my friend Ed was going through a similar crisis of confidence, having ventured on that same transatlantic route to San Francisco with his family. We'd ruthlessly pursued these jobs at the top of the tech pyramid, these roles that were the envy of so many others. "Are we crazy to want to give all of this up?" I asked him.

"We're the lucky ones," Ed replied. "We landed what so many spend their lives chasing, and realized in our thirties that it's not all it's cracked up to be. Many go their whole lives without that insight."

When your brain pulls at one of these existential threads, it's hard knowing just how naked you'll be when it's done. I started to see a signal among the noise, confirming this oasis of success was more of a mirage. Close friends who had done enviably well—CEOs of global agencies, VPs at tech companies—told me how they felt trapped in a bind of their own making. Mortgage payments on the house they stretched to buy, two leased SUVs in the garage, private school tuition for their children to avoid the perceived pitfalls of the public system. One told me, "I can never ever earn less than $500,000 ever again. The house of cards would tumble within months."

The path that brought me to the West Coast was heading in a similar direction. I could make the numbers work—but I'd need to get my head down, grit my teeth, grind it out, and hope for the best. But what would I be giving up along the way? One evening, I was sitting at the kitchen table, settling in for another late night with my demanding mistress Gmail, as my three-year-old daughter was vying to get my attention. I was replying to an absolutely urgent matter so inconsequential it's impossible to recall today. As I looked down, I realized something; in this moment, right now, my daughter thinks I am the most incredible, exciting, smart, brave, strong, and funny human being in the world—alongside her mother, who is all of those things and more. Now was the time to be with her as much as I could. It would have been all too easy to chase the illusion of success I'd been sold, put my head in a laptop, and work myself ragged for a decade before looking up and seeing a teenager whom I didn't recognize, and who no longer had the time of day for her dad.

Defining Your Quality of Life

French playwright Eugène Ionesco once wrote, "It is not the answer that enlightens, but the question." During my time in California and my experience with Ethan, the question had shifted: "What does success mean now?" Society's yardstick was no longer a valid measurement for a life well lived. I didn't know what the answer was, but I knew it had moved away from a big corporate word cloud filled with words like *income*, *trajectory*, and *promotion*, all rendered in a ghastly font.

It became more ethereal, a wispy outline that I needed to fill in for myself. "What kind of life do I want for me and my family?" became a primary focus. That was a question that wasn't easily answered by salary bands and bonus targets. This question led me somewhere different—beyond the pastures of work-life balance, that false dichotomy that elevates your job into equal stature with your existence. I began obsessing over the idea of "quality of life," and how this could be used as a guiding light. While the definition of success can shift, driven by perception of others, quality of life has been used by governments, charities, and organizations across the world to judge the impact and efficacy of the work they do. It comes with a definition widely agreed upon from the World Health Organization: "an individual's perception of their position in life in relation to their goals, expectations, standards and concerns."

When you start looking at life through the lens of quality over quantity, everything shifts. You start to notice all the times we substitute money for presence. There's a reason that corporate America talks incessantly about "compensation." You are being paid to compensate you for all the things you must give up in exchange, the sacrifices you make every day in order to succeed in, and retain, your job. Quality of life isn't about lowering your ambitions—it's about redirecting them. It's a new definition of intention. In order to recontextualize success in terms of quality moments rather than quantity of achievements and dollars, I needed an entirely new approach—allowing me to make decisions that evaluated the whole picture of what makes a life worth living, not just about finding the right job.

This is tough to codify because of the inherent subjectivity in the quality-of-life debate. Your personal list of priorities will be based on different factors than mine. Our definitions are shaped by the deepest grooves of our childhood experiences. What we experience in our youth, for better or worse, becomes our definition of normal, pushing us to either re-create what we had or adamantly pursue its opposite. You may prioritize security and safety if it was lacking in your own childhood, or seek escape and adventure if you grew up in a household where predictability felt suffocating.

And even in breaking from the past and existing in the present, our needs in the moment will differ. What brings me peace and fulfillment might drive you up the wall. You might want to spend all your spare time parachuting from airplanes: an idea of fun to you which terrifies me. The choices that make sense for my family could be completely wrong for yours. But it doesn't matter one iota whether our needs overlap. What matters is that you (hopefully) share a similar set of priorities as your partner. In a just world, you'll end up with a circle of friends who share a life outlook similar to yours. Over time, we tend to find our people—other parents whose values and priorities rhyme with our own, even if they're not Xerox copies. The script keeps evolving, shaped by conversations with friends who nudge us to think differently, along with what we read, listen to, and watch.

A Framework: Toward a Unified Quality of Life for You and Your Family

TL;DR: Define what's important for your family and find an answer that sits in the sweet spot.

When I coach dads, one of the first exercises we do is breaking down their current definition of success: not to judge it, but to put it under the microscope and examine it in detail. Where did these metrics come from? How did they contribute to where you are today? And are they still serving you and your family? Or are they a subtle disguise for the goals of another, leaving you to chase a dream you've inherited rather than one you've intentionally crafted—a false appearance that allows the hamster wheel to masquerade as a career ladder?

Over the last decade I've developed this framework based on conversations I've had, essays I've written, and—most importantly—mistakes I've made. It's not prescriptive: Think of it more like a paper map than a turn-by-turn GPS. It won't tell you exactly where to go, but it will ensure you're heading in the right direction.

I. Defining What Quality of Life Means to You

Task 1: Take a blank piece of paper, go through this list, and make a note of quality-of-life attributes that resonate as being most important to you and your family. This is by no means an exhaustive list. Think of it like a tasting menu. It's been crafted in conversation with other dads, exploring globally recognized markers of quality of life across the world, and my own experience. As you read through these, notice which ones make your heart rate quicken, which ones make you anxious, and which ones make you nod in recognition. Your reactions are data points, nudging you toward what matters most.

- **Connection and Community** How close are you—physically and emotionally—to the people you love? There's a direct correlation between the distance of your immediate family and how often they can help out with you when you need it—the occasional school run, or taking the kids for a day when you need a break. This isn't just about family—friends will play a huge role too. It's about finding your people, your corner of the world where your parenting choices don't make you the weird one.

- **Natural Environment** This isn't just about weather forecasts—it's about how your environment shapes your daily reality. When you wake up every morning and look out your window, is it delight or despair you feel? Can your kids play outside most days or are you trapped indoors for months at a time? I learned this one the hard way growing up in Manchester—summertime meant a brief window of possibility between days-long blights of light drizzle. When you're raising kids, the ability to step outside on a whim, to have impromptu park trips or lazy beach days, isn't just convenience—it's freedom.

- **Economic Reality** This isn't just how much you earn, but what that means in real terms. Can you live well without constant financial anxiety? Are you trading your time for money, or have you found that sweet spot where you can afford what matters without sacrificing everything else? In the Bay Area, I realized that a big number on your paycheck means next to nothing if it all goes to rent, childcare, and thirty-dollar pizzas.

- **Cultural Vitality** What feeds your soul? What keeps you growing, learning, and inspired? You might yearn for a life surrounded by world-class museums or street art, underground music venues, or food markets that expose your palate to brave new worlds. Culture can mean the difference between living in a place and feeling truly alive in it.

- **Autonomy and Freedom** The freedom to shape your days, your decisions, your destiny. This hits different as a parent; it's not about being completely untethered (those days are long gone) but about having enough agency to be the father you want to be. Are you able to be present for moments that matter, and even little ones that don't? Can you make it to school events without having to check Slack for messages from your boss? Can you take a mental health day without guilt? Do you make it home for bath time and bedtime more often than not? Time is a resource we can't make more of. How freely you spend yours might be the truest measure of wealth.

- **Physical Space and Movement** How does your daily environment support or constrain your life? Can you walk to get groceries? Bike with your kids to school? Find quiet when you need it? Does your home feel like a sanctuary or a storage unit? This isn't about square footage—it's about how well your space serves your life.

- **Physical Health** Our generation is rewriting what it means to age: We're the dads who still learn to skate and surf well into their forties, who care about what we eat and how we move. Not because we're chasing eternal youth, but because we want to actively participate in our kids' lives for as long as possible. What good is living a long life if you're too weak to enjoy it? Intrinsically connected to this is the infrastructure that keeps your family well. Do you feel safe letting your kids play outside? Are the structures in place to help you if they get sick? These aren't sexy considerations, but everything else pales in comparison when you need them.

- **Spiritual Connection** This isn't necessarily about organized religion (though it might be). It's your state of mind around life's biggest questions, especially when your kids start asking them. Where do we go when we die? Why are we here? What makes a good life? Maybe you find this in traditional faith, in nature, in philosophy, or in the quiet moments watching your child sleep. I left the church in my teens. Now, raising kids, I find myself creating new rituals, ways of marking life's passages, and fresh language on meaning and purpose.

- **Progressiveness and Diversity** Are there people in your community who look, sound, and think differently than you do? I appreciate this is a lot to wrap up all in one bullet point, as it's so important and covers such a wide range of factors: gender, race, religion, sexual orientation, and more. For those who are not straight white men (or who, like me, are not raising straight white children), this will likely place high up your list. It boils down to a single question: How will the cultural norms of those around you influence and impact your family?

- **Work and Purpose** Not just your job, but how your work fits into your life. Does work energize or drain you? Can you do it on your terms, or are you constantly compromising? How much of yourself does your job demand of you, and is this a fair trade? This may mean traditional success in some stretches of your career, and radical reimagining in others.

- **Educational Environment** This is about more than just schools but the whole learning ecosystem your kids inhabit. Are they growing up in a place that sparks curiosity? That welcomes questions? That makes space for different ways of thinking? I remember my daughter coming home from her school in Barcelona, mixing three languages in one sentence, and realizing she was getting an education I couldn't have dreamed of during my monolingual childhood.

- **Infrastructure and Mobility** The invisible systems that leave you spending your life in flow or friction. Can young people safely get themselves around, or will you be spending your children's teenage years driving them around in Dad's Taxi? Do you spend too many of your waking hours stuck in traffic? Can you sit back and read a book on your commute instead of white-knuckling the steering wheel as you're cut off again? One dad who moved from LA to Barcelona told me, "I'm never buying a car again." Another shared that his quality of life in Copenhagen came down to this: "My kids can bike everywhere safely, and that changes everything."

II. Building Your Own Quality of Life Framework

This is where it gets real. The true power comes from how these elements interact. A fantastic job means little if it keeps you from your kids. Perfect weather doesn't make up for isolation from extended family. The highest-rated schools may not be worth the soul-crushing commute to get there. It's in the balance, the interplay, and the conscious compromises you make that you will find your own definition of a life well lived.

Take your list of attributes and whittle it down to your top three non-negotiables. (You can have four, if you must.) If you're doing this with a partner, each make your own list first, then come together to find where your priorities overlap. This conversation may get uncomfortable. That's okay; the most important discussions usually are.

Task 2: Draw a Venn diagram with three (or four) circles. Label each circle with one of your core quality-of-life attributes. This becomes a way to bring the future into the present, a decision-making framework for life's biggest questions, big hairy ones like:

- Where should we raise our family?
- Is now the right time to start my own business?
- Should I take this new job, even if it means more travel, or keep my current one?
- Should we move closer to family or stay where our careers are thriving?

- Do we need a bigger house, or more time together?
- Should one of us step back from work to be more present at home?

Don't try to answer every question at once. Choose the most pressing one. Map out your options and where they'll sit in the circles. That sweet spot—where all your elements overlap—should be your guide to the right answer. It won't always be possible to land there, but it gives you a clear idea of what you're aiming for. This isn't about seeking perfection but about making conscious choices rather than letting life happen to you. It's about making decisions you can stand behind even when they're hard and modeling for your kids what it looks like to live with intention.

III. How We Did It: Choosing Where to Live

During our time before and during San Francisco, the topic of where we wanted to live was a constant headache. We agonized about the decision. Any family that has moved for any reason—for a job opportunity, to be closer to grandparents, or to just let rip and see what happens—has done the same. My insights gleaned from years inside the hyperambitious tech broligarchy meant that career was no longer a top priority. Our top three quality-of-life elements at this time were (and continue to be) the following:

- **Natural Environment.** I'd grown up in Manchester all my life. Whenever summer came around and the weather got slightly better, I'd be shipped off to Ireland to spend six weeks with my granny in an even starker climate. Even London, as gray as it can be, offered an upgrade. And the golden sunsets of California made me realize that what was important to us was the freedom to live outside as much as we could—so we wanted to optimize for somewhere with great weather all year round.

- **Connection and Community.** California to the UK was a

ten-hour flight, and the jet lag meant it was something you wouldn't do with kids on a regular basis. The grandparents are getting older, and we wanted to be closer to family, and even if that trip was via plane, rather than car, that would still work.

- **Cultural Vitality.** The final factor might have been career, but after leaving Google I was going out on my own, so location wouldn't have an outsized influence on quality of life in terms of where we lived. We wanted to make sure we ended up somewhere culturally rich that would help us feel creatively inspired.

My wife and I mapped these onto the model. Then we started talking about all the places we'd thought about living. Amsterdam was an early contender. It did well in Connection and Culture (two hours from the UK via a number of budget airlines, interesting things going on, a group of friends we already knew) but was a no-go on climate—I didn't want to go back to spending the majority of the year in the rain, and huge swaths of the year hiding with the kids in soft play centers drinking overpriced, bitter coffee. And as hard as it was to say goodbye to the idea of Berghain on my doorstep, Berlin's winters put it in the same place.

Also on the list was Bali. We'd spent a month there during a career sabbatical in 2018. The cost of living? Few places better, anywhere in the world. Natural environment? Stunning, even if it got a little too humid sometimes. Cultural vitality? Well, if you enjoy yoga, surfing, and vegetarian living, there are few better places in the world. But it was so far from family: seventeen hours on a plane, no direct flights to the UK, a rougher ride than living on the West Coast of the United States. Those drawbacks, coupled with worries about extreme weather events, pushed us to look elsewhere. Heading back to London became a front-runner. One of the world's cultural capitals. Huge career opportunities. So many friends that we miss so much. A few hours in the car and we'd be with either set of grandparents. The weather isn't great all year round, but once summer hits, there are few better cities in the world.

But in the end we couldn't shake the idea of Barcelona. What's the difference between two and a half hours in the car and two and a half hours on a plane, really? It's cheaper to fly to Manchester from Barcelona than to take a train from London. We'd spent so many good times there during weekends away, wondering, as so many do, "Maybe we could live here, one day?" So that was it. We moved to Barcelona in 2019. We gave it a year, to see how it would pan out. We've been here ever since. It isn't perfect; nowhere is. It's all a trade-off. But the feeling I get as my plane lands in the city, witnessing the excitement on the faces of the passengers coming here for a brief visit, always confirms it was the right choice. Knowing what matters most to my family, there's nowhere we'd rather be. When I look around at our life, my definition of success has been reset, and it has very little to do with my nine-to-five.

Let's hear it from the dads on…new definitions of success

I left my birth city, NYC, nineteen years ago with one mission: Make it. Ask me what that meant at the time, and I could not tell you. Beyond some vague idea, images of success I'd seen in magazines and on TV, and a dollar amount (maybe a cool million?), I now realize that I had no clue what "making it" actually meant for me. Now I've come to understand that what I intended to achieve after leaving New York all those years ago was perhaps some form of reasonable freedom and peace of mind. Safety, not having to worry about where my next meal or dollar would come from. I've also come to learn that "making it" is different for everyone, primarily being dictated by where you come from, what your upbringing was like, and what your story is. I'm going to try to instill similar values in my daughter. Help her to choose her life goals consciously. It doesn't really matter what they are; as long as she chooses and makes an intentional effort to achieve them I know she'll be okay. **Kervs**

Success in America is born from capitalism and linked as such. It's too bad that it is for most. But I will admit it is changing. Success, to me, is creating something and sharing it. If I can do that with writing, music, and even with building something with my hands alongside my sons, or creating a great dinner, a great moment, a memorable experience. This is success. Building great relationships by creating something shared. **David**

For me success is to be happy. Everything we do is in the search of happiness. We find a good job because the social recognition/income makes us happy. We quit our job to go part time because we would be happier with a more appropriate work-life balance. We build a family because that would make us happy. We move countries because we would be happier in that other country. We buy cars, find a hobby, quit a hobby...all for the same reason. I think that being happy in your personal and professional life would be the meaning of success to me. So if anybody asks me, that would be the answer. Stop and think, "Is it going to make us happier?" **Federico**

Whenever I look outside of my own life, I find myself feeling fairly unsuccessful without even thinking about why I'm feeling like that. I'm talking about reading about and subconsciously comparing myself to people online, in the news, and on LinkedIn. But it's a cliché; as soon as I look at what I have around me at home—wife, son, and time together—I do feel more successful. And, since having a kid, looking at what I have at home has become more and more easy for me. Every time I play with my son it does immediately make me feel like I've done something good with my life, and the older he gets, the more of my life I'm happy moving time from me and my career over to investing my time with him. *Investing* sounds cold, but it's an unconscious thing and that's what it is, it's investing time to have a really good relationship with him. If that means I'm not going to climb the ladder to the top of a big company, then I'm fine with that—actually, *relieved* is a better word. **Marc**

CHAPTER 16

Recruit Your Crew

Loneliness is the suffering of our time. Even if we're surrounded by others, we can feel very alone—we are lonely together.

—Thich Nhat Hanh, *The Art of Communicating*

Old rule: *MAN UP.*
New rule: *Man down!*

Loneliness remains on the rise worldwide, a trend that predates the pandemic. A 2020 study found that more than 61 percent of Americans reported "sometimes" or "always" feeling lonely. In the UK, a 2016 study found that 1 in 10 UK residents felt they lacked a single friend to rely upon, which shot up to 1 in 8 by 2020. One in 5 Brits said they had no one to confide in, which jumped to 1 in 4 for men. Loneliness is more prevalent in the elderly, but it isn't exclusive to them: One study found that a third of adults over forty-five regularly feel lonely; a meta-analysis of 345 studies on loneliness found levels steadily increasing from 1976 to the present day, particularly in young males aged eighteen to twenty-nine. And for as long as those men have been able to pick up an instrument, they've been crooning to the world about how lonely they feel: from

Hank Williams telling the world "I'm So Lonesome I Could Cry" in 1949 to Roy Orbison suggesting in 1961 that "Only the Lonely" could understand his deep sense of solitude. Sometimes these feelings were connected to love and heartbreak, but it was far from a requirement: In 1980, Joy Division shared their sense of "Isolation" on what would be their final album, released posthumously after singer and lead lyricist Ian Curtis took his own life; Purple Mountains and Silver Jews singer David Berman sang about making strangers wherever he went on "All My Happiness Is Gone"; his body was found in his Brooklyn apartment less than a month after the album's release.

Loneliness doesn't cause depression. But it's often one of the first stops on that journey. Governments are doing everything they can to identify and eradicate loneliness, because the knock-on effects are clear: Chronic loneliness is linked to increased rates of anxiety, depression, and suicide; it raises the risk of premature death in numbers that rival those for smoking, obesity, and physical inactivity; and those who feel isolated are 50 percent more likely to develop dementia, are 29 percent more likely to develop heart disease, and have a 32 percent higher risk of a stroke. Policymakers are prioritizing this as a public health emergency: In 2017, US Surgeon General Vivek Murphy declared loneliness a "deadly, invisible epidemic, hiding in plain sight." In 2018 the UK government started publishing an annual report on the topic and appointed its first Minister for Loneliness. Japan followed with a minister of their own the year after.

These social problems are exacerbated when multiplied by the particular male urge to keep quiet and bottle up. The number of American men who said they had "at least 6 close friends" fell from 55 percent to 27 percent between 1990 and 2021. That same study found 15 percent of men reporting having no close friendships at all, a fivefold increase in three decades. It won't come as a surprise to anyone reading this that studies consistently find men less likely to share their personal feelings than women. We don't ask for help, even when we desperately need it. Loneliness exacerbates these feelings in a vicious cycle where they are reinforced and compounded. Support is needed, but it is hard to find and rarely asked for.

Now, atop these shaky foundations, throw a newborn baby into the mix. Picture the man who spent years walking this tightrope of solitude, then losing his grip on everything. Fatherhood can be the beginning of a beautiful new chapter in your life, but openings don't exist without a closing somewhere else; welcoming a baby into your world can kick-start a fundamental reconstruction of every aspect of your life—your sense of self, a shifting understanding of purpose, changing dynamics of key relationships, an altogether alien structure and routine—which means saying goodbye to aspects of "the old days" you realized too late that you took for granted. Like the spontaneity of a few drinks after work. A last-minute decision to catch a movie with your partner, thirty minutes before the showing. An impromptu weekend away, city-breaking with old friends—the same folks you spent most of your adult life with, before having kids. Suddenly, it's all different.

Help is what we need. But modern society puts it further from reach. A genuine sense of connection to community feels like a relic from a bygone era. Robert Putnam's 2000 book *Bowling Alone* documented the decline in community engagement across America, showing how the social capital and small habits that kept society braided together had begun to fray: People still bowled, but teams dissolved; club nights faded; the PTA, union meeting, church social, neighborhood barbecue, and weekly card game all thinned out. All across America, since the 1950s, there has been a steady drop in spending time with neighbors, participating in civic organizations, and socializing with friends. These findings have been echoed in study after study, drawing lines between social disconnection and mental health struggles in high-income countries worldwide.

You may still live close to the friends you grew up with. You may have stayed put but expanded your social circle after becoming one of the first to have kids, searching for others stepping into a similar life stage: learning to live on breadcrumbs of sleep, search history littered with queries that would have seemed perverted a few years earlier. If you moved for work, love, or sheer hedonism, you will have made new friends there. You might have met folks through your hobbies, you probably made friends through your job—transforming colleagues into friends, bonds forged in the fire of tight deadlines, late nights, and asshole bosses, after-work drinks that became a place to make sense of the day you were raising a glass to the death of.

But things get harder when you have kids. You have less time to see the friends you already have, never mind make new ones. There isn't a place where dads just hang out, waiting to befriend others. That's a shame, because the dads you surround yourself with will color your entire fatherhood experience. "You are the average of the five people you spend the most time with." You've no doubt heard this line before, from motivational speaker and self-help guru Jim Rohn. It's a little reductive—it's obviously more than five people, and the things you watch, the books you read, and the places you visit can contribute just as much to the second-order changes we are striving for. But that line remains laden with truth; its simplicity gives it weight. And it lends itself to the parenting experience too: What if, as a father, you're the sum of the five dads you are closest to?

Who'd be in your handful of padres? What type of a father will you become alongside them? Are they a positive influence on your parenting perspective? Do they lead by example, rejoicing in the role a father can play? Are they raising the bar, as you help each other uncover the opportunities for joy, contemplation, and purpose that can come through raising children? Or are they doing the opposite? Does an evening spent with them leave you more exhausted than when you started? Are they constantly complaining about their job, their partner, their kids, how much they dislike being a parent? Are their visions of fatherhood, and the actions they take as dads, in conflict with the father you want to be?

A huge necessary caveat here: If you made it this far, you're fully aware that being a dad can be a rough ride, and I am in no way telling you to cut other men out of your life if they are having a hard time. This chapter is in no way intended as permission to tell friends, "Sorry to hear your dog got run over, you lost your job, your kid is sick, your team sold their best player, and your favorite TV show got canceled, but I'm really not feeling your negative energy right now" before deleting their number. At some point we all need help. But it's important to take steps to protect your own mental well-being, supporting friends while ensuring you don't get pulled under.

My dad crew is a little more than five, but not far off. They're my fatherhood support group, my Dadvisory Board; it's like the Council of Elrond, only with fewer seats, more rings, and better beards. Most of what you read in this book began in conversation with them: a group of us all winging it; assembling our parachutes while hurtling toward the ground together; understanding the dads we want to be while grappling with the models we inherited; kicking the tires on different ways to raise kids; trying to figure out the right way forward and the feeling of a life well lived. Fatherhood is hard. But it is made easier by having a group of men you trust, whom you can open up to, who give you permission to move beyond the banter—that surface-level yakking about football, beers, memes, stocks, and Netflix shows—to a place where you can dig deeper, down toward the bigger issues we wrestle with, all too often on our own.

Who's in Your Dad Crew?

"No one is useless in this world," Charles Dickens wrote, "who lightens the burden of it for anyone else." If you follow the branches of this book, back through their trunk and roots, the original burden I've been obsessed with—since the first day I started writing, and will be until the last—is how hard fatherhood is without effective support structures in place. Fatherhood can, all too often, be an isolating experience. Call it what you want: the male loneliness epidemic, the fatherhood friendship recession—data shows that when men feel disconnected from their local communities, friends, and family, this impacts their physical and mental health, driving undesirable outcomes for all parties involved. Men need each other, but we're doing a terrible job of showing up.

A long time back, I asked dads reading the newsletter: "Who's in your dad crew? Who do you feel comfortable opening up with?" Some were lucky to have become parents at the same time as other friends, like Dalton: "We just found out three couples close to us are expecting for the first time as well. It's exciting to think that I will most definitely have a core group of dad friends to lean on and spend time with." Others found connections through school, daycare, or baby classes. Bonding around hobbies was a familiar theme, like for Marcus: "I have a group of cycling mates, four of us who all take racing bikes pretty seriously while also taking being modern fathers pretty seriously too. Not an easy juggle but a great way to manage stress." And where would a conversation on dad support networks be without the group chat? It was a regular reply, a digital lifeline that came into its own during the pandemic.

When I left Manchester and headed to London, I moved in with the woman who would later become my wife. Through her, I inherited a group of friends, many of whom I'm still close to today. I also made some of my own: often through work, fellow northern escapees who'd moved down to ply their trade in the Big Smoke. When you start in a new city, with a new job there, your office provides a preestablished group of people, roughly your age, all in the same place. During my decade in London, I was lucky enough to end up in two teams filled with exactly the type of people I'd wish to befriend—interesting, with cool side projects, from every corner of the world, great taste in design, music, and cinema, the kind of folks you'd be happy to be delayed at an airport with. They'd already read the books everyone was talking about, had secret recommendations for the best cities, had a take on the current hot internet shit—and maybe a finger in the pie too.

Our next move wouldn't come with preordained friendship groups: We headed toward San Francisco, and we knew a grand total of four people: my wife's cousins and a couple from London. It was even slimmer pickings when we moved to Barcelona. When we arrived here, I knew very few people in the city—just one friend of a friend. Work looked different—I wasn't heading in to an office every day. Four months later, my son was born. Looking back, I can see a clear link between that feeling of loneliness and my depressive episode. Yes, I had friends in other places, and yes, once I opened up and shared that I was struggling, they were a huge support. But I didn't need dozens of peer-reviewed papers to know I needed local friends.

My wife signed up for events where we could meet other families. I came along, often under duress, as we slowly tested the waters, the strange new family friendship dance: What is the other dad like, do the mothers get along, are the kids hanging out and having fun, or does one of their kids look like he's just about to hit one of ours—and began to build our community. I wasn't hugely involved in the early days, but after a slow start I began to be more gregarious in the search for others. The shifts in fatherhood mean an ever-growing number of dads at the school gates, although I struggled there. The biggest barrier was the language—my Spanish wasn't yet up to scratch, and although most of these dads already spoke two languages—Spanish and Catalan—not all spoke a third. It was odd starting to feel these potential friendships out: I distinctly remember the birthday party where I realized the Catalan dad I was trying my best to hold a conversation with was much more my kind of person than the English-speaking one, where conversation came easy but was unfulfilling.

Sometimes I found people. Other times, they found me. I made one friend in the oddest manner. In our first year here, my daughter—who had recently turned five—hit a spell where she didn't want to go to school. She'd get upset in the morning and throw a small-scale protest at whatever the tragedy of the day was: She didn't like her uniform, didn't want to brush her teeth, hated the milk I used on the cereal or the color of the spoon she was forced to eat with. These kinds of snags can be minor battles on a Saturday afternoon but are insurmountable at 7:30 a.m. on a Tuesday, especially during the depths of the first year of her baby brother.

One day, walking out of my door, bleary-eyed, I heard a Californian voice utter: "Well, at least she's in a better mood today than she was yesterday."

What? Who the hell are you? And how are you saying what I'm already thinking? It turns out we regularly left home around the same time—me with my kids, him with his dog—so he noticed the daily struggle. He introduced himself and invited me into a group chat. It was a good way to meet people, especially in the early days when I was finding my feet here. With any open-invite group, it's inevitable you won't agree with everyone, especially one made up of dads from around the world, with different mental models of what they believed a father should be. Cultures would clash in the chat. But, just like dating, you put yourself out there among the many in the hope of finding the right few. And find one I did—if I hadn't joined that group, there's a fair chance you wouldn't be reading this book today.

One great cure for loneliness—especially in a world where you don't go to the office every day—is to fabricate the illusion of working with others. After the pandemic, I started turning up on Friday mornings to hang out with Carles, a friend who owned a local restaurant. I'd plug in the Moccamaster and make coffee for the staff. After a few weeks of this, and seeing no one tackling the box of peas that needed shelling and separating into small, medium, and large piles, I started to make myself useful. Soon I was washing the mushrooms, taking out the trash, choosing the music, shooting the shit—all while picking up an excellent education in local swear words. After a while, I graduated to calamari line chef. Every Friday morning, a few kilograms of squid would arrive straight from the Mediterranean Sea, ice-packed in a white polystyrene box, and I'd get to work prepping it. I got good at it (after massively oversalting it first time around). It scratched my "going to the office" itch—I would head there every Friday, cosplay as a chef for a few hours, and get paid with a bottle of wine at the end of my short shift.

Over the last few years, and during the period of writing this book, my new social hub has become a local coffee shop, and I've made numerous great friends through it—fellow caffeine addicts who would arrive for their hit after the school run. These centers of gravity exist everywhere, attracting the like-minded and giving them a space to collide with one another. Sociologist Ray Oldenburg coined the term *the third place* in his 1989 book *The Great Good Place*. Third places are distinct from the two usual social environments of home (the first place) and work (the second). They're public gathering spots where people can relax, meet others, and build community. Historically, they've been pubs, cafés, barbershops, and community centers—neutral ground where people can connect across different social backgrounds. For dads seeking connection, third places offer neutral territory and built-in conversation starters: The climbing gym provides a shared activity to focus on while conversation develops naturally; the coffee shop creates regular opportunities to see the same faces; the playground becomes a weekly rendezvous point with other parents. In our increasingly isolated world, these third places have become increasingly vital for creating the weak ties that eventually strengthen into meaningful connections. The key is consistency—showing up at the same places, around the same times, allowing familiarity to develop gradually. Your third place will be somewhere you genuinely enjoy being, where the right kind of people (for you) tend to gather, and making it part of your regular routine.

Loneliness can be defined as the gap between the social connections you would like and those you feel you have. If you sit with the word *lonely*, even for a few seconds, you'll begin to feel its effect; a person being alone, against their will, feels like cruelty. Isolation is one of the most severe levels of prison punishment for a reason. And there's a particular flavor of loneliness a father can feel—surrounded by evidence of others, everywhere you look, yet unable to escape the feeling of being, as we say in England, on your tod. I am almost hesitant to talk about it—having a family means being surrounded by love, held in its embrace, yet you still feel the void. It's hard to write that, just as I know it will be hard for some to read it. But, in my entire life, I never felt more lonely than after the birth of my son.

In *The Lonely City*, Olivia Laing wrote: "Loneliness feels like such a shameful experience, so counter to the lives we are supposed to lead, that it becomes increasingly inadmissible, a taboo state whose confession seems destined to cause others to turn and flee." *The Banshees of Inisherin* saw Colin Farrell's Pádraic turning to his sister and telling her: "I am not putting my donkey outside when I'm sad, okay?" It's played for laughs but comes with a rush of empathy. Admitting you feel alone feels humiliating—it triggers feelings reminiscent of high school angst, your nerve endings attuned to perceived popularity, your friend count the primary indicator of social standing. But it's an emotion we need to open up about. Because we all wear it during our life, and we shouldn't be ashamed of it. We need to do a better job at bringing this to the fore, so we can live happy, fulfilled lives and avoid descending into lonely chaos, like those cursed fingerless men on the island of Inisherin.

Meeting People Is Easy

When online spaces are codified as gender neutral, the balance of the community naturally leans female—women are more open in talking about their struggles and seeking help, reassurance, and support in all aspects of their life. So it logically follows that online parenting communities will become dominated by motherhood conversations. These spaces don't exclude men—far from it. But what we've learned over the past two decades—through shifts in attitudes toward race, gender, and intersectionality—is that when you don't intentionally include, you exclude. Fathers enter these spaces and feel like they are not welcome, just as they read gender-neutral parenting books and find helpful advice and guidance but huge swaths that do not resonate. Resources for dads and moms overlap, but the Venn diagram provides a complex web of connections.

I started The New Fatherhood because I wanted a place for men to connect and have these conversations. From the very first time I hit Publish, it was never about me. This was, first and foremost, a community at its heart—a wide tent permitting entry to anyone who felt they were trying to be a father in a way that didn't seem represented anywhere else. A place for dads with feelings who weren't afraid to show 'em, even if they needed a nudge in the right direction first.

The *vulnerability loop* is a term created by Harvard professor Dr. Jeff Polzer. It is a way of deepening relationships and increasing trust between two people. It works like this: Person A takes the risk of being vulnerable—admitting a fear, sharing a struggle, or exposing uncertainty—and offers it to the other. Person B can reject this offer, switching the conversation to more neutral ground ("Great weather we're having" or "Did you see the game last night?"). But if Person B accepts it, this creates the psychological safety for them to reply in kind. This exchange of vulnerability creates trust and deepens connection in a self-reinforcing cycle.

For men—and especially fathers—this loop is particularly powerful because we've been conditioned to avoid vulnerability. We're trained to hide it away in the hope that others won't exploit it at work as they climb over each other on their way to the top. But when one dad admits he's struggling with his toddler's tantrums or confesses his fear that he's not measuring up as a father, it breaks the façade of perfect parenting that so many of us work diligently to maintain. The relief is palpable—suddenly everyone can breathe easier and share their own challenges.

I've seen this happen countless times in the comment threads of essays I've sent. One dad admits to feeling overwhelmed, and the floodgates open. What starts as a simple admission becomes a profound conversation about the realities of modern fatherhood, creating bonds that couldn't form through surface-level discussions about sports or work. I began to see the power of the vulnerability loop in action, being reinforced by dads across the world, as they got real with each other. As the topics of these conversations spread, and their content deepened, they continued in private spaces—less public square, more public house—as hundreds of dads started to congregate in the Dadscord, our Discord community. Something magical kept happening in these spaces: Dads felt like they could open up in ways they previously were unable to. Writing about topics that weren't discussed anywhere near often enough and inviting other dads to share their perspectives created strong social norms in the group—a feeling of safety and the assurance that this was somewhere you could open up, without fear, embarrassment, or shame.

I found in this community of men something I'd been searching for myself—a space to practice the new behaviors I'd been working on, many of which you've read about in this book—and finding others who wanted to do the same. Think of how different you are today from the boy who turned eighteen all those years ago. Each phase of your life that you move into—the friends you jettison and the ones you actively work to keep—creates your sense of reality. New people and places will push you to new mindsets and ways of thinking, but with older relationships, we can become tethered to the people we were, not the ones we want to become. To your high school friends, you might still be that awkward teenager. To your parents, you will always be the child they remember. Surrounding yourself with people who represent where you are today and where you're heading tomorrow will allow you to confidently step into the dad you want to become.

As the newsletter continued to grow, the community became populated with dads in countries and cities I used to point out on a globe as a child. It began to feel like a critical mass of dads was amassing in some places—the London dads were already meeting up for a drink every so often, and a pair of dads in the Dadscord realizing they lived a few miles from each other became a regular occurrence. Digital relationships can provide essential support and community, especially when searching for others pushing against the status quo. But nothing beats meeting up in real life. In 2024, we launched Dadurdays—meetups for dads in thirty cities across the world. Sometimes dads would meet with their kids, hit up a park, and give Mom a break. Other times, it would be a coffee shop or bar without the little ones, actually getting a chance to talk with one another rather than running around a playground, hoping nobody gets smashed in the face by a swing. And now, these dads come together regularly to participate in men's circles, supporting each other in doing the difficult work of personal growth and building emotional resilience together.

"Do men want to talk to each other?" is entirely the wrong question to ask. If we start from the assumption they do, what happens when we instead ask, "How can we make it happen? And what might come because of it?" Dads are—unbelievably and contrary to public opinion—still human beings, and we will continue to search for ways to build community, even if we are terrible at it. My experience has shown me that so many out there are longing for a genuine sense of connection but have no idea where to start. If you can bring enough of us together, all trying to be better in our own way, such a community becomes more than the sum of its parts. "For a bunch of guys I've never met, I've come to value your opinion an awful lot, far more than some of my friends, to be honest," Sam, a Dadscord dad, once shared. "This place has made me feel that I'm not alone in the everyday titanic struggle of raising little *Homo sapiens*, and it's giving me the tools to be a better dad for the next generation," said another.

Each vulnerable exchange between two men is evidence that a renewal is underway. We stand witness to the fundamental shift in fatherhood, forging new models while casting old ones aside: incorporating strength without sacrificing tenderness, conviction without resorting to control, authority grounded in respect rather than fear. This may be the most important work we ever do—not just for ourselves, but for our children. Because they're watching. They're learning how men show up and support each other, how men love. Through the friendships you intentionally build, you're showing them what's possible for their own relationships throughout life. So send that text. Leave that voice message. Make that invitation. Show up at your local playground or coffee shop consistently. The fathers you need are out there, and they're looking for you too. The bridge may feel rickety at first, but with each crossing, it gets stronger, and we get braver. Together, we'll build a world where our sons don't mistake numbness for strength, and our daughters don't mistake silence for love.

Building Your Dadvisory Board

Creating a circle of confidants won't happen overnight. Your crew may start small—perhaps just one other father who gets it, who sees you, who understands the magnitude of what you're trying to accomplish. But that connection can be lifesaving, literally and figuratively. From there, it might grow to three fathers, then five, then a community that sustains you through the roller coaster of raising children.

Here's a road map to getting started:

I. Start with existing connections

Which of your current dad friends share a similar set of values with you? Who might be open to deeper conversations? Sometimes the foundation is already there, waiting to be built upon. It wasn't until the pandemic that the vulnerability loop became active in some of my closest male relationships, allowing us to forge more meaningful relationships.

II. Become a regular

Choose a third place that aligns with your interests and commit to showing up consistently—same coffee shop every Saturday morning, same climbing gym every Thursday night. Go there, break the ice with someone who looks interesting.

III. Find a local dad meetup

Check dadurdays.org and see if there's a dad group near you. If there is, jump in and say hello. Check other online spaces, like Meetup or local Facebook groups to see what dads are doing.

IV. Create something

Can't find the right group of dads? Start something yourself. We've had dads start local Dadurday groups all over the place—it's been built from the ground up to scale anywhere. (Check the appendix for details on how to do it.)

V. Practice vulnerability in small steps

Test the waters—mention a parenting challenge you're facing to friends and see who responds with understanding and opening up rather than shutting the conversation down.

VI. Think "shoulder-to-shoulder" activities

Researchers studying differences in how men and women form friendships found that while women emphasize emotional sharing, men report higher bonding through shared activities. These activities are often performed alongside one another—watching a football game, sitting at a bar, going on a road trip—providing a way to connect and share without the additional pressure of staring directly into their eyes. This insight has driven the popularity of men's sheds across the world: spaces where men can gather under the guise of building and repairing, and connect with other men who are interested in doing the same.

VII. Extend specific invitations

Rather than the vague "We should grab a beer sometime," try "I'm heading to [place] on Thursday at seven p.m. if you'd like to join." Specific invitations are easier to respond to.

VIII. Be the friend you're looking for

Ralph Waldo Emerson once wrote, "The only way to have a friend is to be one." Often the best way to find supportive friendships is to model that behavior yourself. Be the one who checks in and cares.

IX. Normalize the "dad date"

Get comfortable with the potential awkwardness of what feels like "dating" to make friends. The initial discomfort passes quickly when you find the right connections. Use group meetings to avoid awkwardness. Keep the stakes low: A good meetup is low commitment. Some of the best dad hangs have been the times I've told the local dad group,

"I'm heading to this park at ten a.m. on Sunday, roll through if you're free."

X. Use your children as an excuse

Your kids' friendships can be a natural bridge to other parents and can give you an excuse to do things you might otherwise avoid. You're into video games but don't have time to play them anymore? Arrange to hit up an arcade with a bunch of dads and their kids. Want to get your kids into football? Set up a monthly meet-up in a local park. Dads are out there, searching for activities to do with their kids. But like an awkward school disco, we're all desperately waiting for someone else to make the first move.

Building your Dadvisory Board is a marathon, not a sprint. Dads will come and go. Quality connections take time to develop, but the investment pays enormous dividends for your mental health, your relationship with your children, and your overall quality of life.

Let's hear it from the dads on...meeting other dads

We moved from San Francisco to the suburbs during the pandemic and we're still struggling a bit to connect with the community. I often hear about being friends with your kiddo's friends whether you like it or not because you end up hanging out on playdates, the playground, school events. We probably have to take more initiative to put ourselves out there. And just as important is the frequency/consistency in showing up. **Wes**

Going up to another dad and asking him out for a coffee/beer/ playdate feels weird—although I'm pretty sure this is how my wife met some of her mum friends, often combined with a conversation about how they already follow each other on Instagram. Strangely, organizing something bigger feels more natural—maybe less about forcing a relationship between two dads and more of a general solidarity. **Jon**

How open/likely I am to approach another dad on the playground seems pretty variable—I guess it depends on my mood or energy levels at the time. I am a sociable person but I'm really not great at the awkward small talk bit that's often necessary at the start of a new relationship and I find it quite hard work. It seemed to get easier at school age where, in my case at least, there are more dads involved in the school run, some of whom are more willing to make the first move. We've actually got a pretty decent group of pals all within the same catchment area since my daughter started school last year. Thinking about it, over drinks in the pub is probably the most common way I've found shared interests with other men in the past, pre-kids (thinking more about work colleagues here), but diverting a playdate to the pub at 11 a.m. probably isn't the most practical suggestion. I guess we should start thinking of it as a personal development thing and challenge ourselves to push outside our comfort zones and make that first move more often, and see where it takes us. **Adam**

CHAPTER 17

Reboot Your System

It's not the load that breaks you down, it's how you carry it.

—Lena Horne

Old rule: *Fight or flight.*
New rule: *The dad abides.*

When you're stacking your deck of dads, it's useful to have some at the same life stage as you—kids of a similar age that happily play together are one of life's greatest reliefs—but I'd highly recommend roping in dads further along the path too. I've started to think of these men as FOKs: Fathers of Older Kids. A conversation with an old FOK can be enlightening and terrifying in equal measures—a chance to gaze into the crystal ball toward the future of parenting. Martin, a FOK and close friend, once introduced me to the idea of *the Tunnel*—a place where all parents reside while their children are under five. Dads in the Tunnel can cycle through bliss and despair on a turnaround that would give nonparents whiplash. I'd never suggest wishing those early years away, but know that once you're out the other side, it will be different. It won't be any easier, but the problems shift to demanding more of your mind than the early years demanded of your body.

My writing started when I was deep inside the Tunnel. I was making my way out the other side as this book came together, and the brightness was dazzling. Every day, as I look around, I see dads heading into the Tunnel for the first time, and wonder: *Who will these men be when they emerge from the other side?* We know they will have changed, but will it be for the better? Imagine, just for a second, a dad who could reach back through time—like Marty McFly in *Back to the Future*—and send a message to himself all those years ago. What would I have told past Kevin, that fresh-faced young man with zero gray hairs and fewer frown lines on his forehead?

I'd echo the earlier advice, to remember that "this too shall pass." There is no phrase that has become more dependable, has given me more relief, and has helped me weather even the most brutal storm than this one. With very few exceptions, your current battle will not be one you will keep fighting forever. There are times—sleep regressions my soul still bears the scars from, dinner battles that felt like Sisyphus was pushing rigatoni into a little mouth rather than rolling a giant boulder uphill—when this will feel far from the truth. But trust the process, hold your co-parent close, and remember: Things will get better.

But I'd tell him to be careful what he wishes for. We can be so eager for the next milestone, we don't realize how much we'll miss along the way. You'll want your toddler to start talking, before later experiencing the gut-wrenching sadness when they stop saying a phrase in the adorable—but incorrect—way they've always said it. Years ago, we took a trip to Yosemite National Park. My daughter was three years old and she thought we kept saying "Your Semity," so she started calling it "My Semity." My heart aches to think of it. Your kids will get older. You think you won't miss these moments. I promise that you will.

What else would I say to parents on entering the Tunnel? I'd warn them that there will be large swaths of time when their child will develop a complete fixation on a particular fruit, and they'd better hope, for the sake of their bank balance, that it isn't fresh berries. I'd tell them never do something once that you aren't prepared to do a thousand times. It could be the one funny face you pull to stop a meltdown when they're six months old. It could be a game of Dobble, the visual matching game that spent two years as the hottest thing in our house, or it could be Uno, coming back around again. It will be something. Pray you can do it while lying down.

I'd tell my old self to choose his battles. Your son wants to wear a Spider-Man outfit every single day for a month? Go nuts. (Just remember to wash it.) Do you want to be the dad who forced your son into "real clothes" or the one he remembers who rented a Venom outfit so you could spend Halloween chasing each other around "New York City" together? I'd tell him however long you think you need to do anything, double it: Whether it's bedtime, bath time, dinnertime, getting out of the house, taking a walk, or coloring a Marvel printout you found online. The majority of parenting stress comes from forcing my kids to do things according to my timetable. Whenever I can let go of this, I'm a better, happier dad.

Who knows what the younger me would have done with this advice. I see this fresh-faced man often; he regularly peers at me through my inbox. Every time a dad signs up for the newsletter, he is automatically sent a welcome note with a photo at the top: me, my wife, our two kids, and the dog. I often forget this is the first impression many have of me until somebody hits reply and I'm gifted this artifact from the past, this apparition in my inbox. The photo is no longer an accurate representation of our family. It hasn't been for years; it's a relic, a reminder of a time that no longer exists. My hair is grayer now, the dog too. The tiny baby on my lap—still small enough to carry in one arm, his beautiful golden curls yet to sprout forth—is now a young boy. The "entirely defenseless and dependent" phase of raising children is done. The toddler phase, over too. My babies are babies no more. I'm out of the Tunnel now, and it's an odd feeling to stare back into it, thinking about everything that has happened since.

It feels like decades have passed in the intervening years. Becoming a parent, second time around, broke my heart but opened it up, and I came back better. I wore my scars proudly, visible for all to see. I learned who I was, and worked on who I wanted to become. Looking back at those early months is like trying to work my way through blackstrap molasses, reaching out through impenetrable fog. But the feeling can never be forgotten. That dark, heavy weight I carried everywhere I went, rendering me unable to do even the most basic tasks. I can sense it, have learned its patterns, and when the proverbial black dog on my shoulder appears again, I know what I need to do: Reach out and ask for help rather than waiting to be saved. Continue good habits I know will keep me on track, helping me to steady the ship instead of readying the lifeboats.

In *The Ferryman*, the 2023 novel by Justin Cronin, citizens live on the utopian archipelago of Prospera and measure their life satisfaction via monitors embedded in their forearms, their physical health and psychological well-being represented on a scale from 0 to 100. Most characters sit in the 90s; a drop below 80 is cause for concern. As residents get older, and the weight of the world begins to strain upon them, their levels skydive. When that magic number falls below 10, they're forced into retirement, leaving the island with the ferryman, never to return.

My mind has often wandered to the utility of such a device. Might it help me realize I'm falling into a fog, catching me before I notice it myself? What effect would this awareness provide? Maybe I'd shift into better habits earlier, or let loved ones know before its fangs had made their way into my flesh. What if we could subscribe to a live feed of our friends' numbers? You'd know when to reach out and offer support. Instagram would take on a new dimension if well-being numbers were attached to carefully selected highlights.

No matter how hard we try, there will come times when the universe plants us flat on our arse, and sometimes the lag time between it happening and us noticing is far from instantaneous. This will happen before you have children. It will happen after. Your ability to bounce back will entirely depend on the support structures you have in place, the habits and help networks I've spent the last few chapters outlining. It happened when my son was born. It happened again while I was writing this book: a combination of recurring physical illness, work-related stress, and the overwhelming pressure of raising two children. I've noticed the comforting darkness of falling into a funk, its slimy tentacles spreading and infecting everything it touches. If you're feeling it, your particular flavor of funk might flow from any number of sources: intensifying cycles of unbearable news, dark evenings bringing the dreaded cycle of "Is this seasonal affective disorder or something worse," uncertainties around the economy, the increasing cost of everything (apart from salaries, which remain stubbornly flat), the inevitable exhaustion that comes from trying to balance everything and feeling like you're doing a shitty job of it all. These things pile up.

When you've only got yourself to worry about, you can easily sit in your underpants for hours, PlayStation controller in hand, working on your *Call of Duty* K/D ratio before you finally shame yourself into taking a shower. It isn't pretty, but you're the only person paying the price. When you're a dad? You owe it to those around you to get back out, because your funk has a particular aroma that can stink up the whole house. But getting out from under it is hard. There's no silver bullet—just as it's unlikely that one thing got you into this hole, it's unlikely that one thing will get you out.

Complex problems can feel insurmountable and can trick us into demanding complex solutions. But what if the opposite is true? In his 2009 book *The Checklist Manifesto*, writer and surgeon Atul Gawande found that a simple checklist could save lives, detailing how when eight hospitals adopted one before major operations, surgery complications fell 35 percent and deaths almost halved: no new drugs, no new skills, just a better way to remember what matters. He saw this finding echoed beyond hospitals—pilots could prevent crashes by following a simple list before takeoff, building contractors prevent catastrophic failures with preinspection checklists, even Warren Buffett uses an investment checklist to make the right billion-dollar decisions.

Gawande calls these simple systems for difficult problems "required for success under conditions of complexity." Notice he doesn't say they're helpful—he says required. Parenting children, holding down a job, and trying to navigate an entirely different model of fatherhood that shifts beneath our feet? Complexity with a capital *C*. Over the years, I've started to build my own checklist: a self-maintenance manual, a personal well-being toolbox, habits I can lean on to keep me operating at my best or to reach for at a break-glass moment:

- ☐ Am I getting enough sleep?
- ☐ Am I eating well? (Trying to follow Michael Pollan's advice to "Eat food. Not too much. Mostly plants.")
- ☐ Am I drinking enough water? Am I drinking too much alcohol?
- ☐ Am I spending enough time in nature and away from screens?
- ☐ Am I exercising regularly?
- ☐ Am I meditating regularly?
- ☐ Am I listening to music I love? Have I been to the movies lately?
- ☐ Have I spoken to my friends recently? Or at least swapped voice messages?
- ☐ Is what I'm watching, reading, and listening to helping me or hurting me?
- ☐ Do I have a hobby or creative outlet that excites me?

- ☐ Do I have a space where I can show up authentically? Am I able to practice vulnerability with others there?

- ☐ Am I being kind to myself? Am I talking to myself the way I would talk to a close friend?

- ☐ Am I maintaining spiritual practices, whatever form they take?

- ☐ Am I connecting with something larger than myself, through spirituality, nature, or community?

- ☐ Have I taken time to celebrate small wins? Both mine and my family's?

One school day, feeling stuck in a funk, I took my own advice. I dropped the kids off and took advantage of a morning without meetings to venture into the mountains and walk it off. I felt notable resistance all the way up: *You have emails to answer, a book to write, it's going to be too windy up there, your laptop might get stolen even though it's completely hidden in the boot of the car.* I remembered what Steven Pressfield wrote in *The War of Art*: "Resistance is always lying, and always full of shit." I shut these voices off and hiked toward Tibidabo, a hill that sits 512 meters (about a third of a mile) above Barcelona. The views from up there are unparalleled as you look down onto the city's many sights and out toward the glistening Mediterranean Sea. I walked through the Collserola, the mountain range that acts as a backdrop to the city, and pressed play on *In Rainbows*, an album always guaranteed to make me feel better. Bad days will always come—but I'll just lean on my list, feel the sun on my face, and keep putting one foot in front of the other.

Let's hear it from the dads on... pulling yourself out of a funk

I've been feeling better recently because I've pushed myself to be more social, and, importantly, not just online. I reached out to an old friend and we've started golfing again recently. I'm a better-than-average player and enjoy the challenge of trying to improve. It's a decent form of exercise, as long as I walk the course. But it's also a great way to be more present because hitting good shots requires total focus on the task at hand and blocking everything else out in those moments when you hit the ball. It can be frustrating too, of course. But I'm trying to care less about my score and appreciate that I can make the time and can afford to be out there. **Lyle**

Feel this very strongly. I think it's a mix of having a kid being very boring sometimes, getting older and not realizing that I'm not my younger self any more, and probably still quite a bit of postpandemic funk. My therapist says that so many people are feeling like this, so it's not uncommon. That doesn't make it easier. She ended up basically telling me to get a hobby—but I think she's right. I need to reconnect with doing a thing that's just for me and that gives energy rather than taking it. I find that hard for a bunch of reasons as well, but she's right for sure. Hang in there and stay open about it! **Michael**

Celebrate wins, no matter how small. Depression can be like carrying an invisible eight hundred–pound backpack that others may not experience. Some days, just getting out of bed is enough and needs to be celebrated. If my depressive symptoms spiked today—it doesn't mean I am anything negative, it just means it'll be harder to get things done today. No dumber than the last time I did this activity I've done before, it just means it'll be harder today. If I persevere and push through it, eventually I'm going to trend upward. If I get mad at myself and shut down, then I'm ultimately not going to trend upward. Kinda like certain yoga poses—might not be able to do the same stretch two days in a row; my body may just be a different body on a different day, and if I give a good-faith effort then I'll eventually trend in the direction I want to go. **Brian**

Because that's the rub, isn't it? Having kids makes things so much harder—I mean they're great and all, we can all agree on that—but having zero free time, being constantly tired, and the distancing that happens with friends means that we're making these changes with a massive handicap. There does need to be a shift in mindset. And better fatherhood role models too, people that you can see working it out in the best way. Just like Kevin, I base a lot of my aspirations for parenting on Bandit Heeler. **Jon**

EPILOGUE

Wholehearted Cooperation with the Inevitable

> *I urge you to please notice when you are happy, and exclaim or murmur or think at some point, "If this isn't nice, I don't know what is."*
>
> —Kurt Vonnegut

As I write this, in the early months of 2025, *Bluey* is arguably the biggest entertainment property in the world. Bloomberg reports that it contributes to 29 percent of all Disney+ streaming time—more than *Star Wars* and its galaxy far far away, the entire Marvel Cinematic Universe and its dozens of spin-off TV shows, and the iconic archive of children's movies from Pixar and Disney. Bandit and Chilli are carrying the House of Mouse on their shoulders. Why is it so popular? Because kids love it. But I'd wager a huge part is because parents love it too. As just like all the books, shows, and movies I've spent hundreds of pages banging on about, you get out of *Bluey* what you put in. You may see it as an opportunity for seven minutes of silence and the chance to get something—anything—done around the house, and there's nothing wrong with that. But the show rewards deeper viewing. On closer inspection, the Heeler family become a pack of emotional support animals, gently resting their heads on your lap and looking up with loving eyes when times get hard. In many years of writing about this show, reader comments are consistently 80 percent positive and 20 percent negative—every time I raise the topic, it's guaranteed that at least one dad will email with an angry tirade, accusing Bandit of setting unrealistic expectations for dads, annoyed that he is placing the bar for fatherhood somewhere unreachable. My reply? Thank fuck someone is raising it, even if it has to be a blue cattle dog from Australia.

Bandit Heeler is a poster child for New Fatherhood. Joe Brumm—showrunner and father of two—refuses to sugarcoat the life of a parent in order to protect the kids. He shows Bandit as someone who struggles, who doesn't have all the answers, who is figuring it out as he goes, with the added pressure of two children constantly demanding he drop everything and play with them. *Bluey* accurately paints parenthood as exhausting—kids relentlessly vie for your attention, and anytime you want a moment to yourself, forget about it. But through those tired eyes, we find gratitude for what we have on the path—sometimes simple, often not—to becoming a better parent. While this gig isn't the easiest, or the best paid, few can be more rewarding.

Most shows aimed at children aim to teach the little ones a lesson. *Bluey* aims its arrow right at the heart of the parent while ensuring kids will still enjoy the ride. I've learned more about being a better dad from watching Bandit roll around in the grass with his kids than anything TV has ever offered. In their world, work doesn't define you. In fact, only the most eagle-eyed viewers will have noticed what Bluey's parents do for work: Bandit is an archaeologist while his wife, Chilli, works in airport security. (Bandit digs up bones. Chilli sniffs suitcases. I told you, this show got levels.) It invites us, through the Trojan horse of a kids' cartoon, to glimpse toward something else, using our children as a lens to see the world from entirely new perspectives. In one memorable episode, Bandit plays "Born Yesterday" with the kids, acting like it's his first day on the planet. He knows nothing and must learn about the world for the first time. During the game, he is filled with childlike wonder, adopting what Zen Buddhists call *shoshin*: the beginner's mind. He ends the day holding a leaf toward the sun and marveling at the tiny universe contained within, the worries of the day disappearing into the ether as his wife looks on from the kitchen and wonders whether he's been microdosing too hard.

Bluey is a constant topic of conversation among The New Fatherhood dads. They tell me, "It's made me more intentional about the dad I want to be," "It helped me be more present in the lives of my kids," and "It reminds me to take every opportunity I can to play with them." One dad told me, "I often find myself thinking of Bandit when I'm busy and my daughter wants my attention." Far from being threatened by a cartoon dog—I mean, listen to yourself—they're asking how they can bring some of that Big Dog Energy into their own homes. The rising tide of New Fatherhood lifts all boats, and today's modern dad sees Bandit as a model to strive toward—if not every day, then at least on his best ones. Welcome to a brave new world of fatherhood.

During the denouement of the third season, Bandit becomes preoccupied: sitting on the beach with his family, but mentally checked out. It soon transpires that he is on the cusp of a huge change—having been offered a new job, for more money, but one that requires the Heeler family to pack up and leave Brisbane. In the season's penultimate episode, "The Sign," Bluey finds out that they're moving and arrives at school telling her friends, close to tears, that they're leaving. Bluey's teacher, Calypso, reaches for a children's book titled *The Farmer* and begins to read it to them:

> *There was a farmer who owned a beautiful horse, but one day, his horse ran away.*
>
> *Upon hearing the news, his neighbors came to visit.*
>
> *"That's such bad luck," they said.*
>
> *"We'll see," replied the farmer.*

The very next morning, his horse came back and brought three wild horses with it.

"Wow," said the neighbors, "that's such good luck."

"We'll see," replied the farmer.

The next day, his son tried riding one of the wild horses, but it threw him off and he hurt his leg. The neighbors said, "That's bad luck."

"We'll see," said the farmer.

The next day, soldiers came to the village and made all the young men join the army, but they didn't take the farmer's son because his leg was hurt.

"That's such good luck," said the neighbors.

"We'll see," said the farmer.

When the story ends, a dozen puppies look toward their teacher and pepper her with entirely accurate kid questions: "Is that it?" "What happens next?" "What were the horses' names?" For my own children watching, their questions were similar. But for the adults paying attention, more existential queries were implied. As great as *Bluey*'s writers are, they didn't create this story. Both Shia LeBeouf and Philip Seymour Hoffman—one of our generation's finest actors—have told it on film. Its telling goes back 2,200 years at least. It is a Chinese parable called "The Old Man Who Lost His Horse (but It Turned Out for the Best)," rooted in Taoist thinking: a school of philosophy encouraging followers to exist in harmony with the universe through passivity, calmness, and nonstrife.

Like any good parable, it houses many interpretations. The initial read is a familiar idea: "Every cloud has a silver lining." But on deeper inspection, that idea doesn't hold: The horse returns with three more—becoming a silver cloud with a gray lining—and still, the farmer withholds judgment. It is beyond a retelling of "a blessing in disguise." It is bigger than both: a lesson on the constant flow between what we perceive to be good and bad, and the liberation on offer when we move beyond these binary options. The use of the parable in this episode is intentional—as Bluey listens, Bandit wonders how this career move will alter the trajectory of his life and that of his family. How can he know whether it's the right move to make? What if he makes the wrong decision? Such moments are fraught with tension as we agonize over a fork in the road, trying to minimize regret while maximizing our chance of happiness. But what if, instead of obsessing about the outcome, we said, "We'll see," giving space to allow the next right action to present itself?

Anthony de Mello was a Jesuit priest, born in Mumbai, who briefly studied philosophy in Barcelona before returning to India. His somewhat unorthodox background of growing up Indian and Catholic—in what was British-occupied Mumbai—influenced his worldview and led to writings that intertwined Catholicism, Hinduism, Buddhism, and Taoism. These writings caused consternation among the church, with Pope Benedict XVI posthumously decreeing that de Mello's views "are incompatible with the Catholic faith and can cause grave harm." So, of course, I went to hunt these books down. It was page 22 in his 1992 book *One Minute Nonsense* that stopped me in my tracks:

"What is the secret of your serenity?"
Said the Master, "Wholehearted cooperation with the inevitable."

I copied those last five words down onto a Post-it note, and stuck it on the speaker beside my desk. It has remained there since. "Wholehearted cooperation with the inevitable" is how we see the world as the farmer does: Whatever happens will happen, and what will be will be; the more you fight it, the more turmoil you will put yourself through. Whatever you resist, persists. Instead, lean toward acceptance over refusal, and a daily practice to live a life less affected by Lady Luck's capricious twists.

The human brain excels at pattern recognition. Over centuries, we have developed ways to efficiently and effectively identify relationships, categorize information, and infer predictions based on past experiences and data. Humanity has pushed itself forward by doing this in the fields of mathematics, art, and science—we push ourselves forward by doing the same. I've started to see this particular pattern repeated in the years since I stuck that Post-it onto my desk. Cormac McCarthy took a (very on-brand) pessimistic perspective in *No Country for Old Men*, when Uncle Ellis told Sheriff Ed Tom Bell, "You never know what worse luck your bad luck has saved you from." In *Meditations*, Marcus Aurelius famously wrote, "The happiness of your life depends upon the quality of your thoughts." French writer Anaïs Nin suggested, "We don't see things as they are; we see them as *we* are." And in *Dune*, Paul Atreides returns to Caladan to share his insight after living with the Fremen: "Be prepared to appreciate what you meet."

"I Don't Mind What Happens"

We look at our troubles in one of two ways: *externally caused*, where our misfortunes are due to the actions of others—that boss who passed you over for a promotion, your kids who won't listen as you tell them to put their shoes on in the morning, that close friend or family member who did "the thing" again, just like you knew they would. That sense of injustice has a strong pull. Its fire can feel warm and familiar. On the other end of the scale are *internally caused* sources of strife—where we place the blame entirely at our own door, ruminating on wrong decisions or opportunities missed.

A few years back, I read Stephen Mitchell's translation of the Bhagavad Gita. It was a book that, like *The Tibetan Book of the Dead*, loomed large in the internet rabbit holes where I regularly found myself. I married into a Hindu family, we are raising our children with an understanding and appreciation for this profound religion, and I was curious to read a book that extended family members had held dear during their long lives. It sits next to where I write, dog-eared and sticky-tab-laden. Open to a random page, point at a passage, and it will offer a way to rip you out of your current river of thinking and deposit you on the banks of somewhere new. One section fundamentally shifted my perspective on how I think about success and the feeling of being defined by the work that I do: "You have the right to work, but for the work's sake only. You have no right to the fruits of work. Desire for the fruits of work must never be your motive in working."

In *A New Earth*, Eckhart Tolle tells a story about Jiddu Krishnamurti, the Indian philosopher, writer, and spiritual teacher:

> *At one of his talks in the later part of his life, Krishnamurti surprised his audience by saying, "Do you want to know my secret?" Everyone became very alert. Many people in the audience had been coming to listen to him for twenty or thirty years and still failed to grasp the essence of his teaching. Finally, after all these years, the master would give them the key to understanding. "This is my secret," he said. "I don't mind what happens."*

So why am I attempting to land this book of almost eighty thousand words with a seemingly haphazard collection of *Bluey* transcriptions, quotes from dead priests and spiritual thinkers, and suggestions to spend even more of your hard-earned cash on books? Because from this side of fatherhood—ten years in as I write this, approaching the steep incline of life with teenagers—I know that this is how fatherhood feels: a series of clues that didn't make sense at the time, but when carefully fed and nurtured with attention, and given the time to notice the connections between them, might eventually coalesce into more than the sum of their parts. It's impossible to predict exactly what people, places, conversations, experiences, and cultural touchstones will deepen and transform your worldview over the years of your life. This book is littered with evidence of mine—artifacts that act as mental mile markers, showing me how I arrived here. These are what will most influence how you feel on any given day, and the path you'll follow for years to come. I knew I wasn't alone in looking for other dads, searching for a port of calm in the storm of fatherhood. I found them, and they found me, and that's why this book is filled with so many of their words, and not just mine. Because while *Bluey* can be a nice way to pass the time it takes to soft boil an egg, it can also be something more. It's just one of many jumping-off points for curious parents searching for answers to the great unknown. And if you can only pay attention to these little moments—rather than those shiny rectangles that tempt us in newer and more cunning ways all the time—you can pin these clues to your mental corkboard, link them together with red string, and use fatherhood as a vector toward a happier, more fulfilled life.

Fatherhood can be a challenge, but it also offers us limitless opportunities for joy and a sense of meaning. Maybe being a dad isn't the route to enlightenment—but what if it is? And what if, in order to get there, we'd need to break the chains tying us down, dismantle the old rules, and create The New Fatherhood, together?

The puzzle is waiting to be solved. All you need is the right pieces.

I hope this book points you toward them.

ACKNOWLEDGMENTS

The time between signing the dotted line to write this book and delivering the initial manuscript was nine months. The fact that this was the same length of time that it takes a fertilized egg to turn into a squirming, crying baby wasn't lost on me. The first trimester was relatively chill: reading, researching, regurgitating. The second trimester was, as it is for many soon-to-be parents, when the panic kicked in. And the third trimester was an all-hands-on-deck period to finally birth this baby into the wild. Little did I know that, just like having a baby, the hard work was yet to come.

"Dads don't read!" was what I was told from agents and publishers as I pitched this book. I knew this wasn't the case: There were thousands of dads reading the newsletter every week, looking to fatherhood as a lens to ask—and attempt to answer—life's biggest questions, searching for others on the same quest. Men weren't avoiding parenting books because they didn't read—they were avoiding fatherhood books because nothing spoke to their experience. But my agent, Jim Levine, has been fighting the fatherhood fight since I was in diapers, and he understood immediately why it was necessary and what needed to be done to make it happen. From the first moment I spoke with my editor, Diana Ventimiglia at Grand Central Publishing, she understood the vision and has helped shape this book into what it became. I consider myself beyond blessed to have had these two in my corner for my first foray into publishing. And to the rest of the team at Grand Central Publishing and Hachette who helped turn this idea into reality: Fred Francis, who entertained every newbie publishing question I could throw at him (and I threw a lot); Jim Datz, who knew exactly how this book had to show up on the shelves; Amy J. Schneider, whose thoughtful edits helped bridge the transatlantic language barrier; and to the wider team of Nana Twumasi, Jessica McKenzie, Lauren Sum, and Rachel Rodriguez.

If you saw this book on the shelf and picked it up thinking "ooooh, this looks lovely," then that's due to the tireless work of Johnny Selman, Chris Schroeder, John Paul Chirdon, and the rest of the extraordinary crew at Selman, who have crafted the look and feel of *The New Fatherhood* from the very early days. And it was a pleasure to include the illustrations of Tony Johnson inside the book, who was my partner-in-crime in the early days of the newsletter, when we'd publish an essay with a companion illustration every week. He helped create a visual language that became a calling card for my work and pushed me to write better. That period was a little intense; let's not do that again. If you weren't horrified when glancing at my author photo on the back cover, that's down to the fantastic work of Paroma Basu.

To my dadvisory board, who were instrumental in helping me work through conundrums that ultimately became the chapters you've read: Gareth, Cristian, Graeme, Kam, Nic *and* Nick, Toph, Kiko, Hana, Na'im, Wes, Ed, Rodrigo, Shabby, and no doubt many others that I'll regret forgetting to mention here in years to come. Thank you for your counsel, and may we continue to rely on each other until we're well beyond the long days and short years of raising children.

Behind every book is a patchwork quilt of invisible support that makes it possible. Getting this book over the line would have been nearly impossible without my in-laws, Sonal and Dhiren, who spent hot summer days with the kids while I hid away in a coworking space. Carmen, Carles, and Becca provided one of the most beautiful corners of Catalunya to write part of this book. Maria and Clara provided another, and kept the coffee topped up. I am indebted to those who navigated the waters of the publishing world before me and provided insight, direction, and encouragement: Simone Stolzoff, Armin Brott, Paul Millerd, Daniel Pink, and Anne-Laure Le Cunff. Justin Li was the first friend I opened up to when I was struggling, and I've never regretted it—he became a sounding board for so many of these ideas. And a special thank-you to Aaron Shulman, without whom you almost certainly wouldn't be reading this, a great friend before, during, and (thankfully) after this process, and a true book whisperer—my favorite parts are covered in his fingerprints.

Thanks to Maria Lee, Gareth Clark-Jones, and Alan Bader, who provided professional guidance on the paternal postpartum depression assessment tool, and to the many psychologists, counselors, and therapists across the world who have worked with dads seeking help through the TNF therapy fund.

To all the dads who have felt seen and heard as they come under the umbrella of *The New Fatherhood*: Thank you for helping push fatherhood forward together. I'm encouraged and inspired by the hundreds of dads who commented, emailed, and contributed over the years, many of whom you've read here. To the Dadscord dads, who continue to show up for each other as we push ourselves to be the best men we can be—without taking life too seriously along the way. And to all the other fascinating parents this project has brought me into the orbit of. Thank you. I am forever grateful to every person who has shared my writing with other dads over the years in the hope that it may illuminate a path forward or a way out of a dark corner—a tradition I hope will continue with this book. If you've read it and liked it, please spread the word.

To my sisters, Sinead and Claire, who have shown me the enduring strength of the sibling bond and how a shared childhood can bring you closer as you grow older. To my parents, Mary and Kevin, who instilled in me a work ethic that proved essential during the writing of this book and who always encouraged me to follow my curiosities, never knowing where they would lead. Mum: I got to tell you that I was going to write this book, and we laughed together, and cried together, knowing that you'd never get to read it. I know you'd love it, and we miss you every day.

To my two wonderful children, Padme and Bodhi, who will no doubt read this one day and have questions of their own. I will always be happy to answer them. Sorry your dad had to hide away in a room for months and tell you to leave him alone in order to write a book about being a better father. Finally, this book is possible only due to the encouragement, selflessness, and support of my wife, Sejal: the first person to entertain many of these thoughts, the very first sign-up for the newsletter, my biggest cheerleader from the start. May our adventures continue for decades to come. I love you.

RECOMMENDED READING

It says something that the only fatherhood book I buy as a gift for expectant dads has never changed: *The Expectant Father* by Armin Brott. Now in its fifth edition, it remains the go-to guide for dads-to-be. There is no topic uncovered, no stone left unturned. Reading Brott feels like discussing parenthood with a seasoned dad who has seen it all before and can tell you everything that matters. It was first published in 1995. It was almost old enough to drink when I first read it in 2014, and it remains indispensable today.

There are other great fatherhood books, but they're products of seeing the world through the lens of fatherhood rather than focused solely on the act of being a dad. Many of our finest male writers have pointed their acute senses—and formidable talent—toward the topic after becoming parents. Ta-Nehisi Coates's *Between the World and Me* is one heavyweight sharing how his worldview changed after becoming a father; Michael Lewis's *Home Game* is another. Rob Delaney's moving memoir, *A Heart That Works,* tells the story of his son Henry's birth, life, and untimely death, and what it means to learn to live with grief and open your heart in new ways. And no conversation on fatherhood literature would be complete without touching upon Karl Ove Knausgaard's six-book magnum opus, *My Struggle,* which laid the groundwork for a more open, honest conversation around fatherhood and demonstrated an uncanny ability to find beauty in the existential mundanity of being a stay-at-home parent.

Widening beyond fatherhood to the parenting genre: *The Whole-Brain Child* by Daniel J. Siegel and Tina Payne Bryson is one parenting book I return to regularly; its framework is never far from mind in a fiery parenting moment. *Your Baby, Week by Week* is an absolute must during year one, a period when we could time baby milestones almost to the minute, providing daily reassurance that whatever our precious bundle was doing RIGHT NOW was normal, and we had nothing to worry about. Philippa Perry's *The Book You Wish Your Parents Had Read* may be the most accurate book title I've ever encountered. And I'm still miffed that Emily Oster didn't write *Cribsheet* in 2014, before the birth of my first—that might have saved significant time, pain, sleepless nights, and general anxiety. There are some phenomenal books by mothers for mothers that should be required reading for dads: *Mothers: An Essay on Love and Cruelty* by Jacqueline Rose, *I'll Show Myself Out* by Jessi Klein, and *A Life's Work* by Rachel Cusk are three amongst many that are well worth your time—books that make women feel seen and heard. I've been reading fatherhood books for the best part of a decade, and I'm still searching for one to provide a similar feeling.

Your perspective on the world will color your perspective on fatherhood, and a book is a tried and tested way to change your view. This book is a reflection of where I am today and is indebted to the writing of so many others: *Waking Up* by Sam Harris, *Why Buddhism is True* by Robert Wright, and the collective works of Pema Chödrön (especially *When Things Fall Apart*) are three inputs that shifted my spiritual center. Michael Pollan's *How to Change Your Mind* is the first point of call for any dad looking to explore psychedelic therapy to break down barriers preventing them from being a better parent. *Four Thousand Weeks* by Oliver Burkeman, *The Good Enough Job* by Simone Stolzoff, *The Pathless Path* by Paul Millerd, and *From Strength to Strength* by Arthur C. Brooks are all great jumping-off points for rethinking your relationship with success, productivity, and career prestige.

I could have recommended dozens more, but the team at the publishers are waving at me, tapping their watches and page counters, and telling me we're out of space.

MORE FROM *THE NEW FATHERHOOD*

Still want more? You're insatiable. I just wrote a whole book, gimme a minute.

There are a few newsletter pieces I've referenced throughout: a list of books I'll miss reading to my kids, kids' TV shows that won't make you want to gouge your eyes out, reflections on having another child, why you should be reading more motherhood memoirs, and more. These resources, and many others, are available at **next.thenewfatherhood.org**

To access the paternal postpartum depression assessment tool, visit **checkup.thenewfatherhood.org**

Ten percent of every dollar I make from this book will go into The New Fatherhood Therapy Fund: a direct-action venture to help dads struggling with their mental health get access to therapy, regardless of where they are, what healthcare plan they're on, or how much money they have. If you are a dad who needs help, or would like to contribute to cover the cost of therapy for a father in need, go to **newfatherhood.fund**

Over the past decade, I've coached dozens of dads who were looking to navigate moments of transition and intentionally build lives where fulfillment, family, and focus work in harmony. If you've enjoyed reading this book and are curious about working together, you can find out more at **kevinmaguire.coach.** You can apply to be part of the group coaching program REBOOT, a twice yearly program with community and care at its heart, for men done with performative success and ready for real change. Details can be found at **reboot.thenewfatherhood.org**

If you're looking for ~~hot single~~ dads in your area, take a peek at **dadurdays.org.** At the time of writing, we had dads in twenty-seven cities looking to hang out. Come in, say hello, and meet dads like you near you. If there isn't a group in your vicinity, scroll to the bottom of the page and find all the details you need to start your own.

Finally, if you're still not ready to leave and want to head back to where this all began, sign up for the weekly newsletter at **thenewfatherhood.org**

See you in the Dadscord: **join.thenewfatherhood.org**

NOTES

INTRODUCTION. When Fatherhood Doesn't Go to Plan

4 written about a doctor struggling to connect with his second child Margaret Jaworski, "Oh Baby: Postpartum Depression in Men Is Real, Science Says," HealthCentral, March 28, 2018, updated August 26, 2022, https://www.healthcentral.com/condition/depression/postpartum-depression-in-men.

10 Homer Simpson was still strangling his son Dory Jackson, "Homer Simpson Declares He Won't Strangle Bart Anymore on *The Simpsons*: 'Times Have Changed!,'" *People*, November 6, 2023, https://people.com/the-simpsons-homer-promises-not-to-strangle-bart-8391071.

Chapter 1. The Case for Abundancy

22 Bloomberg reported that we spent $6.3 trillion on wellness across the world "Global Wellness Industry Is Now Worth $6.3 Trillion," *Bloomberg News*, November 5, 2024, https://www.bloomberg.com/news/articles/2024-11-05/global-wellness-industry-is-now-worth-6-3-trillion.

22 "It may be a thankless job" Jim Gaffigan, *Dad Is Fat* (Crown Archetype, 2013), 46.

23 around 40 percent of dads don't take the full amount of paternity leave offered Jessica Grose, "Why Dads Don't Take Parental Leave," *New York Times*, February 19, 2020, https://www.nytimes.com/2020/02/19/parenting/why-dads-dont-take-parental-leave.html.

23 less than a third of dads in the UK took any Olivia Petter, "Fewer Than Third of New Fathers Take Paternity Leave, Research Suggests," *The Independent*, July 8, 2019, https://www.independent.co.uk/life-style/health-and-families/paternity-leave-new-fathers-less-third-not-taking-a8992086.html.

23 One Swedish study Anita Heshmati et al., "The Effect of Parental Leave on Parents' Mental Health: A Systematic Review," *The Lancet Public Health* 8 (2023): e57–e75.

23 the University of Oslo Andreas Kotsadam and Henning Finseraas, "Causal Effects of Parental Leave on Adolescents' Household Work," *Social Forces* 92, no. 1 (2013): 329–351, https://doi.org/10.1093/sf/sot044.

Chapter 2. The History of Fatherhood

30 most children were typically weaned at seven months old Sid Perkins, "Infant Tooth Reveals Neanderthal Breastfeeding Habits," *Nature*, May 22, 2013, https://doi.org/10.1038

/nature.2013.13047.

31 79 percent of sixty-three historical societies had evidence of female hunters Cara E. Wall-Scheffler et al., "Women's Contribution to the Hunt Across Ethnographic Contexts," *PLOS One* 18, no. 7 (2023): e0287101, https://doi.org/10.1371/journal.pone.0287101.

32 "The traditional way of raising sons, which lasted for thousands and thousands of years" Robert Bly, *Iron John: A Book About Men* (Element Books, 1993), 19.

33 "By the middle of the twentieth century, a massive change had taken place" Bly, *Iron John*, 100.

33 a 1928 book John B. Watson (with Rosalie N. Rayner), *Psychological Care of Infant and Child* (Norton, 1928).

34 "By taking control and teaching them to control their emotions" Michael Pearl and Debi Pearl, *To Train Up a Child: Turning the Hearts of the Fathers to the Children* (No Greater Joy Ministries, 1994), 26–27.

34 "everything the light touches will be yours" *The Lion King*, dir. Roger Allers and Rob Minkoff (Walt Disney Pictures, 1994).

34 As writer Stephen Marche eloquently noted in 2014 Stephen Marche, "Manifesto of the New Fatherhood," *Esquire*, June 13, 2014, https://www.esquire.com/lifestyle/news/a28987/manifesto-of-the-new-fatherhood-0614.

39 fathers' brains develop enhanced neural responses Ting Li et al., "Explaining Individual Variation in Paternal Brain Responses to Infant Cries," *Physiology & Behavior* 193 (2018): 43–54, https://doi.org/10.1016/j.physbeh.2017.12.033.

39 Research on primary-caregiving gay dads Eyal Abraham et al., "Father's Brain Is Sensitive to Childcare Experiences," *Proceedings of the National Academy of Sciences* 111, no. 27 (2014): 9792–9797, https://doi.org/10.1073/pnas.1402569111.

39 A 2011 study from Northwestern University Lee T. Gettler et al., "Longitudinal Evidence That Fatherhood Decreases Testosterone in Human Males," *Proceedings of the National Academy of Sciences* 108, no. 39 (2011): 16194–16199, https://doi.org/10.1073/pnas.1105403108.

41 In the United States, 29 percent of married opposite-sex couples Richard Fry et al., "In a Growing Share of U.S. Marriages, Husbands and Wives Earn About the Same," Pew Research Center, April 13, 2023, https://www.pewresearch.org/social-trends/2023/04/13/in-a-growing-share-of-u-s-marriages-husbands-and-wives-earn-about-the-same.

Chapter 3. The Odds Are Against You

46 A 2018 University of Cambridge study into the empathy quotient (EQ) Varun Warrier et al., "Genome-Wide Analyses of Self-Reported Empathy: Correlations with Autism, Schizophrenia, and Anorexia Nervosa," *Translational Psychiatry* 8, no. 1 (2018): Article 35, https://doi.org/10.1038/s41398-017-0082-6.

48 correctly identifying 70 to 85 percent of mothers who are experiencing depression J. L. Cox et al., "Detection of Postnatal Depression: Development of the 10-Item Edinburgh Postnatal Depression Scale," *British Journal of Psychiatry* 150, no. 6 (June 1987): 782–786, https://doi.org/10.1192/bjp.150.6.782.

48 a 39 percent reduction in postpartum depression rates Elizabeth O'Connor et al., "Interventions to Prevent Perinatal Depression: Evidence Report and Systematic Review for the US Preventive Services Task Force," *JAMA* 321, no. 6 (2019): 588, https://doi.org/10.1001/jama.2018.20865.

49 affecting anywhere between 1 and 25 percent of dads Janice H. Goodman, “Paternal Postpartum Depression, Its Relationship to Maternal Postpartum Depression, and Implications for Family Health,” *Journal of Advanced Nursing* 45, no. 1 (January 2004): 26–35, https://doi.org/10.1046/j.1365-2648.2003.02857.x.

49 A 2022 meta-analysis, looking at over twenty thousand men Wen-Wang Rao et al., “Prevalence of Prenatal and Postpartum Depression in Fathers: A Comprehensive Meta-Analysis of Observational Surveys,” *Journal of Affective Disorders* 263 (February 15, 2020): 491–499, https://doi.org/10.1016/j.jad.2019.10.030.

49 Forty-eight percent of parents say Natalie Kerr, “Modern Parenting Is Bad for Your Health,” *Psychology Today*, updated September 25, 2024, https://www.psychologytoday.com/us/blog/social-influence/202409/modern-parenting-is-bad-for-your-health.

52 “catnip” for people with depression Julie Muncy, “Depression and the Solace of ‘Grinding’ in Online Games,” *Wired*, July 24, 2019, https://www.wired.com/story/videogame-grinding-depression.

Chapter 4. Breaking the Cycle

60 90 percent of US parents reported using corporal punishment Jennifer E. Lansford and Kenneth A. Dodge, “Cultural Norms for Adult Corporal Punishment of Children: A Review of the Psychological Research,” *Parenting: Science and Practice* 8, no. 3 (2008): 257–270, https://doi.org/10.1080/15295190802204843.

60 A landmark 2012 paper in the *Canadian Medical Association Journal* Joan E. Durrant and Ron Ensom, “Physical Punishment of Children: Lessons from 20 Years of Research,” *Canadian Medical Association Journal* 184, no. 12 (2012): 1373–1377, https://doi.org/10.1503/cmaj.101314.

61 The campaign’s television advertisements National Society for the Prevention of Cruelty to Children, “NSPCC ‘Full Stop’ Compilation,” YouTube video, October 16, 2019, https://www.youtube.com/watch?v=ZHZxcoRQZlY.

61 “All of humanity’s problems stem from man’s inability to sit quietly in a room alone” Blaise Pascal, *Pensées*, trans. A. J. Krailsheimer (Penguin Classics, 2005), fragment [136].

61 parents who admitted to using physical violence as punishment David Finkelhor, “Trends in Adverse Childhood Experiences (ACEs) in the United States,” *Journal of Child and Family Studies* 28 (2019): 316–322, https://doi.org/10.1007/s10826-019-01426-4.

61 with more than two-thirds of adults now saying it is never acceptable NSPCC, “Give Children Equal Protection from Assault,” May 1, 2024, https://www.nspcc.org.uk/keeping-children-safe/our-campaigns/give-children-equal-protection-from-assault.

62 “Britain was the last developed country” Marina Warner, *Into the Dangerous World: Some Reflections on Childhood and Its Costs* (Chatto & Windus, 1989).

62 “I can imagine that someday we will regard our children” Alice Miller, *For Your Own Good: Hidden Cruelty in Child-Rearing and the Roots of Violence*, trans. Hildegarde Hannum and Hunter Hannum (Farrar, Straus and Giroux, 2002).

63 “I am alive, I have my own children” Karl Ove Knausgaard, *Boyhood Island (My Struggle, Book 3)*, trans. Don Bartlett (Harvill Secker, 2014), 248.

64 “Awakening is frequently described as a journey” Pema Chödrön, *When Things Fall Apart: Heart Advice for Difficult Times* (HarperCollins, 2004), 91.

65 "All that was left was emotion, and it was stark" Karl Ove Knausgaard, *A Man in Love (My Struggle, Book 2)*, trans. Don Bartlett (Vintage Books, 2013).

67 "The father of a two-year-old talks about turning on the television" Chödrön, *When Things Fall Apart*, 86.

69 "an intimate metaphoric narrative of loss and recovery" Bonnie Kemske, *Kintsugi: The Poetic Mend* (Herbert Press, 2021), 12.

69 "The world breaks everyone and afterward many are strong at the broken places" Ernest Hemingway, *A Farewell to Arms* (Scribner, 1929), 120.

70 If harm is inherited Philip Larkin, "This Be the Verse," in *Collected Poems* (Farrar, Straus and Giroux, 2001).

Chapter 5. You Are Not Your Job

78 had an average of twelve jobs throughout their entire careers US Bureau of Labor Statistics, "Number of Jobs, Labor Market Experience, Marital Status, and Health for Those Born 1957–1964," news release USDL-25-1322, August 26, 2025, https://www.bls.gov/news.release/nlsoy.nr0.htm.

82 was driving one-third of the value of the US stock market Lewis Krauskopf, "US Stock Market Concentration Risks Come to Fore as Megacaps Report Earnings," Reuters, July 23, 2025, https://www.reuters.com/business/autos-transportation/us-stock-market-concentration-risks-come-fore-megacaps-report-earnings-2025-07-23/.

84 "Greed, for lack of a better word, is good" *Wall Street*, dir. Oliver Stone (20th Century Fox, 1987).

85 "Fuck you! That's my name!" *Glengarry Glen Ross*, dir. James Foley (New Line Cinema, 1992).

86 found that money does bring happiness Daniel Kahneman and Angus Deaton, "High Income Improves Evaluation of Life but Not Emotional Well-Being," *Proceedings of the National Academy of Sciences* 107, no. 38 (2010): 16489–16493, https://doi.org/10.1073/pnas.1011492107.

86 Newer research disputed this finding Matthew A. Killingsworth et al., "Income and Emotional Well-Being: A Conflict Resolved," *Proceedings of the National Academy of Sciences* 120, no. 10 (2023): e2208661120, https://doi.org/10.1073/pnas.2208661120.

87 a salary of $104,400 would classify you as living below the poverty line California Department of Housing and Community Development, "State Income Limits," June 6, 2023, https://web.archive.org/web/20230626072321/https://www.hcd.ca.gov/sites/default/files/docs/grants-and-funding/income-limits-2023.pdf.

87 the average cost of raising a family in the city "Cost of Living in San Francisco, California," Numbeo (mid-2025 snapshot), https://www.numbeo.com/cost-of-living/in/San-Francisco.

87 published a study on "enough" Paul G. Bain and Renata Bongiorno, "Evidence from 33 Countries Challenges the Assumption of Unlimited Wants," *Nature Sustainability* (2022): 669–673, https://doi.org/10.1038/s41893-022-00902-y.

88 in 2023, it was 8.8x Rozi Jones, "Income to House Price Ratio More Than Doubles Since the ['] 70s," *Financial Reporter*, July 5, 2023, https://www.financialreporter.co.uk/income-to-house-price-ratio-more-than-doubles-since-the-70s.html.

88 almost a decade to save up for a down payment Rupert Jones, "First-Time Homebuyers Now Need Nearly 10 Years to Save a Deposit, Research Finds," *The Guardian*,

July 3, 2023, https://www.theguardian.com/money/2023/jul/03/first-time-homebuyers-now-need-nearly-10-years-to-save-a-deposit-research-finds.

90 "The goals on that first mountain" David Brooks, *The Second Mountain: The Quest for a Moral Life* (Allen Lane, 2019), xii.

Chapter 6. A Higher Power

97 "Fuck off back to France, you dirty French bastard" "When Manchester United's Eric Cantona Attacked a Fan (Crystal Palace, Rewind 1995)," ESPN, January 22, 2015, https://www.espn.com/soccer/story/_/id/37411974/when-manchester-united-eric-cantona-attacked-fan-crystal-palace-rewind-1995.

99 eventually see the loss of 3,500 lives in Ireland and the United Kingdom across three decades Joanne McEvoy, *The Politics of Northern Ireland* (Edinburgh University Press, 2008).

101 among the quarter of married Americans from different faiths Pew Research Center, "Religious Intermarriage," February 26, 2025, https://www.pewresearch.org/religion/2025/02/26/religious-intermarriage/.

101 *Going to Pieces Without Falling Apart* Mark Epstein, *Going to Pieces Without Falling Apart: A Buddhist Perspective on Wholeness* (Broadway Books/Harmony, 1998/1999), 118.

101 "trying to understand God is like a dog trying to understand the internet" Pete Holmes, "Rainn Wilson | You Made It Weird with Pete Holmes," YouTube video, May 17, 2023, at 1:29:46, https://www.youtube.com/watch?v=lx07z9m2eRo.

102 three in ten US adults are now "religiously unaffiliated" "About Three-in-Ten U.S. Adults Are Now Religiously Unaffiliated," Pew Research Center, December 14, 2021, https://www.pewresearch.org/religion/2021/12/14/about-three-in-ten-u-s-adults-are-now-religiously-unaffiliated.

102 predicted to fall below 50 percent of the population by 2070 "Modeling the Future of Religion in America," Pew Research Center, September 13, 2022, https://www.pewresearch.org/religion/2022/09/13/modeling-the-future-of-religion-in-america.

102 more people now believe in ghosts than God "British People More Likely to Believe in Ghosts Than a Creator," YouGov, March 26, 2016, https://yougov.co.uk/topics/politics/articles-reports/2016/03/26/o-we-of-little-faith.

102 "most Americans aren't happy that religion is declining" "Most Americans Think Religion's Influence Is Declining—and That's Not a Good Thing, Poll Says," Fox News, https://www.foxnews.com/media/most-americans-think-religions-influence-declining-not-good-thing-poll-says.

102 "Christians increasingly being persecuted worldwide" "Christians Increasingly Being Persecuted Worldwide as Modern, Historical Factors Converge," Fox News, https://www.foxnews.com/world/christians-increasingly-persecuted-worldwide-modern-historical-factors-converge.

103 increased by 17 percent in the years 2007 to 2014 "Americans May Be Getting Less Religious, but Feelings of Spirituality Are on the Rise," Pew Research Center, January 21, 2016, https://www.pewresearch.org/fact-tank/2016/01/21/americans-spirituality.

103 increased from 19 percent to 27 percent in the five years running up to 2017 "More Americans Now Say They're Spiritual but Not Religious," Pew Research Center, September 6, 2017, https://www.pewresearch.org/fact-tank/2017/09/06/more-americans-now-say-theyre-spiritual-but-not-religious.

105 "If you are in a transitional state in your life" Arthur C. Brooks, *From Strength to Strength: Finding Success, Happiness, and Deep Purpose in the Second Half of Life* (Bloomsbury, 2022), 155.

107 "There is no such thing as not worshipping" David Foster Wallace, *This Is Water: Some Thoughts, Delivered on a Significant Occasion, About Living a Compassionate Life* (Little, Brown, 2009).

Chapter 7. The Point of Parenting

112 "The unexamined life is not worth living" Plato, *The Apology of Socrates*, ed. and trans. Nicholas Denyer (Cambridge University Press, 2019), 38a.

112 having children decreases your well-being Maike Luhmann et al., "Subjective Well-Being and Adaptation to Life Events: A Meta-Analysis," *Journal of Personality and Social Psychology* 102, no. 3 (2012): 592–615, https://doi.org/10.1037/a0025948.

112 makes you less happy in your marriage Jean M. Twenge et al., "Parenthood and Marital Satisfaction: A Meta-Analytic Review," *Journal of Marriage and Family* 65, no. 3 (2003): 574–583, https://doi.org/10.1111/j.1741-3737.2003.00574.x.

112 62 percent of parents admitting "Parenting in America Today," Pew Research Center, January 24, 2023, https://www.pewresearch.org/social-trends/2023/01/24/parenting-in-america-today/.

112 satisfying your immediate needs Roy F. Baumeister et al., "Some Key Differences Between a Happy Life and a Meaningful Life," *Journal of Positive Psychology* 8, no. 6 (2013): 505–516, https://doi.org/10.1080/17439760.2013.830764.

113 parents reported significantly higher levels of meaning in life S. Katherine Nelson et al., "The Pains and Pleasures of Parenting: When, Why, and How Is Parenthood Associated with More or Less Well-Being?," *Psychological Bulletin* 140, no. 3 (2014): 846–895, https://doi.org/10.1037/a0035444.

113 parents spent more time thinking about the meaning of life than nonparents Nelson et al., "The Pains and Pleasures of Parenting."

114 Darwin could clearly see positives Maria Popova, "Charles Darwin on the Love of Life, the Value of Children, and the Beauty of Marriage," *The Marginalian*, August 14, 2012, https://www.themarginalian.org/2012/08/14/darwin-list-pros-and-cons-of-marriage.

114 "He that has wife and children has given hostages to fortune" Francis Bacon, "Of Marriage and Single Life," in *The Essays of Francis Bacon* (Kessinger, 2010).

115 "There is no more sombre enemy of good art than the pram in the hall." Cyril Connolly, *Enemies of Promise* (University of Chicago Press, 2008).

115 the number of nonparents who never want children doubled over the last two decades "The Experiences of U.S. Adults Who Don't Have Children," Pew Research Center, July 25, 2024, https://www.pewresearch.org/social-trends/2024/07/25/the-experiences-of-u-s-adults-who-dont-have-children.

116 "If I had followed the great man's advice" Michael Chabon, *Pops: Fatherhood in Pieces* (HarperCollins, 2018), 46.

117 "Rather than being 'the enemy of art'" Austin Kleon, "The Pram in the Hall," austinkleon.com, October 27, 2016, https://austinkleon.com/2016/10/27/the-pram-in-the-hall.

117 Scholars have suggested that it was becoming a father "Darwin in Letters, 1851–1855: Death of a Daughter," Darwin Correspondence Project (University of Cambridge), accessed October 7, 2025, https://www.darwinproject.ac.uk/letters/darwins-life-letters/darwin-letters-1851-1855-death-daughter.

Chapter 8. All You Need Is Time

122 we experience losses as if they were twice as large Amos Tversky and Daniel Kahneman, "Advances in Prospect Theory: Cumulative Representation of Uncertainty," *Journal of Risk and Uncertainty* 5 (1992): 297–323, https://doi.org/10.1007/BF00122574.

130 babies begin to understand it around age six to nine months Elika Bergelson and Daniel Swingley, "At 6–9 Months, Human Infants Know the Meanings of Many Common Nouns," *Proceedings of the National Academy of Sciences* 109, no. 9 (2012): 3253–3258, https://doi.org/10.1073/pnas.1113380109.

130 they won't stop what they're doing in response to the word until they hit twelve to eighteen months Grazyna Kochanska et al., "The Development of Self-Regulation in the First Four Years of Life," *Child Development* 72, no. 4 (2001): 1091–1111, https://doi.org/10.1111/1467-8624.00336.

131 as Gay Hendricks puts it Gay Hendricks, *The Big Leap: Conquer Your Hidden Fear and Take Life to the Next Level* (HarperOne, 2010).

Chapter 9. Health Is Wealth

136 "Pain is inevitable. Suffering is optional." Haruki Murakami, *What I Talk About When I Talk About Running*, trans. Philip Gabriel (Vintage Books, 2007).

136 "the battle going on in your mind" John E. Sarno, *Healing Back Pain: The Mind-Body Connection* (Warner Books, 1991).

137 Half of men haven't seen a medical professional for six months "Why Do Men Seek Healthcare Less Often Than Women?," *Numan*, accessed August 27, 2025, https://www.numan.com/mens-health/why-do-men-seek-healthcare-less-often-than-women.

137 A 2022 study of one thousand American men "Two-Thirds of Men Think They're Naturally Healthier Than Others," EurekAlert! news release, May 23, 2022, https://www.eurekalert.org/news-releases/954176.

137 the infamous 1986 study I. A. McCormick et al., "Comparative Perceptions of Driver Ability—a Confirmation and Expansion," *Accident Analysis & Prevention* 18, no. 3 (1986): 205–208, https://doi.org/10.1016/0001-4575(86)90004-7.

139 In Puerto Rico, researchers spent 2017 conducting a groundbreaking program Beatriz Salvesen von Essen et al., "Opportunities to Address Men's Health During the Perinatal Period—Puerto Rico, 2017," *Morbidity and Mortality Weekly Report* 69, nos. 51–52 (January 1, 2021): 1638–1641, https://doi.org/10.15585/mmwr.mm695152a2.

139 In 2022, a hospital in the suburbs of Paris Hélène Farge et al., "Implementing a Prenatal Health Screening Intervention for Future Fathers in Montreuil, France," *BMC Public Health* (2024): 2414, https://doi.org/10.1186/s12889-024-20388-x.

142 "one wild and precious life" Mary Oliver, "The Summer Day," in *House of Light* (Beacon Press, 1992).

143 "True life is lived only where these tiny, tiny, infinitesimally small changes occur" Leo Tolstoy, "Why Do Men Stupefy Themselves?" (1890), chap. 4, Marxists Internet Archive, accessed August 27, 2025, https://www.marxists.org/archive/tolstoy/1890/why-do-men-stupefy-themselves/chapter-4.html.

Chapter 10. The Mental Toll of Raising Children

149 One in four men will deal with a mental health episode World Health Organization, *The World Health Report 2001: Mental Health—New Understanding, New Hope* (WHO, 2001).

151 The first year after the birth of a child is when new parents are particularly at risk S. Dave et al., "Incidence of Maternal and Paternal Depression in Primary Care: A Cohort Study Using Linked Routine Data," *Archives of Pediatrics & Adolescent Medicine* 164, no. 11 (2010): 1038–1044, https://doi.org/10.1001/archpediatrics.2010.184.

151 Younger and first-time dads are most susceptible Craig F. Garfield et al., "A Longitudinal Study of Paternal Mental Health During Transition to Fatherhood as Young Adults," *Pediatrics* 133, no. 5 (2014): 836–843, https://doi.org/10.1542/peds.2013-3262.

151 those with a partner experiencing depression Judy H. Goodman, "Paternal Postpartum Depression, Its Relationship to Maternal Postpartum Depression, and Implications for Family Health," *Journal of Advanced Nursing* 45, no. 1 (2004): 26–35, https://doi.org/10.1046/j.1365-2648.2003.02857.x.

151 21 percent of dads will have experienced a depressive episode S. Dave et al., "Incidence of Maternal and Paternal Depression in Primary Care."

151 children are 43 percent more likely to develop depression later in life Sinead Brophy et al., "Timing of Parental Depression on Risk of Child Depression and Poor Educational Outcomes: A Population-Based Routine Data Cohort Study from Born in Wales, UK," *PLOS One* 16, no. 11 (2021): e0258966, https://doi.org/10.1371/journal.pone.0258966.

151 Depression is linked with more hostile and violent parenting Karlen Lyons-Ruth et al., "Parental Depression and Child Attachment: Hostile and Helpless Profiles of Parent and Child Behavior Among Families at Risk," in *Children of Depressed Parents: Mechanisms of Risk and Implications for Treatment*, ed. S. H. Goodman and I. H. Gotlib (American Psychological Association, 2002), 89–120, https://doi.org/10.1037/10449-004.

151 poorer academic performance R. J. Lacey et al., "Parental Mental Health and Child Outcomes—a Multimorbidity Perspective," *eClinicalMedicine* 32 (2021): 101000, https://doi.org/10.1016/j.eclinm.2021.101000.

151 diagnoses of suicidality for new mothers tripling since the pandemic Catherine K. Ettman et al., "Prevalence of Depression Symptoms in US Adults Before and During the COVID-19 Pandemic," *JAMA Network Open* 3, no. 9 (2020): e2019686, https://doi.org/10.1001/jamanetworkopen.2020.19686.

152 a man is four times as likely to kill himself as a woman is National Center for Health Statistics, "Suicide Mortality in the United States, 1999–2019," *NCHS Data Brief no. 398* (February 2021), https://doi.org/10.15620/cdc:101761.

152 62 percent of male suicides occur on the first known attempt Erkki T. Isometsä and Jouko K. Lönnqvist, "Suicide Attempts Preceding Completed Suicide," *British Journal of Psychiatry* 173, no. 6 (1998): 531–535, https://doi.org/10.1192/bjp.173.6.531.

152 up to forty-seven times as likely to show suicide warning signs Luciana Quevedo et al., "Risk of Suicide and Mixed Episode in Men in the Postpartum Period," *Journal of Affective Disorders* 132, nos. 1–2 (2011): 243–246, https://doi.org/10.1016/j.jad.2011.01.004.

154 "This guy's walking down the street" "Noël," *The West Wing*, season 2, episode 10, teleplay by Aaron Sorkin, story by Peter Parnell, directed by Thomas Schlamme, aired December 13, 2000 (NBC).

Chapter 11. Reframe the Present

164 "Noticing means thinking with all your senses" Verlyn Klinkenborg, *Several Short Sentences About Writing* (Knopf, 2012), 39.

165 twenty-seven distinct emotions that Berkeley researchers identified Alan S. Cowen and Dacher Keltner, "Self-Report Captures 27 Distinct Categories of Emotion Bridged by Continuous Gradients," *Proceedings of the National Academy of Sciences* 114, no. 38 (2017): E7900–E7909, https://doi.org/10.1073/pnas.1702247114.

169 "Human freedom involves our capacity to pause between the stimulus and response" Rollo May, *The Courage to Create* (Norton, 1994), 100.

170 "When you're doing something, you should reflect on the possibility" William B. Irvine, "The Last Time Meditation," *The Stoic Path* (audio lesson, Waking Up mobile app), WakingUp Course, accessed August 23, 2025, https://dynamic.wakingup.com/course/CO4EB3F99.

172 "responsible for producing many of the characteristics" Daniel J. Siegel and Tina Payne Bryson, *The Whole-Brain Child: 12 Revolutionary Strategies to Nurture Your Child's Developing Mind* (Delacorte Press, 2011).

173 "By integrating your implicit and explicit memories" Siegel and Bryson, *The Whole-Brain Child.*

Chapter 12. Rewire Your Brain

178 "Learn to be calm and you will always be happy" Paramahansa Yogananda, *Man's Eternal Quest: Collected Talks and Essays on Realizing God in Daily Life* (Self-Realization Fellowship, 2017).

178 It reduces anxiety and stress Elizabeth A. Hoge et al., "Randomized Controlled Trial of Mindfulness Meditation for Generalized Anxiety Disorder: Effects on Anxiety and Stress Reactivity," *Journal of Clinical Psychiatry* 74 (2013), https://doi.org/10.4088/JCP.12m08083.

178 decreases negative self-beliefs while improving emotion regulation Philippe R. Goldin and James J. Gross, "Effects of Mindfulness-Based Stress Reduction (MBSR) on Emotion Regulation in Social Anxiety Disorder," *Emotion* 10 (2010): 83–91, https://doi.org/10.1037/a0018441.

178 improves attention Yi-Yuan Tang et al., "Short-Term Meditation Training Improves Attention and Self-Regulation," *Proceedings of the National Academy of Sciences* 104, no. 43 (2007): 17152–17156, https://doi.org/10.1073/pnas.0707678104.

178 reducing age-related cognitive decline Joanna Marciniak et al., "Effect of Meditation on Cognitive Functions in Context of Aging and Neurodegenerative Diseases," *Frontiers in Behavioral Neuroscience* 8 (2014): 17, https://doi.org/10.3389/fnbeh.2014.00017.

178 helps inform better choices and overrule cognitive biases Andrew C. Hafenbrack et al., "Debiasing the Mind Through Meditation: Mindfulness and the Sunk-Cost Bias," *Psychological Science* 25 (2014): 369–376, https://doi.org/10.1177/0956797613503853.

179 helps you live longer and age slower Becca R. Levy et al., "Longevity Increased by Positive Self-Perceptions of Aging," *Journal of Personality and Social Psychology* 83 (2002): 261–270, https://doi.org/10.1037/0022-3514.83.2.261.

179 reduces pain Fadel Zeidan et al., "Brain Mechanisms Supporting the Modulation of Pain by Mindfulness Meditation," *Journal of Neuroscience* 31 (2011): 5540–5548, https://doi.org/10.1523/JNEUROSCI.5791-10.2011.

179 insomnia Jason C. Ong et al., "A Randomized Controlled Trial of Mindfulness Meditation for Chronic Insomnia," *Journal of Clinical Psychology* 64 (2008): 123–138, https://doi.org/10.1002/jclp.20736.

179 blood pressure, heart rate, and the likelihood of heart attacks David S. Schneider et al., "Stress Reduction in the Secondary Prevention of Cardiovascular Disease: Randomized,

Controlled Trial of Transcendental Meditation and Health Education in Blacks," *Journal of Human Hypertension* 19 (2005): 725–734, https://doi.org/10.1038/sj.jhh.1002275.

179 increases happiness by encouraging us to "live in the moment" Judson A. Brewer et al., "Meditation Experience Is Associated with Differences in Default Mode Network Activity and Connectivity," *Proceedings of the National Academy of Sciences* 108, no. 50 (2011): 20254–20259, https://doi.org/10.1073/pnas.1112029108.

179 powered by the DMN Y. Luo et al., "Resting-State Functional Connectivity of the Default Mode Network Associated with Happiness," *Social Cognitive and Affective Neuroscience* 11 (2016): 516–524, https://doi.org/10.1093/scan/nsv132.

180 "You can't stop the waves, but you can learn to surf" Jon Kabat-Zinn, *Wherever You Go, There You Are: Mindfulness Meditation in Everyday Life* (Hachette, 2005).

182 "The thing about meditation is you become more and more you" David Lynch, *Catching the Big Fish: Meditation, Consciousness, and Creativity*, 10th anniversary ed. (TarcherPerigee, 2016).

Chapter 13. Reconsider Reality

191 dancing with mushrooms sprouting out of their bodies Colin Marshall, "Algerian Cave Paintings Suggest Humans Did Magic Mushrooms 9,000 Years Ago," Open Culture, January 27, 2021, https://www.openculture.com/2021/01/algerian-cave-paintings-suggest-humans-did-magic-mushrooms-9000-years-ago.html.

191 scholars arguing they played a formative part Michael James Winkelman, "Psychedelics in History and World Religions (Editorial)," *Journal of Psychedelic Studies* 3, no. 3 (2019): 97–99, https://doi.org/10.1556/2054.2019.021.

191 "turn on, tune in, drop out" Timothy Leary, "Turn on, tune in, drop out," used publicly in 1966–1967 (e.g., Human Be-In) and as the title of his 1967 spoken-word LP.

191 "It was a little like being shown a door in a familiar room" Michael Pollan, *How to Change Your Mind: What the New Science of Psychedelics Teaches Us About Consciousness, Dying, Addiction, Depression, and Transcendence* (Penguin Press, 2018), 12.

192 "what the microscope is for biology or the telescope is for astronomy" Stanislav Grof, *LSD Psychotherapy* (Multidisciplinary Association for Psychedelic Studies; originally Ronin, 1980), 297.

192 psychedelics reduce the noise and disrupt the integrity of the DMN Robin L. Carhart-Harris et al., "Neural Correlates of the Psychedelic State as Determined by fMRI Studies with Psilocybin," *Proceedings of the National Academy of Sciences* 109, no. 6 (2012): 2138–2143, https://doi.org/10.1073/pnas.1119598109.

192 one near-death experience Christopher Timmermann et al., "DMT Models the Near-Death Experience," *Frontiers in Psychology* 9 (2018): 1424, https://doi.org/10.3389/fpsyg.2018.01424.

193 what researchers have termed REBUS Robin L. Carhart-Harris and Karl J. Friston, "REBUS and the Anarchic Brain: Toward a Unified Model of the Brain Action of Psychedelics," *Pharmacological Reviews* 71, no. 3 (2019): 316–344, https://doi.org/10.1124/pr.118.017160.

193 comparable results to traditional antidepressants Alan K. Davis et al., "Effects of Psilocybin-Assisted Therapy on Major Depressive Disorder: A Randomized Clinical Trial," *JAMA Psychiatry* 78, no. 5 (2021): 481–489, https://doi.org/10.1001/jamapsychiatry.2020.3285.

193 unlike traditional SSRIs (selective serotonin reuptake inhibitors) that can cause a general emotional blunting Leor Roseman et al., "Increased Amygdala Responses to

Emotional Faces After Psilocybin for Treatment-Resistant Depression," *Neuropharmacology* 142 (2018): 263–269, https://doi.org/10.1016/j.neuropharm.2017.12.041.

193 help cancer patients manage overwhelming emotions in end-of-life anxiety and depression Stephen Ross et al., "Rapid and Sustained Symptom Reduction Following Psilocybin Treatment for Anxiety and Depression in Patients with Life-Threatening Cancer: A Randomized Controlled Trial," *Journal of Psychopharmacology* 30, no. 12 (2016): 1165–1180, https://doi.org/10.1177/0269881116675513.

193 Seventy-one percent of people who took psilocybin for major depressive disorder Davis et al., "Effects of Psilocybin-Assisted Therapy on Major Depressive Disorder."

193 an oft-cited report on mystical experiences Roland R. Griffiths et al., "Mystical-Type Experiences Occasioned by Psilocybin Mediate the Attribution of Personal Meaning and Spiritual Significance 14 Months Later," *Journal of Psychopharmacology* 22, no. 6 (2008): 621–632, https://doi.org/10.1177/0269881108094300.

193 "even if further research finds psilocybin only 50% as effective" Ezra Klein, "Can Magic Mushrooms Heal Us?," *New York Times*, March 18, 2021, https://www.nytimes.com/2021/03/18/opinion/oregon-psychedelic-therapy.html.

194 Public data on Google searches indicates a 450 percent increase George Danias and Jacob Appel, "Public Interest in Psilocybin and Psychedelic Therapy in the Context of the COVID-19 Pandemic: Google Trends Analysis," *JMIR Formative Research* 7 (December 2023): e43850, https://doi.org/10.2196/43850.

Chapter 14. Rewild Your Attention

201 "If you input wrong figures, will the right answers come out?" Charles Babbage, *Passages from the Life of a Philosopher* (Longman, Green, Longman, Roberts, & Green, 1864), chap. 5 ("Difference Engine No. 1"), 67, Project Gutenberg, https://www.gutenberg.org/ebooks/57532.

202 giving the angry-reaction emoji five times the weight Shraddha Chakradhar, "More Internal Documents Show How Facebook's Algorithm Prioritized Anger and Posts That Triggered It," Nieman Journalism Lab, October 26, 2021, https://www.niemanlab.org/2021/10/more-internal-documents-show-how-facebooks-algorithm-prioritized-anger-and-posts-that-triggered-it.

202 we respond physiologically to news based on how negative it is Stuart Soroka et al., "Cross-National Evidence of a Negativity Bias in Psychophysiological Reactions to News," *Proceedings of the National Academy of Sciences* 116, no. 38 (2019): 18888–18892, https://doi.org/10.1073/pnas.1908369116.

202 Manufactured outrage has become the primary currency of digital spaces Claire E. Robertson et al., "Negativity Drives Online News Consumption," *Nature Human Behaviour* 7 (2023): 1003–1012, https://doi.org/10.1038/s41562-023-01538-4.

202 cable news saw a 25 percent rise in revenue during 2017 "US Ad Market Grows by 3.7% in 2017," Standard Media Index, press release, January 23, 2018, https://www.globenewswire.com/news-release/2018/01/23/1299410/0/en/US-Ad-Market-Grows-3-7-in-2017-New-Data-from-Standard-Media-Index.html.

204 it leads to two hundred thousand human lifetimes wasted every day Aza Raskin, quoted in *The Telegraph*, "We Lost Control of Our Creations," May 10, 2019, https://www.telegraph.co.uk/technology/2019/05/10/lost-control-creations-silicon-valley-heretic-mission-make-big.

204 "Tell me with whom you consort" Johann Wolfgang von Goethe, *Wilhelm Meisters Wanderjahre*, "Betrachtungen im Sinne der Wanderer" (Kunst, Ethisches, Natur), in Projekt Gutenberg-DE edition, accessed August 23, 2025, https://www.projekt-gutenberg.org/goethe/meisterw/mstw212.html.

204 "rewilding your attention" Tom Critchlow, post on X (formerly Twitter), July 10, 2021, https://x.com/tomcritchlow/status/1413867323144933378.

204 "If you want to have wilder, curiouser thoughts" Clive Thompson, "A Quick Primer on 'Rewilding Your Attention,'" Medium, July 12, 2021, https://clivethompson.medium.com/a-quick-primer-on-rewilding-your-attention-892af77c7bca.

204 "The mind is a garden; what we decide to grow there will determine our prosperity" Yung Pueblo, *Inward* (Andrews McMeel, 2018).

204 "one must cultivate one's own garden" Voltaire, *Candide, ou l'Optimisme* (1759), chap. 30.

204 "I am a compost heap" Ann Patchett, "The Getaway Car," in *This Is the Story of a Happy Marriage* (Harper, 2013).

205 coined the term *outrage porn* in 2009 Tim Kreider, "Isn't It Outrageous?" *New York Times*, July 14, 2009, https://opinionator.blogs.nytimes.com/2009/07/14/isnt-it-outrageous.

Chapter 15. Redefine Success

213 "It is not the answer that enlightens, but the question." Eugène Ionesco, *Découvertes* (Éditions d'Art Albert Skira, 1969), 16.

Chapter 16. Recruit Your Crew

225 Loneliness remains on the rise worldwide Louise C. Hawkley et al., "Loneliness: A Social Pain with Public Health Relevance," *Nature Reviews Psychology* 2 (2023): 389–404, https://doi.org/10.1038/s44159-022-00124-1.

225 more than 61 percent of Americans "Loneliness and the Workplace: 2020 U.S. Report," Cigna, 2020, https://www.cigna.com/static/www-cigna-com/docs/about-us/newsroom/studies-and-reports/combatting-loneliness/cigna-2020-loneliness-report.pdf.

225 1 in 10 UK residents felt they lacked a single friend to rely upon Relate & Relationships Scotland, press release summarizing "You're Not Alone—the Quality of the UK's Social Relationships," March 1, 2017, https://www.relate.org.uk/get-help/loneliness-rising-1-8-adults-have-no-close-friends.

225 jumped to 1 in 4 for men Matthew Smith, "One in Five Britons Have Nobody to Open Up to About Problems," YouGov, April 18, 2019, https://yougov.co.uk/topics/society/articles-reports/2019/04/19/one-five-britons-have-nobody-open-about-problems.

225 a third of adults over forty-five regularly feel lonely "Social Isolation and Loneliness in Older Adults: Opportunities for the Health Care System," *National Academies of Sciences, Engineering, and Medicine* (National Academies Press, 2020), https://doi.org/10.17226/25663.

225 a meta-analysis of 345 studies on loneliness Susanne Buecker et al., "Is Loneliness in Emerging Adults Increasing over Time? A Preregistered Cross-Temporal Meta-Analysis and Systematic Review," *Psychological Bulletin* 147, no. 8 (2021): 787–805, https://doi.org/10.1037/bul0000332.

226 increased rates of anxiety, depression, and suicide Farhana Mann et al., "Loneliness and the Onset of New Mental Health Problems in the General Population," *Social Psychiatry and Psychiatric Epidemiology* 57, no. 11 (2022): 2161–2178, https://doi.org/10.1007/s00127-022-02261-7.

226 numbers that rival those for smoking, obesity, and physical inactivity Maike Luhmann et al., "Loneliness Across Time and Space," *Nature Reviews Psychology* 2 (2022): 9–23, https://doi.org/10.1038/s44159-022-00124-1.

226 50 percent more likely to develop dementia Jisca S. Kuiper et al., "Social Relationships and Risk of Dementia: A Systematic Review and Meta-Analysis of Longitudinal Cohort Studies," *Ageing Research Reviews* 22 (July 2015): 39–57, https://doi.org/10.1016/j.arr.2015.04.006.

226 29 percent more likely to develop heart disease Nicole K. Valtorta et al., "Loneliness and Social Isolation as Risk Factors for Coronary Heart Disease and Stroke: Systematic Review and Meta-Analysis of Longitudinal Observational Studies," *Heart* 102, no. 13 (2016): 1009–1016, https://doi.org/10.1136/heartjnl-2015-308790.

226 an annual report on the topic UK Department for Culture, Media & Sport, "Tackling Loneliness: Annual Report—the Third Year," 2022, https://www.gov.uk/government/publications/loneliness-annual-report-the-third-year.

226 "at least 6 close friends" Daniel A. Cox, "Men's Social Circles Are Shrinking," Survey Center on American Life, June 29, 2021, https://www.americansurveycenter.org/why-mens-social-circles-are-shrinking/.

227 social capital and small habits Robert D. Putnam, *Bowling Alone: The Collapse and Revival of American Community* (Simon & Schuster, 2000).

227 These findings have been echoed in study after study Siu Long Lee et al., "The Association Between Loneliness and Depressive Symptoms Among Adults Aged 50 Years and Older: A 12-Year Population-Based Cohort Study," *The Lancet Psychiatry* 8, no. 1 (2021): 48–57, https://doi.org/10.1016/S2215-0366(20)30383-7.

228 "You are the average of the five people you spend the most time with" Jack Canfield and Janet Switzer, *The Success Principles: How to Get from Where You Are to Where You Want to Be* (HarperCollins, 2005). (Quote credited to Jim Rohn.)

229 "No one is useless in this world" Charles Dickens, *Our Mutual Friend*, Book III, chap. 9 (Oxford University Press, 2009).

233 coined the term *the third place* Ray Oldenburg, *The Great Good Place* (Marlowe, 1989).

234 "Loneliness feels like such a shameful experience" Olivia Laing, *The Lonely City: Adventures in the Art of Being Alone* (Canongate, 2016), 25.

234 "I am not putting my donkey outside when I'm sad" *The Banshees of Inisherin*, dir. Martin McDonagh (Searchlight Pictures, 2022).

235 The *vulnerability loop* Daniel Coyle, "How Showing Vulnerability Helps Build a Stronger Team," TED Ideas, February 20, 2018, https://ideas.ted.com/how-showing-vulnerability-helps-build-a-stronger-team.

239 differences in how men and women form friendships Rosalind Aukett et al., "Gender Differences in Friendship Patterns," *Sex Roles* 19 (1988): 57–66, https://doi.org/10.1007/BF00292464.

239 men's sheds across the world D. Kelly et al., "Men's Sheds: A Conceptual Exploration of the Causal Pathways for Health and Well-Being," *Health & Social Care in the Community* 27, no. 5 (2019): 1147–1157, https://doi.org/10.1111/hsc.12765.

239 "The only way to have a friend is to be one" Ralph Waldo Emerson, "Friendship," in *Essays: First Series* (1841), Project Gutenberg, https://www.gutenberg.org/ebooks/2944.

Chapter 17. Reboot Your System

246 citizens live on the utopian archipelago of Prospera Justin Cronin, *The Ferryman* (Ballantine Books, 2023).

247 a simple checklist could save lives Atul Gawande, *The Checklist Manifesto: How to Get Things Right* (Profile Books, 2011).

249 "Resistance is always lying, and always full of shit." Steven Pressfield, *The War of Art: Break Through the Blocks and Win Your Inner Creative Battles* (Black Irish Entertainment, 2012), 9.

Epilogue. Wholehearted Cooperation with the Inevitable

253 29 percent of all Disney+ streaming time Lucas Shaw, "How *Bluey* Became a $2 Billion Smash Hit—with an Uncertain Future," *Bloomberg Businessweek*, April 3, 2024, https://www.bloomberg.com/news/features/2024-04-03/is-bluey-ending-disney-s-worried-biggest-kids-show-ever-is-at-risk.

255 "There was a farmer who owned a beautiful horse" *Bluey*, "The Sign," season 3, episode 49, written by Joe Brumm, directed by Richard Jeffery and Joe Brumm, aired April 14, 2024 on ABC Kids (Australia).

257 posthumously decreeing that de Mello's views "are incompatible with the Catholic faith" "Congregation for the Doctrine of the Faith: Notification Concerning the Writings of Father Anthony de Mello, S.J.," June 24, 1998, The Vatican, https://www.vatican.va/roman_curia/congregations/cfaith/documents/rc_con_cfaith_doc_19980624_demello_en.html.

257 "What is the secret of your serenity?" Anthony de Mello, *One Minute Nonsense* (Gujarat Sahitya Prakash, 2003), 22.

258 "You never know what worse luck your bad luck has saved you from" *No Country for Old Men*, dir. Joel and Ethan Coen (Miramax/Paramount Vantage, 2007).

258 "The happiness of your life depends upon the quality of your thoughts" Marcus Aurelius, *Meditations*, trans. Martin Hammond (Penguin Classics, 2006), 5.16.

258 "We don't see things as they are" Anaïs Nin, *Seduction of the Minotaur* (Swallow Press, 1961).

258 "Be prepared to appreciate what you meet" Frank Herbert, *Dune* (New English Library, 1982).

259 "You have the right to work, but for the work's sake only" *Bhagavad Gita: A New Translation*, trans. Stephen Mitchell (Three Rivers Press, 2002), 2.47.

259 At one of his talks in the later part of his life Eckhart Tolle, *A New Earth: Awakening to Your Life's Purpose* (Penguin, 2006), 199.

INDEX

ABOUT THE AUTHOR

Kevin Maguire is dad-in-chief at *The New Fatherhood.* His writing has been featured in *Esquire* and Emily Oster's *ParentData,* and he has appeared on podcasts with Daniel Pink, Oliver Burkeman, Jon Klassen, and more. He works as an executive coach with CEOs, CMOs, and VPs of Fortune 500 companies like Amazon, Netflix, and Google as they navigate the intersections of career and family. He lives in Barcelona with his wife and two children.